JANE AUSTEN'S INSPIRATION

JANE AUSTEN'S INSPIRATION
BELOVED FRIEND ANNE LEFROY

JUDITH STOVE

PEN & SWORD
HISTORY

AN IMPRINT OF PEN & SWORD BOOKS LTD
YORKSHIRE - PHILADELPHIA

First published in Great Britain in 2019 by
PEN AND SWORD HISTORY
An imprint of
Pen & Sword Books Ltd
Yorkshire – Philadelphia

Typeset in Times New Roman 11.5/14 by
Aura Technology and Software Services, India
Printed and bound in the UK by TJ International

Pen & Sword Books Limited incorporates the imprints of Atlas, Archaeology,
Aviation, Discovery, Family History, Fiction, History, Maritime, Military,
Military Classics, Politics, Select, Transport, True Crime, Air World,
Frontline Publishing, Leo Cooper, Remember When, Seaforth Publishing,
The Praetorian Press, Wharncliffe Local History, Wharncliffe Transport,
Wharncliffe True Crime and White Owl.

For a complete list of Pen & Sword titles please contact
PEN & SWORD BOOKS LIMITED
47 Church Street, Barnsley, South Yorkshire, S70 2AS, England
E-mail: enquiries@pen-and-sword.co.uk
Website: www.pen-and-sword.co.uk

Or
PEN AND SWORD BOOKS
1950 Lawrence Rd, Havertown, PA 19083, USA
E-mail: Uspen-and-sword@casematepublishers.com
Website: www.penandswordbooks.com

Contents

Introduction

It was with surprise, in 2015, while preparing a talk about Jane Austen's friend Anne Brydges Lefroy (1747/8–1804), that I learned that Anne has no Wikipedia entry, usually the first resort for inquiry. Online articles were sketchy, while no full-length study had apparently appeared.

It is true that Anne Lefroy has tended to be obscured, not only by her famous friend, but by her loud, overbearing, eccentric and long-winded brother, Samuel Egerton Brydges (1762–1837). As will become clear, Samuel's legacy is a mixed one; but he was, at least, a devoted brother to his talented sister.

Anne Lefroy continued to write verse and prose after her marriage to the Reverend George Lefroy, Rector of Ashe in Hampshire. She was a devoted clergyman's wife, but she was far from quiet and submissive. Anne took a keen interest in matters such as the ongoing conflict with Napoleon, the new practice of vaccination, and legal matters. Her mind was active and inquiring, and she balanced many roles in her busy life.

With ever-growing interest in women writers of the 'long eighteenth century', along with unprecedented interest in every aspect of Jane Austen's life and times, there is a gap in the record. While naturally her sister Cassandra was Jane Austen's closest and dearest friend, the role of other female friendships in her life and work has perhaps not received the attention which one might have expected. Anne Lefroy died in 1804; another Anne, the Godmersham governess Anne Sharp, became, in the years following, another close friend of the author. While Anne Sharp has begun to receive some critical attention, this book is the first attempt to provide the same for Anne Lefroy.

The study of male writers and their literary circles is an ancient one. The study of female writers and their networks, so often illustrated by letter-writing, has only in recent years taken off as a comparable pursuit. In the belief that study of great writers is enriched through awareness of their social and artistic contexts, this book will examine the life and works of Anne Brydges Lefroy, the woman who was arguably a role model for the writer second only to Shakespeare in English literature.

Parents and siblings of Anne Brydges Lefroy

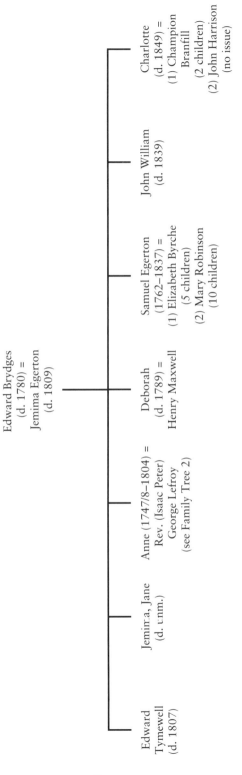

Edward Brydges
(d. 1780) =
Jemima Egerton
(d. 1809)

Edward
Tymewell
(d. 1807)

Jemima, Jane
(d. unm.)

Anne (1747/8–1804) =
Rev. (Isaac Peter)
George Lefroy
(see Family Tree 2)

Deborah
(d. 1789) =
Henry Maxwell

Samuel Egerton
(1762–1837) =
(1) Elizabeth Byrche
(5 children)
(2) Mary Robinson
(10 children)

John William
(d. 1839)

Charlotte
(d. 1849) =
(1) Champion
Branfill
(2 children)
(2) John Harrison
(no issue)

Children of Anne Brydges Lefroy and Rev. George Lefroy

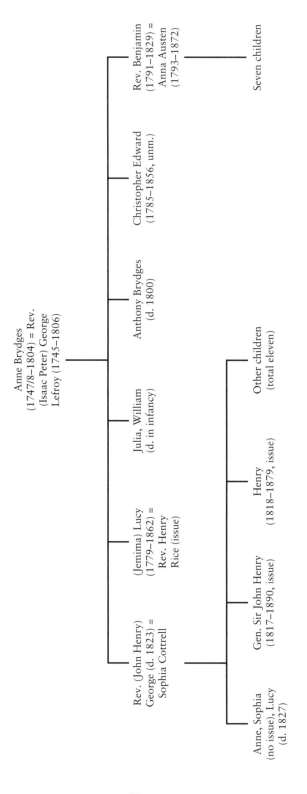

Anne Brydges
(1747/8–1804) = Rev.
(Isaac Peter) George
Lefroy (1745–1806)

Rev. (John Henry)
George (d. 1823) =
Sophia Cottrell

(Jemima) Lucy
(1779–1862) =
Rev. Henry
Rice (issue)

Julia, William
(d. in infancy)

Anthony Brydges
(d. 1800)

Christopher Edward
(1785–1856, unm.)

Rev. Benjamin
(1791–1829) =
Anna Austen
(1793–1872)

Seven children

Anne, Sophia
(no issue), Lucy
(d. 1827)

Gen. Sir John Henry
(1817–1890, issue)

Henry
(1818–1879, issue)

Other children
(total eleven)

Part One

The Austen Connection

Chapter 1

Jane/Anne

Readers of Jane Austen's novels love her work partly because of the great emotional power with which she expresses love, most notably in her last novel *Persuasion* (1818). In that novel, Anne Elliot's and Captain Wentworth's love for each other has survived years of separation and family opposition, and their reunion, the climax of the novel, is probably the most satisfying in English fiction.

Yet the most emotional work of Jane Austen in her own voice was not to be found in her surviving letters. It is her 1808 poem in memory of her friend, Anne Brydges Lefroy, who had died four years earlier, after falling from a horse. Few commentators have thought it worthwhile to discuss the poem; fewer still to consider in detail what it suggests about the nature of the relationship between the two women over more than fifteen years (from the late 1780s until Anne's death in 1804).

Anne Lefroy was much older than Jane Austen; she was aged about 40 when Jane was in her teens. When Jane was 20, she met and seems to have fallen in love with Anne's husband's nephew, Tom Lefroy. Did Anne Lefroy play the part of a Lady Russell from *Persuasion*, in encouraging the young man and young woman to separate because of worldly considerations? Did Jane's dear friend bring sadness into her life?

First, it is important to look at Jane Austen's records of the events. Tom Lefroy is mentioned in the very first letter of Jane Austen's which survives, that of 9-10 January 1796. Jane was just 20 years old, and this is the letter in which she tells her sister Cassandra about the young man with whom she has been spending time over Christmas 1795: Tom Lefroy.

Thomas-Langlois Lefroy (1776–1869) was the son of George Lefroy's brother, Anthony-Peter (1742–1819). Anthony rose to the rank of lieutenant colonel in the British Army, and lived in Ireland. He married Anne Gardiner and had eleven children, of whom Tom was the sixth, coming after five daughters.[1]

Tom's full name is clearly a respectful nod to Anthony's Langlois uncles, most significantly Benjamin, who wielded considerable influence within the clan. Tom came from Dublin to Ashe to visit his uncle George and family, before undertaking law studies at Lincoln's Inn in London.[2]

Tom's subsequent career in the law was to be stellar, but there is evidence that his academic performance had already been impressive. At Trinity College, Dublin, which he had entered at the age of 14: 'Every academic honour, premiums, certificates, a moderatorship, and finally, in 1795, the gold medal of his class, attended his progress.'[3]

In a very famous passage, Jane tells Cassandra that she and Tom showed disregard for the conventions by sitting out dances together:

> Imagine to yourself everything most profligate and shocking in the way of dancing and sitting down together.[4]

Their growing friendship had apparently been noticed, and not necessarily in a good way. Jane goes on:

> He is so excessively laughed at about me at Ashe, that he is ashamed of coming to Steventon, and ran away when we called on Mrs Lefroy a few days ago.

Jane seems here to be trying to dismiss her evident feelings for Tom. Some encouragement occurred while she was still writing the same letter:

> After I had written the above, we received a visit from Mr Tom Lefroy and his cousin George. The latter is really very well-behaved now; and as for the other, he has but one fault, which time, will, I trust, entirely remove – it is that his morning coat is a great deal too light. He is a very great admirer of Tom Jones, and therefore wears the same coloured clothes, I imagine, which he did when he was wounded.[5]

Jane and Cassandra seem, at an earlier stage, to have agreed that George Lefroy junior was badly behaved (although probably he was simply cheeky, in the manner of pre-teen boys).

In her notes to this letter, Deirdre Le Faye cites the passage from Henry Fielding's *The History of Tom Jones, a Foundling,* to which Jane Austen refers:

As soon as the sergeant was departed, Jones rose from his bed, and dressed himself entirely, putting on even his coat, which, as its colour was white, showed very visibly the streams of blood which had flowed down it.[6]

Tom Jones' injury had been caused by a bottle thrown at his head during a rowdy encounter in the army mess, when Tom thought that the name of his beloved, Sophia Western, had been uttered disrespectfully. It was a mock-heroic setting, with the injury not incurred in battle, but as a result of Tom's heightened, and naïve, sense of honour. For Jane Austen to have thought of the scene indicates her feelings of interest, affection and honour for the other Tom, Tom Lefroy, but also her keen sense of the mock-heroic.

It would appear that even before this, Cassandra had already offered some kind of warning to her sister about becoming a public spectacle in her flirtation with Tom.[7] Jane had written: 'You scold me so much in the nice long letter which I have this moment received from you, that I am almost afraid to tell you how my Irish friend and I behaved...'[8]

It is significant that a letter from Jane to Cassandra is missing after this one, dated 12 or 13 January 1796.[9] It is safe to infer, as Jon Spence did, that Cassandra destroyed letters relating to this time.[10] Jane expected it to become more than a flirtation. In her next (her second) surviving letter, she writes:

Our party to Ashe tomorrow night will consist of [cousin] Edward Cooper, James (for a Ball is nothing without him), Buller, who is now staying with us, & I – I look forward with great impatience to it, as I rather expect to receive an offer from my friend in the course of the evening. I shall refuse him, however, unless he promises to give away his white Coat.[11]

Yet how serious was Jane Austen, here? Her context, as usual, is satirical. She manages to include a shot at her widowed brother James, who was not in general the most affable of men, but who at this time was passing through a phase of extreme sociability, no doubt with a view to attracting a second wife.

'Buller' was the Reverend Richard Buller (1776–1806), who had been a pupil of the Reverend George Austen at Steventon, and was of an age to be thought, other things being equal, to have a possible interest in Jane. Yet other things were not equal. Jane's partiality for Tom Lefroy over any other potential admirer was highly visible.

Tell Mary [Lloyd, soon to become that second wife of James Austen] that I make over Mr Heartley & all his Estate to her for her sole use and Benefit in future, & not only him, but all my other Admirers into the bargain wherever she can find them, even the kiss which C[harles] Powlett wanted to give me, as I mean to confine myself in future to Mr Tom Lefroy, for whom I donot [*sic*] care sixpence. Assure her also as a last & indubitable proof of Warren's indifference to me, that he actually drew that Gentleman's picture for me, & delivered it to me without a Sigh.[12]

Here Austen, mimicking the style of a will and testament, names no fewer than three other possible admirers: Mr Heartley; Charles Powlett; and 'Warren'. Deirdre Le Faye, the world authority on Jane Austen's letters, has been unable to identify Mr Heartley except as 'Possibly a member of the Hartley family, of Bucklebury, Berks.'[13]

Charles Powlett is identified by Deirdre Le Faye as a child of Percy Powlett, one of the illegitimate sons of the third Duke of Bolton, also Charles Powlett or Paulet (1685–1754). The Bolton family lived at Hackwood Park, near Ashe, and later family members became friends of the Lefroys.

The number of Charles Powletts in the extended family is certainly confusing. This Charles (b.c. 1765–1834) was brought up at Hackwood Park by his uncle, also Charles (1728–1809). He failed to graduate, but still took orders and held several Bolton family livings. At the time of Jane Austen's early letters, this Charles Powlett was rector of Itchenstoke, Hampshire, some fourteen miles from Ashe.[14]

On the other hand, at this time Lord Bolton (Thomas Orde-Powlett) and Lady Bolton had a young son, inevitably called Charles Powlett, born in the second half of the 1780s, who would have been old enough to demand a kiss from Jane Austen in 1796.[15] Whichever the Charles Powlett to whom 20-year-old Jane refers – the one ten years older than herself, or the one six or seven years younger – both are clearly joke-worthy.

This leaves Mr Warren. This man has been identified by Deirdre Le Faye as John-Willing Warren (1771–c.1831). He had probably been a pupil of the Reverend George Austen at Steventon, then was a friend of James Austen at Oxford, contributing to James and Henry Austen's magazine *The Loiterer*.[16] Jane Austen's familiar use of his surname, as with 'Buller', indicates a long-term family friendship; it was a way in which women mimicked male address to each other, reserved for very close friends (we note that in *Emma*, the heroine resents Mrs Elton referring to the master of Donwell Abbey as 'Knightley'). John Warren must have been attached to Jane Austen to draw for her a picture of Tom Lefroy.

Jane concludes this letter with a hopeful note:

> *Friday.* At length the Day is come on which I am to flirt my last with Tom Lefroy, & when you receive this it will be over. – My tears flow as I write, at the melancholy idea.[17]

As we know, no offer came from Tom Lefroy, either at that meeting, or subsequently. The next surviving letter is from London, address simply given as 'Cork Street'. The only Austen connection known at Cork Street was Benjamin Langlois, the Reverend George Lefroy's uncle, so it has been reasonably conjectured that the Austens were staying with him.[18]

However, a great deal more has been made of this than simply their acquaintance through the Lefroys. Jon Spence thought it 'unusual' that the Austens would be staying with Benjamin Langlois.[19] Spence thought that it indicated a special relationship between Jane and Tom, possibly fostered by Anne:

> Perhaps [Anne] herself felt betrayed, especially if she had had a hand in arranging the meeting in Cork Street.[20]

Yet we do not know even if Jane Austen met Tom at Cork Street. The invitation could have been simply from Benjamin Langlois to honoured friends of his nephew the Rector of Ashe, and Tom may not have been there at the time. Jane Austen's letter does not indicate that he was. She opens with a typically funny declaration, but we are not to take it as suggesting anything about actual sexual conduct.

> Here I am once more in this Scene of Dissipation & vice,
> and I begin already to find my Morals corrupted.[21]

Pace what Spence clearly wished (without being explicit) to imply, this is simply Jane-speak for being in London.

Deirdre Le Faye notes that there are letters missing following this one.[22] Letters 4 through 7 were dated September 1796. Letter 8 is from April 1798.

On the next occasion we hear about Tom Lefroy, it is obliquely, and without reference to his name. This is from November 1798, over two years later. During the hiatus of letters, Cassandra had, in the early months of 1797, received the sad news of the death of her fiancé Thomas Fowle (1765–1797). This will have made a difference to Jane Austen's manner in discussing affairs of the heart. It may be that Jane was the Marianne of the pair, bemoaning the loss of her one-time lover, and Cassandra the Elinor, suffering in silence over the permanent loss of hers.

After letters resume in April 1798, there are two from October (Letters 9 and 10); some further missing letters; then this (Letter 11), from 17-18 November.

> Mrs Lefroy did come last Wednesday, and the Harwoods came likewise, but very considerately paid their visit before Mrs Lefroy's arrival, with whom, in spite of interruptions both from my father and James, I was enough alone to hear all that was interesting, which you will easily credit when I tell you that of her nephew she said nothing at all, and of her friend very little.[23]

Jane adds:

> She did not once mention the name of the former to <u>me</u>, and I was too proud to make any enquiries; but on my father's

afterwards asking where he was, I learnt that he was gone back to London in his way to Ireland, where he is called to the Bar and means to practise.[24]

Her father's otherwise clumsy, indeed cringe-worthy, conversational interventions produced a useful result for Jane, if only in confirming what she had been too proud to ask. (The Reverend George Austen was probably as concerned for his daughter's future as she could have been, and, like many a father before or since, did not realise or care how embarrassing he was.) And this is the end of Jane Austen's recorded utterances about Tom Lefroy.

The 'friend' of Anne's that she did mention was, it appears, the Reverend Samuel Blackall (1770–1842).[25] Blackall had apparently stayed with the Lefroys the previous Christmas, and had shown interest in Jane.[26] He now wrote to Anne, however, no doubt with a view to her transmitting this information to Jane, to indicate that he was not in a position to wed. Jane writes:

[Anne Lefroy] showed me a letter which she had received from her friend a few weeks ago … towards the end of which was a sentence to this effect: 'I am very sorry to hear of Mrs Austen's illness. It would give me particular pleasure to have an opportunity of improving my acquaintance with that family – with a hope of creating to myself a nearer interest. But at present I cannot indulge any expectation of it.' This is rational enough; there is less love and more sense in it than sometimes appeared before, and I am very well satisfied. It will all go on exceedingly well, and decline away in a very reasonable manner. There seems no likelihood of his coming into Hampshire this Christmas, and it is therefore most probable that our indifference will soon be mutual, unless his regard, which appeared to spring from knowing nothing of me at first, is best supported by never seeing me.[27]

To quote Richard III: 'Was ever woman in this humour woo'd? Was ever woman in this humour won?'[28] Who but Jane Austen could respond so frankly, brutally, and amusingly to Samuel Blackall's half-hearted,

8

retailed-at-second-hand suit? Jane was, of course, correct; Samuel Blackall's rational passion faded away, and we find him, in 1813, marrying a woman called Susannah Lewis (1780–1844).[29]

Now we need to consider the role of Anne Lefroy in the abortive relationship of Jane and Tom. It is unfortunate that Anne's surviving letters only begin in 1800, four years after the flirtation, so we do not have first-hand evidence about her view of the events.

There are two contrasting views of Anne's role: (1) that, having introduced Jane and Tom, Anne and the Reverend George Lefroy were dismayed to see an intimacy develop, and took steps to separate them (this is broadly the view expressed by Deirdre Le Faye[30] and implied by Claire Tomalin[31]); (2) that Anne promoted the relationship and was disappointed by Tom's evasion and decampment (the view promoted by Jon Spence[32]).

The surviving family sources for what Anne may or may not have thought are, themselves, conflicting. Spence quoted Mary Lloyd Austen, James' second wife, as believing that Anne had sent Tom to London to get him away from Jane, before things could develop seriously. The family sources for what Anne's attitude may have been were Mary and James' daughter Caroline's recollection, in a letter to her brother James-Edward Austen Leigh of the late 1860s, that:

> It was a disappointment, but Mrs Lefroy sent the gentleman [Tom] off at the end of a *very* few weeks, that no more mischief might be done.

Anna Austen, who married Ben Lefroy in 1814, had – at least by the time her half-brother James Edward Austen-Leigh was preparing material for his biographical work on Jane Austen in 1869 – come to the view, perhaps inherited through Ben (who had died in 1829), or from George junior, that both Anne and the Reverend George had disapproved of Tom's treatment of Jane.

Anna wrote to James-Edward's wife Emma:

> *But* when I came to hear again & again, from those who were old enough to remember, how the Mother [Anne] had disliked Tom Lefroy because he had behaved so ill to Jane Austen, with sometimes the additional weight of the

Father's condemnation, what could I think *then*? ... First, the youth of the Parties – secondly, that Mrs Lefroy, charming woman as she was, & warm in her feelings, was also partial in her judgments – Thirdly – that for other causes, too long to enter upon, she not improbably set out with a prejudice against the Gentleman, & would have distrusted [him] had there been no Jane Austen in the case.[33]

Anna here may have been hinting at some bad feeling between the Irish Lefroys and the Reverend George, possibly concerning relations with Benjamin Langlois. Otherwise it would be hard to understand why Anne would have had a prejudice against her husband's nephew.

Spence himself disbelieved any account in which Anne is shown as ultimately opposing the match, as he was committed to a deliberate meeting, possibly engineered by Anne, between the pair at Cork Street.[34] Spence went further. He speculated:

The sad truth may be that three warm, romantic, impulsive people – Jane, Tom and Mrs Lefroy – got swept away by their feelings, and their enthusiasm and optimism were misplaced.[35]

Anne Lefroy was warm, but hardly romantic or impulsive: she was not young when she married the Reverend George, and none of her letters suggest that she was likely to have been 'swept away by her feelings'. The same can be said for Jane Austen. About Tom Lefroy, we have no way of knowing, but he certainly does not seem to have been overly romantic.

Hazel Jones, in *Jane Austen and Marriage* (2009), manages to have it both ways. She writes, conventionally enough, that:

[Tom's] aunt and uncle had seen sufficient to unsettle them, and Tom was sent back to London.

Yet she continues:

Mrs Lefroy in particular blamed Tom for behaving thoughtlessly towards a young woman whom he knew he was in no position to marry.[36]

However counterintuitive, this composite view of Jones' is as compelling as any other pure conjecture. It would not be surprising that Anne was *both* dismayed about the apparent progress of the relationship between Tom and Jane, but, given its existence, disappointed and annoyed that Tom failed to follow through with a proposal. The matter of whether Tom was in a position to marry was settled only a year later when he proposed to, and was accepted by, Mary Paul, sister of a friend.[37]

Contrary to Spence's view, it is unlikely that Anne attempted to set up a meeting at the house of Benjamin Langlois in Cork Street. The formidable Benjamin Langlois, it appears, disposed matters, and the Lefroy clan did as they were bid.

Cork Street appears to have been a terrifying destination for the young. Anne writes in September 1800 (in her earliest surviving letter):

> George [junior, then 18] will go to Cork St he is not much delighted with the scheme as you may suppose.[38]

The reason for this reluctance becomes clear from a letter written by Benjamin Langlois himself. He had undertaken to coach George junior for university. Mr Langlois (as even Anne continued to call him) had no very high opinion of poor George's abilities, although he approved of his work ethic:

> The studies [at Cork Street] have been principally classical …
> I have decided that this youth shall not go [to Oxford] till he is pretty well grounded in the first elements both of Euclid & Algebra. This is my great object at present, & … I never saw a better disposed or more laborious lad at his age …

On the other hand, added Mr Langlois:

> The only thing that displeases me in my good George's letter, is the very diffident or rather mean opinion he has of his own abilities. Though they may not be transcendent, they are *very very* far from being deficient, & his application brings them *above* the common level…[39]

There is something grim, almost sinister, in Mr Langlois' emphatic repetition of 'very'. In the summer of 1801, it appeared poor George would again be sacrificed to Cork Street:

> About 3 o'Clock George came home he looks very well & is in good spirits I dread very much Mr Langlois's insisting upon his spending some time in town but your father will have the goodness to get him off if possible.[40]

Anne's brother Samuel Egerton Brydges was to describe his brother-in-law's uncle Benjamin Langlois, ironically showing a low view of *his* talents:

> A good and benevolent old man, with much diplomatic experience, but most fatiguingly ceremonious, with abilities not much above the common.[41]

Benjamin Langlois was a formal, old, confirmed bachelor, but Anne's tone of dread on George's behalf suggests something worse than mere tediousness. In any event, it seems very unlikely that Cork Street will have been a congenial scene for Anne to engineer a lovers' meeting.

The Tom Lefroy episode occurred many years after Anne and Jane (then a young girl) first became friends. Claire Tomalin, whose 1997 biography of Jane Austen was ground-breaking, laments that we do not have more detail about the early days of the relationship between Anne and Jane.

> While Jane's adult letters mention Mrs Lefroy as hostess or fellow guest, and we hear of her calling on the Austens for informal conversation, no solid picture of her character or of the exchanges between the young woman and the clever child appears; we have to take on trust the way in which she demonstrated her early friendship.[42]

To some extent, we are forced to read back the relationship from Jane Austen's famous lament for Anne, written four years after her death in 1804 (reproduced in a later chapter). In this poem, Jane indicates that Anne had singled her out, as a young girl, for support and encouragement:

Can ought enhance such Goodness? – Yes, to me,
Her partial favour from my earliest years
Consummates all. –Ah! Give me yet to see
Her Smile of Love – the Vision disappears...[43]

This is the most emotional that Jane Austen, *in propria persona*, ever gets. By contrast, in her (surviving) letters to Cassandra, her tone is almost uniformly light-hearted and mocking of both herself and others. Clearly, not only did Jane appreciate Anne's interest and involvement, but she felt that Anne had singled her out with kindness.

There was, however, a major asymmetry in the friendship, not only because of the age difference between them. Anne was not really a 'young woman' in the 1780s; she was about 40 in March 1787. Jane was 11 in that year, turning 12 in December 1787. We can only assume that Anne encouraged Jane in her writing, the brilliant juvenilia she was to produce in her teens, but we have no direct evidence about this. Further, Anne was the wife of the Rector of Ashe; a mother; a friend of the Boltons: Jane was simply one of the Miss Austens, and not even the elder of those.

Against the emotional power of Jane's lament must be set the surviving evidence from both Jane's letters about Anne, and Anne's letters about Jane. These are very far from expressing deep attachment. In the surviving 161 letters from Jane Austen collected in Deirdre Le Faye's standard edition, Le Faye lists only eleven references to Anne Lefroy.

Letter 1, 10 January 1796: '[Tom Lefroy] ran away when we called on Mrs Lefroy a few days ago.'[44]

Letter 11, 17-18 November 1798, as discussed above, the letter in which Anne's visit is described, with Jane's reluctance to bring up the subject of Tom.[45]

Letter 14, 18-19 December 1798: 'I took care to tell Mrs Lefroy of your calling on her Mother, & she seemed pleased with it.' Cassandra was at Godmersham, some twenty miles west of Wootton. It may have involved some effort for Cassandra to have called on the widowed Jemima Brydges; perhaps it was en route to Godmersham, rather than a special journey. Jane does not seem sure about Anne's reaction ('she seemed pleased'), so the whole effect here is rather less satisfactory than might have been expected.[46]

Yet it is Anne's anticipated absence from an upcoming ball which makes Jane, later in the same letter, irritated with both herself and the world:

> I expect a very stupid Ball, there will be nobody worth dancing with, & nobody worth talking to but Catherine [Bigg]; for I beleive [*sic*] Mrs Lefroy will not be there; Lucy [Lefroy] is to go with Mrs Russell.[47]

So clearly Jane still relied on Anne for interesting local conversation.

Letter 15, 24-26 December 1798, describes the said ball. Jane lists her partners, including George Lefroy junior, and notes with surprise that she enjoyed dancing all twenty dances on the night.

> My black Cap was openly admired by Mrs Lefroy, & secretly I imagine by every body else in the room.[48]

Here, evidently, Anne has gone out of her way to compliment Jane, evidence of her desire to make people happy.

Letter 16, 28 December 1798. In a letter otherwise full of the news of the promotion of brother Frank to Commander of the sloop *Petterel* ('If you don't buy a muslin Gown now on the strength of this Money [an allowance from the Rev George Austen], & Frank's promotion, I shall never forgive You'), Jane adds another kind thought from Anne:

> Mrs Lefroy has just sent me word that Lady Dortchester means to invite me to her Ball on the 8th of January, which tho' an humble Blessing compared with what the last page records, I do not consider as any Calamity.[49]

Here Anne seems to have been passing on a compliment, rather than giving it herself. Characteristically, Anne evidently values the patronage of Lady Dortchester on Jane's behalf. Presumably this is Lady Dorchester, born Maria Howard, wife of Guy Carleton, first Baron Dorchester (1724–1808), governor of Quebec. He had been Wolfe's quartermaster-general in the Quebec action of 1759, and subsequently served in several campaigns. His daughter Maria was married to William Orde-Powlett, second Baron Bolton (1782–1850), so the connection may have been made through Anne's friends the Hackwood family.[50]

Perhaps both this, and the kind comment about Jane's cap, are of a pattern of gradual atonement for whatever role Anne may have played in separating Tom from his entanglement. They may even indicate some regret for having played such a role.

Letter 18, 21–23 January 1799. Jane's letter is full of her brother Charles Austen, who has been staying at Steventon but was now on his way to his ship, the *Tamar*; 19-year-old Charles had made a stir among the Austen friends and neighbours:

> Martha [Lloyd] writes me word that Charles was very much admired at Kintbury, and Mrs Lefroy never saw anyone so much improved in her life, and thinks him handsomer than Henry. He appears to far more advantage here than he did at Godmersham, not surrounded by strangers and neither oppressed by a pain in his face or powder in his hair.[51]

This, again, sounds rather as though Anne may have been attempting to appease Jane by flattering Charles, although it might be questionable whether any disparagement of Henry would invite favour with Jane. It is also rather faint praise to consider Charles 'much improved,' indicating some (unspecified) previous deficiencies (rather as Jane and Cassandra had found George junior 'well-behaved now' in 1796).

This can only be speculation, but Jane's next reference to Anne is decidedly lukewarm.

Letter 20, 2 June 1799:

> I am quite pleased with Martha & Mrs Lefroy for wanting the pattern of our Caps, but I am not so well pleased with Your giving it to them –. Some wish, some prevailing Wish is necessary to the animation of everybody's Mind, & in gratifying this, You leave them to form some other which will not probably be half so innocent.[52]

Even if we allow for Jane's humorous approach, there would appear to be a distinct residue of resentment here, almost of suspicion about the motivations of Martha and Anne. This would gel with the impression given by the previous references, in which Anne almost seems to flatter Jane.

Letter 24, 1 November 1800. Jane describes Lord and Lady Portsmouth's ball. Three groups of friends – the Harwoods, Mrs Bramston, and Anne – had offered to convey Jane to the ball. This was, again, a flattering attention on their part.

Conversation between Jane and Anne had revealed:

> A deaf Miss Fonnereau is at Ashe, which has prevented Mrs Lefroy's going to Worting or Basingstoke during the absence of Mr Lefroy.[53]

Miss Fonnereau will have been a connection of the Lefroys' old Livorno business associate, also of Huguenot origin, Henry Fonnereau. Deirdre Le Faye identifies one branch of the Fonnereau family as having lived at Reading, and possibly another at Wargrave, Berkshire (the village immortalised as the scene of Lord Barrymore's theatre, described in Part Two).[54]

Letter 31, 14-16 January 1801. Jane writes to Godmersham clearly in response to a letter from Cassandra:

> Mrs Milles flatters herself falsely; it has never been Mrs Rice's wish to have her son settled near herself – & there is now a hope entertained of her relenting in favour of Deane. Mrs Lefroy & her son in law were here yesterday; she tries not to be sanguine, but he was in excellent Spirits. – I rather wish they may have the Curacy. It will be an amusement to Mary to superintend their Household management, & abuse them for expense, especially as Mrs L[efroy] means to advise them to put their washing out.[55]

Mrs Sarah Rice (1755–1841) was the mother of Henry Rice, who was to marry Lucy Lefroy six months after this letter (so was not, technically, yet the son-in-law of Anne). Jane is contradicting the theory of Mrs Milles, a Canterbury connection, that Mrs Rice wished her son and his wife-to-be to settle near her in Kent.[56] The question, rather, was whether Henry Rice would be allocated the curacy of Deane, which duly occurred. As Rector of Steventon at that period, James Austen would have some supervision over the curate of Deane. This is why Jane relishes the thought of James' wife Mary casting a disapproving eye upon Lucy and Henry's lavish housekeeping. Anne's advice to the couple to put their washing out, to have it washed by a professional washerwoman, may indicate a desire to 'keep up appearances'.

Jane's comment about the differing demeanours of Anne and Henry Rice is revealing. Henry Rice was perpetually sanguine: his high spirits and evident charm had captivated Anne from an early period. Yet presumably she saw more obstacles in the future than he did, and thus tried to moderate his restless optimism.

The comment also reveals the perceptiveness of Jane as a writer. It was her intuition for interpreting the feelings and personalities of others which would help to lend greatness to her novels. She is observing Anne, here, as a character, not necessarily as a friend.

That was the last reference in Jane Austen's letters to Anne during the latter's lifetime. The next (and last) letter in which she is mentioned is from November 1813, nearly nine years after Anne's death, in which Jane, then staying at Godmersham, met Charlotte Harrison, one of Anne's sisters. Anne's youngest surviving sibling Charlotte Brydges (1765–1849) had married first Champion Branfill (d. 1792), with whom she had a son and a daughter, Jemima-Elizabeth; and secondly John Harrison (d. 1818), with whom she had no children.[57]

Letter 96, 6-7 November 1813.

> When the Concert was over, Mrs Harrison & I found each other out & had a a [*sic*] very comfortable little complimentary friendly Chat. She is a sweet Woman, still quite a sweet Woman in herself, & so like her Sister! – I could almost have thought I was speaking to Mrs Lefroy. – She introduced me to her Daughter, whom I think pretty, but most dutifully inferior to La Mere Beauté.[58]

It must have been a strange, almost spiritual experience for Jane to meet somebody whose resemblance to the long-deceased Anne was so intense.

Jane Austen's 1808 poem showed that any resentment she may have felt about the part played by Anne in ending the Tom Lefroy affair had long since been softened, with only deep love and respect for Anne remaining. By the time Jane Austen came to write *Persuasion*, towards the end of her own life, she had the insight and the consummate skill to portray Lady Russell as a loving, misguided, but ultimately sympathetic, actor in the drama of Anne Elliot and Captain Wentworth.

Chapter 2

Anne/Jane

If the references in Jane Austen's letters to Anne are limited and less emotional than we might expect, the same – only more so – can be said of Anne's references to Jane.

In a letter to her second surviving son, Christopher Edward, who was in his mid-teens, learning the ropes in Richard Clarke's law office in Newport, Isle of Wight, Anne wrote:

> Wednesday… the Miss Austens spent the day here – next week they mean to return to Bath & after that I suppose it will be long before they again visit Steventon.[1]

Since the early months of 1801, with the retirement of the Reverend George Austen, the Austen family had been exploring options for living in Bath. In June they took a tenancy of 4 Sydney Place, Bath, before setting off on a tour in Devonshire and later returning to Hampshire, visiting Manydown and Ashe.[2] Anne, therefore, is commenting on the fact that the Austens are now permanently, it would appear, removed from the immediate neighbourhood. It is difficult not to notice that she does not appear unduly concerned about the prospect. The fact that Cassandra and Jane spent the whole day with her, however, perhaps suggests the mutual desire for relaxed conversation prior to a lasting separation.

Another, presumably shorter, leave-taking visit took place at Steventon on the following Saturday 3 October.

> We dined at James Austens to take our leave of Mr & Miss Austens who are to return to Bath on Monday next –[3]

The next reference in Anne's letters is not until October 1803. Cassandra and Jane came to stay with George and Anne Lefroy.

Miss Austens have been with me these two or three days & I believe stay till Monday next I am now surrounded by my School & with the three Ladies in the room I can therefore only add Love from all...[4]

In writing that she was 'surrounded by [her] School,' Anne appears to mean that she had her village students working in the room as she wrote. If so, she may have made use of the Miss Austens as additional teachers for her village school, so they will have had to work for their accommodation. It is interesting to think of Jane Austen in the role of a teacher. Unlike her friend Anne Sharp, the governess of her nieces and nephews at Godmersham (children of her brother Edward Austen Knight), Jane had never quite been reduced financially to seeking paid teaching work. Nor was she, like the Rector's wife Anne Lefroy, expected to teach as a parish responsibility. Yet from what we know of her popularity with her nieces and nephews – who recalled the stories she told and the games she played with them – she would probably have been a successful teacher.

As Jane had grown up, their relationship will have changed; she was no longer the precocious child or the potential relative-by-marriage, but on a different footing, perhaps one with more authority. Within fourteen months after this visit, however, Anne was dead, and there could be no more development in their friendship; only nostalgia for what was, and disappointment for what might have been.

The Austen family members who appear most regularly in Anne's letters are the Reverend James Austen and his wife Mary. This is partly because of the fraternal relationship between James and George Lefroy, as Rectors of neighbouring parishes, but also because both James and Anne were always out and about, visiting friends and parishioners. In the hot June of 1801, Anne writes:

In the evening Rice drove Lucy to Basingstoke Mr L[efroy] rode the Poney, & I drove the Donky up the Lanes by Overton, as we returned we met J[ames] Austen who had been to call at Freefolk, & heard that John Portal was so ill that he had been obliged to leave home immediately, & was gone to Winchester to consult Dr Littlehales & from thence meant to proceed to the Isle of Wight for sea air-[5]

John Littlehales was a physician who had practised in Winchester for many years. He is commemorated by a memorial in Winchester Cathedral which includes a sculpture of the Good Samaritan, and records Littlehales' generosity, goodness to the poor, and the extent of his practice. He died in 1810 aged 57.[6]

There are several records of dining with James Austen or meeting the James Austens at dinners with other guests. In the summer of 1803, when all of southern England was in a fever of anticipation of an invasion by Napoleon, George Lefroy junior and James Austen joined forces in recruiting a local volunteer unit. Anne wrote to Christopher Edward:

> We found George [Lefroy junior] in a great bustle he & John Harwood & James Austen have been round the parishes of Ashe Deane Steventon & Hannington they have got a list of near 100 names your father & Holder have subscribed 50 pds each & John Harwood George & James Austen 10 each towards the expenses of raising this Company...[7]

In July 1803 James Austen was 38, so not likely to take part in paramilitary activities himself, but keen to contribute to a cause which, briefly, roused national and local energy among all groups in the community.

It was in her capacity as the village teacher and rector's wife that Anne took a particular interest in the fate of Robert Simmons, a local boy who had joined the navy and was serving with Charles Austen on the ship *Endymion*, under the Austens' relative Sir Thomas Williams. On 29 May 1801 she writes:

> I received today a message from Charles Austen to inform us that Bob: Simmons had turned out such a Thief that he had been obliged to dismiss him from his service, & reduce him to a common Sailor, & that Sir T[homas] Williams had ordered him the severest whipping, he had ever inflicted upon any man under his command; I am afraid he is incorrigibly bad – I will not mention this in the family lest his poor mother should hear it, & perhaps it may never reach her ears, the boy may not live to return, or if he does she may before he arrives, be taken from the evil that awaits her here – Charles Austen is going to Egypt, (at least so

he supposes) the Endymion is going out with sealed orders which are not be opened till they have passed the Lizard –[8]

Even allowing for Charles Austen's youth and inexperience, his lax approach to national security, or at very least his indiscretion – in speculating to friends about the contents of his commander's sealed orders – is surprising. Anne was forwarding these speculations to Christopher Edward on the Isle of Wight, and he no doubt passed them on to his employer Richard Clarke and others.

On the other hand, Charles may have been following orders in disseminating a deliberately misleading theory about the *Endymion*'s movements. Jane Austen noted that the ship had arrived in Portsmouth from its previous voyage on Sunday 24 May. On Wednesday 27 May she writes to Cassandra a similar account as Anne to Christopher Edward:

> The Endymion has already received orders for taking Troops to Egypt – which I should not like at all if I did not trust to Charles' being removed from her somehow or other before she sails. He knows nothing of his own destination he says, – but desires me to write directly as the Endymion will probably sail in 3 or 4 days.[9]

This sounds a little obscure, and perhaps we may give Charles the credit of muddying the waters about his own ultimate role at least. Or perhaps Charles already felt himself above such details as 'loose lips sink ships'. A year earlier, he had played a key role in the *Endymion*'s series of successful actions in capturing four enemy vessels, including his own capture, with a small group of men, of a privateer, *Le Scipio*.[10]

Bob Simmons' corporal punishment was particularly severe. Anne writes on 3 March 1802:

> I forgot to mention that Charles Austen told me that Bob: Simmons had behaved very well since his whipping which was uncommonly severe he had the honor to suffer in the presence of Prince Augustus who chose to stay upon deck & be a spectator of his punishment –[11]

It is unlikely that the presence of Prince Augustus (1773–1843) contributed much to the occasion. The Prince Augustus Frederick, Duke of Sussex, was known chiefly for having contracted an unauthorised marriage in Rome in 1793, subsequently annulled as he was under age and did not have his father's permission. He and Lady Augusta Murray then married at the highly fashionable St George's, Hanover Square, after banns were called to announce the occasion. This was an unusual proceeding, perhaps reflecting some remorse about their previous secret elopement; for members of the middle and upper classes, marriages usually took place by licence, a more private proceeding than 'banns', which meant a public announcement in church.[12]

Charles' account of Bob Simmons' distressing conduct in the service may ultimately have contributed to Jane Austen's masterly depiction of the late Richard Musgrove, whom Captain Wentworth in *Persuasion* (1818) did his best to mentor, with no success; a hopeless lad whose mother, nonetheless, is convinced that he was merely unlucky in his naval service.

At any rate, Charles seems to have regarded Anne Lefroy as something of a confidante. As well as discussing the Simmons case with her, he told her about another shipboard scandal. In March 1802, Charles Austen was on a brief leave:

[He] had got a few days leave of absence from his Ship in order to appear as a witness to speak to the good character of Lieut:nt Lutwich who is to be tried at Winchester for the murder of a Sailor by striking him with the tiller of the Boat so as to fracture his skull –[13]

The account of the case in the *Hampshire Chronicle* gave the following version of events:

The circumstances were that Lieutenant [Henry] Lutwedge, having been sent ashore with a boat crew of 12, then received a note from his Captain to return to the ship [HMS *Resistance*] immediately. Lutwedge ordered the men into the boat but most were in liquor. Lutwedge told them to pull hard as the wind and tide were against them but one seaman, Fagan, took no notice as he was drunk. Lutwedge struck him on the arm and on the head and he fell. Two sailors carried him on board and put him in his hammock but next morning he was found to be dead. Rumours spread that he had been murdered. Several naval officers gave Lutwedge excellent character references.

Lutwedge was convicted of manslaughter, then sentenced to pay a fine of £100, and to be imprisoned for three months.[14] Anne will have been very interested, as one of her hobbies was to attend the Winchester Assizes and hear the matters tried:

> [Henry] Rice drove me in his curricle to Winchester as I like hearing some of the Trials at the Law [Assize] in the Justices Box...[15]

It is also possible that Anne took a particular interest in conversing with Charles Austen, because he was young enough to be some kind of a substitute for her absent sons Christopher Edward and Ben. Clearly, Henry Rice also fulfilled this role to an extent.

It is certainly noteworthy that we read much more about Charles than about his sisters Jane or Cassandra in Anne's letters. However, Anne was also targeting her subject matter to what she thought would interest 16-year-old Christopher Edward: bad behaviour, flogging, murder charges, and naval movements fitted the bill, whereas literary or religious discussion with Jane Austen would not have appealed.

There may be another factor at play. We have seen how much Anne valued the friendship of the Boltons and the patronage of Lady Dorchester. There is also the remark from the waspish Benjamin Langlois, in his instructions to his executors:

> I leave to Mrs George Lefroy my triple magnifying glass mounted in mother-of-pearl and set in silver gilt, which at the same time that it may be useful to her in her botanical amusements, may recall to her mind one who since he had the honor [sic] of being allied to her, has much valued many of her excellent qualities as a warm friend, an affectionate wife, and a tender mother, and though he has often lamented the excess so prejudicial with respect to the advancement of

her sons in life, to which her maternal affection has been carried, he could not help respecting the motive.[16]

In other words, Anne was perceived to flatter the great in her desire for the worldly advancement of her sons. On this basis the Austens, and particularly the female Austens, were not important enough to merit as much attention as the Boltons and their ilk. Despite her verses regularly, and conventionally, decrying worldly status and success in favour of virtue and religion, it does appear as if Anne had a streak of that family failing, a tendency to overvalue and flatter those of noble rank. It was certainly the prevailing flaw of her brother, Samuel Egerton Brydges, and will be discussed in Part Two.

If we wish to enter into the world of Jane Austen and Anne Lefroy, we need to survey their family history in the way that their contemporaries would have. For women, in particular, who had no professions and often brought little wealth to a marriage, lineage was a form of inheritance and a source of pride. Part Two of this book will sketch out that family background which was of such vital importance to clans such as the Brydges, the Langlois, and the Lefroys.

This kind of survey has been well and thoroughly performed for Jane Austen by her biographers; notably Claire Tomalin in her 1997 work and, in a number of important books, Deirdre Le Faye. The late Jon Spence also made a considerable contribution with *A Century of Wills from Jane Austen's family 1705–1806* (published by the Jane Austen Society of Australia in 2001). It is the purpose of Part Two of this book to cover this essential background for Anne Lefroy. If we wish to understand the woman who inspired Jane Austen's most explicitly emotional expressions, we should look at the places and the people among whom Anne Brydges Lefroy grew up, married, and lived.

Part Two

Anne Before Jane

Chapter 3

Egertons and Brydges:
The Castlehaven Scandal

Anne was the eldest child of Edward Brydges of Wootton Court in Kent, and his wife Jemima, née Egerton, a daughter of the Reverend William Egerton of Penshurst, also in Kent. The Reverend William was of noble descent. His grandfather was John Egerton (1623–1686), the second Earl of Bridgewater.

The first Earl of Bridgewater, John Egerton (1579–1649) was married to Lady Frances Stanley, a daughter of the Earl of Derby. Lady Frances and her sister Anne Stanley were direct descendants of Henry VIII's sister Mary Tudor, and thus were potential claimants to the English throne.

Despite these royal connections, the Egertons and Stanleys found themselves in one of the most scandalous episodes in the history of the British nobility. Because of these events, Anne Stanley herself – a foremother of Anne Brydges Lefroy's – has found an increasingly important place in women's legal history.

In 1608, she married Gray Brydges (c. 1579–1621), fifth Baron Chandos of Sudeley (a peerage which will make numerous appearances in this book). They had at least five children. Chandos died suddenly in 1621.

Anne Stanley's second husband was Mervyn Touchet (1593–1631), Earl of Castlehaven, also previously married with children. One of Anne's daughters, Elizabeth (probably aged only about 13) was married to one of Castlehaven's sons, Lord Audley. In 1630, Lord Audley made sensational claims to the Privy Council that his father was planning to disown his own children and had encouraged a servant, Giles Brodway, to rape his wife, Anne, and make her pregnant. It was also alleged that servants had been urged to rape young Elizabeth.

Rape within marriage did not exist as an offence; Castlehaven's crime was ordering and enabling Anne's and Elizabeth's rapes by others. The countess said that her rape was the final act in a marriage which had been abusive from the start.[1]

Witnesses gave evidence that Castlehaven had had sexual relations with servants of both sexes. Formally charged with rape and sodomy, he was tried in a hearing which lasted only one day. Anne did not give evidence. Castlehaven was found guilty and beheaded in May 1631 on Tower Hill, maintaining his innocence. Giles Brodway was found guilty of rape and also beheaded; Lawrence Fitzpatrick, another servant with whom Castlehaven had had a relationship, was found guilty of sodomy and also put to death.

Anne Stanley lived on money saved from her first marriage, as well as support from her mother and brothers-in-law, and withdrew from public life. She died in 1647.

It has been conjectured that the poet John Milton's masque, *Comus* (1634) refers to the Castlehaven case. Its first performance was before Anne Brydges' direct ancestor John Egerton, the first Earl of Bridgewater and brother-in-law of Anne Stanley. Egerton family members acted parts in the masque. It has been conjectured that *Comus*, a work with a strong emphasis on chastity, was an attempt to restore some virtue to the house of Egerton. *Comus* is also important because of the special status of Milton, the leading Protestant English poet, in the cultural and literary inheritance of the eighteenth century, and therefore of relevance to Anne Brydges.

The opening address of *Comus* sets the scene. An Attendant Spirit describes the genesis of Comus, son of Dionysus through a union with the enchantress Circe. Circe was known from Homer's *Odyssey* as the magician who turned Odysseus' sailors into animals, and, in parallel, we are told, intemperance leads people into the guise of beasts.[2] Enter Comus:

> Comus enters with a Charming Rod in one hand, his Glass in the other, with him a rout of Monsters headed like sundry sorts of wilde Beasts, but otherwise like Men and Women, their Apparel glistering, they com in making a riotous and unruly noise, with Torches in their hands.[3]

Among other deities, Comus calls upon Cotytto: 'Hail Goddesse of Nocturnal sport / Dark vail'd Cotytto' (lines 128–129). In ancient Greek culture, Cotytto was a Thracian goddess. Her rites, which in time became established in Athens, involved extreme sexual activity combined with consumption of alcohol.[4] In the context of the Egerton masque, this mention of Cotytto and her ritual is very likely to refer to the recent horrific scandal. The fact that Cotytto was one persona of Persephone, who was raped by the underworld god Hades, is also probably a reference to the Castlehaven crimes.

As the revellers move on, a Lady wanders in, played in the first performance by the earl's teenage daughter Alice Egerton. She muses:

> A thousand fantasies
> Begin to throng into my memory
> Of calling shapes and beckning [sic] shadows dire...
> (lines 205–7).

Here, too, there seems to be a sense of recent disaster. Comus, overhearing, is struck by her beauty and innocence, and offers to escort her to safety in a 'loyal cottage.' She responds:

> Shepherd I take thy word,
> And trust thy honest offer'd courtesie,
> Which oft is sooner found in lowly sheds
> With smoaky rafters, than in tapstry [sic] Halls
> And Courts of Princes, where it first was nam'd,
> And yet is most pretended... (lines 321–326)

Again, it would appear that the contrast between the nobility of the Egerton-Stanleys and the bizarre nature of the scandal is being pointed up.

The Lady's brothers (played in the first performance by Alice Egerton's younger brothers) discuss what might have befallen her. They conclude that their sister's chastity will have lent her a hidden strength to withstand whatever violence might have been offered:

> [Eld. Bro] My sister is not so defenceless left
> As you imagine, she has a hidden strength
> Which you remember not.

> [2 Bro] What hidden strength,
> Unless the strength of Heav'n, if you mean that?
> [Eld. Bro] I mean that too, but yet a hidden strength
> Which if Heav'n gave it, may be term'd her own:
> 'Tis chastity, my brother, chastity:
> She that has that, is clad in compleat steel… (lines 414–421).

Suddenly eloquent, the rustic Brother cites the powers of Diana, virgin goddess of the hunt, and of Minerva, with the Gorgon's head on her shield, as evidence of the prophylactic quality of virginity.

Without entering into a cultural history of the concept of chastity – which could take up a book on its own – it is important to realise that within it, was a belief that women were, in part, responsible for any sexual violence which they might suffer. The Brother's next statements make it clear that a woman who takes part in sexual activity is effectively de-souled.

> But when lust
> By unchaste looks, loose gestures, and foul talk,
> But most by leud [*sic*] and lavish act of sin,
> Lets in defilement to the inward parts,
> The soul grows clotted by contagion,
> Imbodies, and imbrutes, till she quite loose
> The divine property of her first being… (lines 463–469).

With the assistance of the Attendant Spirit, and Sabrina the spirit of the Severn River, the Brothers rescue their sister from the captivity of Comus. Sabrina lends both local geographical colour and a link with the classical world, as she was supposed to have been the granddaughter of the Roman Brutus, through his son Locrinus, legendary King of England, and hence descended from the people of Troy.[5]

Milton scholars since the 1970s have been divided about the extent to which the Castlehaven scandal lay in the background of *Comus*. Barbara Breasted in 1971 first explored the issues in detail, followed by Rosemary Karmelich Mundhenk in 1975.[6] Others push back, expressing a view that the Castlehaven crimes were simply too horrifying to have been referenced, literally, in the mouths of the young Egertons.

In 1987 John Creaser put forward such a view, citing Jane Austen's *Mansfield Park* (1814), which features the same awkwardness about well-brought-up young ladies uttering sexually suggestive lines while acting a part in a play. Yet Creaser also acknowledged that Milton 'dealt most adroitly with an invidious issue'. In other words, even if not directly referenced, the Castlehaven horrors were the unspoken elephant in the room.

The importance of the case to women's history was highlighted, perhaps inadvertently, by Creaser. In terms reminiscent of much less enlightened times than 1987, he described the Stanley women (Anne and her daughter Elizabeth, both victims of rape) as 'corrupted and inured to their violation'.[7] This, in case it has to be spelt out, is victim-blaming of a classical kind.

It is also surprising that it took until 2002 for the critic Ross Leasure to point out that the depiction of Comus as a sexually-ambiguous figure meant that it was therefore very likely to have been intended to stand as a portrait (if not a caricature) of the Earl of Castlehaven. Comus, like the earl, clearly represents a predator to people of both sexes – even those as young as the Lady and her brothers. It was not only young Alice who had to utter sexually suggestive lines; as indicated earlier, her primary-school aged brothers were obliged to discuss the merits of virginity. Viewed in this light, it seems clear that the masque was, in some way, a literal 'acting out', an exposure, of the family scandal.[8]

Cynthia Herrup, the principal historian of the Castlehaven case, has emphasised the extent to which the earl's crimes went beyond instances of rape and sodomy; they exposed a radical failure by an English lord to act his proper role as a patriarch. He violated, rather than protected, his household. This aspect assists in explaining the fact that he was convicted on the evidence of women and servants, not witnesses whose testimony would normally wield much social weight against the status of an earl.[9] The scandal also touched on corruption within the monarchy. Anne Stanley Brydges Touchet and Frances Stanley Egerton were of royal blood. Not only that, but the earl's homosexual relationships recalled a little too closely the affairs of King James I with his male partners, including George Villiers.[10]

The Castlehaven affair, with its elements of radical betrayal, rape in marriage, child rape, violence, and same-sex relationships, represented the kind of family episode which later Egertons and Brydges wished entirely to erase. It was never entirely scrubbed from the record (during the eighteenth and early nineteenth century it appeared in several editions of legal reference works on state trials), but has received attention in recent years as part of a focus on women's and LGTBI history. Homosexual acts between consenting adult men were decriminalised under the Sexual Offences Act 1967, while it was not until 1991 that rape in marriage formally became a crime in Britain. Until made redundant by legislation, 'Castlehaven' was the leading case behind an injured wife's right to testify.[11]

John Egerton the second earl's third son, Thomas Egerton of Tatton Park (b. 1651), was the maternal great-grandfather of Anne Brydges Lefroy. Thomas' third son, William Egerton, was born in 1682. Anne's brother Samuel Egerton Brydges (1762–1837), who edited and reissued *Collins' Peerage*, may have done so in part to celebrate his own Egerton ancestry. In that work, Samuel happily reports this epitaph account of his and Anne's maternal grandfather, on his tomb in the church at Penshurst, Kent:

Here lies the body of William Egerton, L.L.D. He was grandson of John, [second] Earl of Bridgewater, but received less honour from his noble descent, than from his own personal qualifications; for he had a strong memory, and most excellent parts, both which were greatly improved by a learned education; and as his birth gave him an opportunity of being brought up and living in the best company; so he made a suitable improvement from it, happily mixing the knowledge of the scholar with the politeness of the gentleman. He had talents peculiarly fitted for conversation; for, with a great vivacity, he had a command and fluency of words, which he well knew how to express to such advantage, as might make him either entertaining or instructive. Thus accomplished, it is no wonder he was distinguished in his profession; being made chaplain to two succeeding Kings, rector of Penshurst, and All-hallows, Lombard-street, chancellor and prebendary of Hereford, and prebendary of Canterbury. He left behind him two daughters and one son, by Anne, daughter of Sir Francis Head, Bart. who caused this marble to be laid down as a slender testimony of her gratitude and affection to the memory of the best of husbands. He died February 26th, 1737, aet. fifty-five.[12]

A prebendary is a senior clergyman who has an administrative role connected with an Anglican or Roman Catholic cathedral.

The lavishness of this biography of William contrasts with the sparing account of his widow, Anne Head Egerton (d. 1778). As was usual for a woman, the emphasis is on duty and agreeableness, not on talent or achievement.

> Near this place lieth the body of Anne, relict of William Egerton, L.L.D. She died March 5th, 1778, aged seventy-four. The constant tenor of her life was the best preparation for death, as she was eminently distinguished for discharging every duty in life in the most amiable manner, and upon the purest motives. All her knew her, loved and revered her, and must sooner or later be happy, if they follow her example.[13]

William and Anne's children were John (b.c. 1723), Charlotte (b.c. 1727) and Anne's mother Jemima (b.c. 1728).[14] John tragically contracted smallpox while on a visit to the London house of his maternal uncle, Sir Francis Head. He died from the illness, aged only 17, in November 1740.[15]

The loss of young John Egerton was commemorated in a lengthy poem by his friend Osmund Beauvoir (d. 1789), Doctor of Divinity and at one time a 'master of the free-school at Canterbury', which may or may not be the same King's School where several Brydges and Lefroys attended.[16] Samuel Egerton Brydges quoted the entire elegy with relish, but a sample will suffice here.

> Elegy, to the memory of John Egerton, Esq. who died November 1740, aet. seventeen. By Dr. Osmund Beauvoir.
> Permit, blest shade, the pious Muse to pay
> This humble tribute of the mournful lay;
> With artless grief thy hopeless fate to mourn,
> With widow'd cypress shade thy hallow'd urn;
> With short liv'd flowers to deck thy verdant grave-
> What more can she bestow, or you receive!...[17]

This tragic death of her uncle in his teens was probably a motivating factor in Anne Brydges Lefroy's project, discussed in a later chapter, of vaccinating family, friends and community members against smallpox, once a vaccine was developed by Edward Jenner later in the century. It was also a constant reminder of the fragility of young life, a fact of which Anne would constantly be aware.

The death of their brother left Charlotte and Jemima as the co-heirs to their father's estate. Charlotte married William Hammond of St Albans Court, Kent, and died in 1770. Their son, also William, inherited St Albans Court.[18]

Jemima married Edward Brydges, of Wootton Court, also in Kent. Samuel Egerton Brydges, whose view of his family background was forever coloured by his sense of his own utter superiority to his surroundings, was later to describe his and Anne's father in the following unflattering terms:

> a stern-minded man, a severe reasoner and a man of business, but grave and unimaginative.[19]

In the second volume of his autobiography, Samuel gives a few more hints about his father's personality: he had been a keen sportsman in his youth (in the sense of shooting sports), and he was not such a passionate Whig as some of his neighbours.[20]

Edward Brydges, who worked in family businesses in Canterbury, had co-inherited Wootton Court with his brother John. Passing through various families over many centuries, the manor of Wootton was bequeathed in 1704 to their father John Bridges. After John's death in 1712, his surviving elder sons both inherited, and resided together at Wootton Court.[21] Edward Brydges was described as having retired to Wootton at a young age, 'to enjoy the tranquillity of a country life.'[22] The Brydges family background will be described in more detail in the chapter 'Samuel's Claim', covering Samuel Egerton Brydges' attempts to allege noble ancestry on his father's side.

John Brydges, unmarried, died in April 1780; Edward Brydges, married to Jemima and having numerous children, survived his brother only by months, dying in November 1780.[23]

Anne was the eldest of Edward and Jemima's surviving children. Her christening is recorded as having taken place on 22 March 1747.[24] Many siblings followed. Edward Timewell (or Tymewell) was born in 1749;[25] Jane in 1750; John in 1752 (died in infancy); Deborah in 1755; John Egerton in 1758 (also died in infancy); Charlotte Jemima, known as Jemima, in 1759; Samuel Egerton in 1762; John William Head in 1764; and Charlotte, born 1766.[26]

We know little about the life of Edward and Jemima and their family at Wootton, but it seems to have been very quiet indeed. At the time of their marriage, in 1747, the passage from the hall to the kitchen at Wootton was given a renovation with some fresh wallpaper. We learn this from evidence given by Jemima in a much later House of Lords Privileges Committee hearing, relative to Samuel's pretensions to a peerage.[27] 'Very ancient', that is apparently Tudor, elements were said to have survived within the fabric of Wootton Court.[28]

Wootton was certainly retired, indeed remote. In the year 800, Cenulf, King of Mercia, and his wife Cengitha, gave the ploughlands of 'Geddinge and Wodetone' to Archbishop Athelard.[29] A survey of Kent published in 1800 gives a sense of the isolation of the small and ancient parish of Wootton.

> The parish of Wootton lies very obscurely and unfrequented, among the high mountainous hills of the eastern part of Kent, and like the adjoining parishes is much covered with frequent coppice wood. The soil is … very poor, consisting of chalk, or an unfertile red earth, but both covered with quantities of sharp flint stones. The village, called Wootton-street, containing about eight houses, lies on very high ground, nearly in the middle of it, having the parsonage on one side of it, and the court lodge and church on the other.[30]

An engraving from the late eighteenth century shows a Georgian mansion with a protruding portico, any pretensions to elegance offset by the two shepherds pasturing a small flock just out the front.[31] It must have been as quiet a place to spend a childhood as can be imagined.

An agricultural report on Kent was published in 1796, prepared by John Boys, who was a farmer at Betteshanger, a parish to the west of Deal, and some ten miles north-east from Wootton.[32] His account of the country can assist us to envisage the Kent in which Anne and her siblings grew up.

Readers of Jane Austen's letters will recall her ironic references to her visits to her brother Edward Austen Knight, at Godmersham, as sojourns in 'East Kent wealth.'[33] She was apparently referencing a local Kent saying, quoted in the agricultural report:

> The inhabitants divide the county [Kent] into three parts, East, Middle, and West Kent; and, according to the ancient

provincial adage, West Kent is healthy, but not wealthy; East Kent is wealthy, but not healthy; but Middle Kent is both healthy and wealthy.[34]

If Godmersham counted as East Kent, then Wootton must have qualified even more readily, as it is some twenty miles to the east of Godmersham (further by road, as indicated by Google Maps).

As an indicator of the relative climate of this part of Kent, we read that the harvest was early, by mid-July, in the northern parts such as the Isle of Sheppey; a week or so later, in the stretch between Canterbury and Dover, in which Wootton lies; and a week later still in the colder areas to the south-west.[35]

The soils were chalky and often poor. There were also patches of bog.[36] In the later eighteenth century, Kent lagged behind other counties in the enclosure of common lands. John Boys complained that,

> Our commons for live stock are generally much covered with furze, thorns, brakes, or heath, with a mixture of plots of poor grass-land; the cattle and sheep feeding upon them, are of course in a half-starved state … There have been some exertions for accomplishing a division and enclosure of an extensive common in East Kent, within these few years; which failed for want of unanimity among the persons concerned.[37]

It is hard to reconcile these comments with East Kent's reputation for wealth. Kent's proximity to London meant that local prices were closely tied to those at Smithfield or Mark Lane markets. John Boys quotes prices for December 1795 of mutton 6*d* per lb, bacon 8*d* per lb, 'good Cheshire cheese' 7*d* per lb; potatoes 8 to 10*s* a sack of 200 lb, and so on.[38]

The collection of tithes, the privilege of exacting a tenth of farm revenues for the benefit of the local clergy, apparently caused resentment among the Kent farmers, more so than in other parts of England:

> An unfortunate circumstance which I found to be corroborated, about that time, by the low estimation in which the clergy were held, at market meeting, by the higher

class of occupiers, in that County; – comparatively, I mean, with what I have observed, in the rest of the kingdom.[39]

Growing of hops for beer was already an industry in Kent. Woodlands in East Kent furnished timber for shipbuilding, but most commonly poles for growing hops.[40] Barley, beans, and wheat were also grown.[41]

A farm worker's day ran from six in the morning till eleven, then from one o'clock to six in the evening, with a half hour break for breakfast if not eaten before work. Boys reports contemporary farm wages. A wagoner (with his own wagon) could earn from £10–13 a year including board. If married, and living off site, his wage was reduced to 10s per week. Women could earn 8d to 10d per day for weeding. 'Children, from ten to thirteen years old, 6d.' Boys adds that rural wages had doubled in the previous thirty years (i.e. since the 1760s).[42] Rural labourers and their families lived on bread, made from locally grown wheat, and bacon, most families fattening a pig over winter.[43]

In the eighteenth century, Wootton Court was apparently the centre of an estate of 600 acres, including parkland planted with specimen trees.[44] It presumably had tenant farmers and generated income, but there seems little specific information about this aspect of the property's history. Samuel Egerton Brydges, who could no doubt have provided this kind of data in his autobiographical works, failed to do so, no doubt because he thought such details beneath him.

Edward Brydges lived here in peace and seclusion, but the repeated deaths of Anne's younger siblings must have caused great grief. In the church at Wootton are memorial stones to two of her younger brothers.

On a Small white flat stone. John Egerton. Son of Edward and Jemima Bridges, ob. 27 Feb. 1758. Aged 1 Month.
On Another. John, Son of Edwd. and Jemima Bridges, ob. 26 of Mar. 1753. Aged 7 Months.[45]

Without naming her, Samuel wrote about his sister Anne:

My eldest sister was fourteen years and a half older than me: she had an exquisite taste for poetry, and could almost repeat the chief English poets by heart, especially Milton, Pope,

Collins, Gray, and the poetical passages of Shakespeare; and she composed easy verses herself with great facility.

Samuel added, since after all his subject was himself:

It is probable that her conversation and example contributed greatly to my early bent to poetry.[46]

Anne's occupations, then, were reading, writing, and helping to educate her numerous younger siblings. During the winter, the young Brydges would attend parties, dances and assemblies held in Canterbury. Dances were held every fortnight, and a 1779 letter from Lady Head, Anne's maternal great-aunt, suggests that even on turning 30, Anne was much admired at these gatherings:

Canterbury is gayer than ever, dancing once a fortnight, cards and routs all the week round; some people complain of being tired; but still go on. You have more compliments from hence than would fill this paper…[47]

Jane Head was at this stage 84 years old; John Lefroy reports that she 'first saw the light under William and Mary.'[48] William and Mary's co-regency lasted from 1688 to 1694, so Jane Head represented a relic from the seventeenth century – albeit one apparently very much alive.

Anne also spent considerable time on needlework, as women were expected to be able to make clothes for themselves and for others (for the needy, if not for their own family members). Anne was also a keen artist, painting works depicting insects and flowers.[49] According to the 1868 account published by her grandson Sir John Henry Lefroy (1817–1890), Anne was seen as 'charming and gifted.' Portraits indicated that most important of female attributes, 'the attractions of her person'.[50]

For his part, Samuel added:

My sister was one of the most amiable and eloquent women I ever knew, and was universally beloved and admired … She was fond of society, and was the life of every party into which she entered.[51]

The Lefroy family historian, John Lefroy, was less than flattering about Anne's surviving verses. In a comment which he must have felt was ungracious enough to be relegated to a footnote, he judged:

> Chris.[topher] Edward Lefroy collected and printed these verses, which, however, judged by the standard of the present day, do not entitle their author to any high place among female poets.[52]

Sir John was perhaps thinking of the female poets of the mid-nineteenth century: Elizabeth Barrett Browning (1806–1861) or Christina Rossetti (1830–1894). While Sir John could certainly perceive the stylistic differences wrought by a hundred years, it is striking that in her verses, Anne Brydges Lefroy examined some of the same themes which were to preoccupy the female poets of the next century; death, and resignation under hardship, are prominent. It is time to look at the verses which survive from Anne's youth, in the poetic context in which they were written, not to judge them by the creative norms of a century later.

Chapter 4

Poems of a Sister

Several years after Anne Lefroy died, her son Christopher Edward collected a number of her poems and published them in a private edition. Few copies of this book (1812) survive. On the title page, Christopher Edward points out that many of the poems were written by Anne early in her life:

> *Carmina Domestica*; or Poems on Several Occasions, (the Majority written in the early Part of Life), by Mrs Lefroy, of Ashe, in the county of Southampton, now printed, with some others, by her Son.[1]

Christopher Edward added epigraphs by Cowper and Xenophon. The Cowper extract reads:

> My boast is not that I deduce my birth,
> From loins enthroned, or rulers of the Earth;
> But higher far my proud pretensions rise,
> The son of Parents passed into the Skies.

The extract is from 'On the receipt of my Mother's picture out of Norfolk, the gift of my cousin, Ann Bodham' (1798). It was a highly evocative and influential work, giving voice to a profound nostalgia for childhood. Its recollection of a mother untimely deceased clearly possessed significance for Christopher Edward.

It is worth back-tracking for a moment to revisit the poets of the mid-eighteenth century, whose poems formed a large element of the mental furniture of educated people such as the Brydges family, but whose works are today known only to specialists. Samuel Egerton Brydges wrote that Anne was familiar with Milton, Pope, Collins, and Gray, as well as Shakespeare.

John Milton (1608–1674), we have already met, as the author of *Comus*. Milton's most famous work, *Paradise Lost* (1667), dealt with the fall of Adam and Eve from Eden, and of Satan from Heaven to Hell. The epic is in blank verse, a style which became strongly associated with Milton's verse.

For the modern reader, Milton, at least in his trademark epic, is the least accessible of the classic English poets. The themes of Satan, Original Sin, and female untrustworthiness (exemplified in Eve) are too particular to their era, and to Milton's own preoccupations as a Puritan ideologue. His shorter works, however, such as 'Methought I saw my late Espoused Saint', or 'Song on May Morning', or *Comus*, are far more readily appreciated; it is probably they, rather than *Paradise Lost*, which exerted such a key influence on poets of the next two centuries. The blank verse of *Paradise Lost* can seem less focused; the short pieces are supple, direct, and personal in tone.

That Milton may not have been a personal favourite of Jane Austen can perhaps be gauged by the fact that the only two mentions of him in her letters seem neutral, at best. The earlier is in her account of having met Stephen Lushington, Member of Parliament for Canterbury, while staying at Godmersham:

> Now I must speak of <u>him</u> – & I like him very much. I am sure he is clever & a Man of Taste. He got a vol. of Milton last night & spoke of it with Warmth. – He is quite an M.P. – very smiling, with an exceeding good address, & readiness of Language. – I am rather in love with him. – I dare say he is ambitious & insincere.[2]

Austen's implication is surely that Lushington was trying to show off with the Milton. Her other reference is in a letter to Anna Austen, in which she is attempting to make a tactful but still useful critique of her niece's writing:

> Newton Priors is really a Nonpareil. – Milton wd have given his eyes to have thought of it.[3]

The joke here, of course, is that Milton was actually blind. It sounds as if Austen was treating the second-greatest of national poets with something less than the reverence he might have been due, as the acknowledged prince of English Protestant letters.

Alexander Pope (1688–1744) was largely self-educated, but a published poet from a young age. His moral and philosophical poems, such as the *Essay on Man* (1733–34) became widely known. Pope's later satires were more controversial, including personal attacks, and it was probably the moral works which were commonplace in the Brydges household.

William Collins (1721–1759), in his own way, was as representative of his age as Milton was of his. Religious preoccupations had given way to broadly sociological ones. As it was for his older contemporary Montesquieu, for Collins the variety to be found in earthly human life was a more engrossing theme than the speculative denizens of Heaven and Hell which Milton had conjured up.

Collins' breakthrough work was the *Persian Eclogues* (1742), in which the shepherds and cameleers of Baghdad, while traversing the 'dreary Desarts', discourse – improbably perhaps – on love and virtue in English rhyming pentameter. Authenticity is applied through the use of footnotes: 'That these Flowers are found in very great Abundance in some of the provinces of Persia; see the *Modern History* of the ingenious Mr Salmon.'[4] The tone may be conveyed, in short, through the opening couplet of Eclogue the Fourth:

> In fair Circassia, where to Love inclin'd,
> Each Swain was blest, for ev'ry Maid was kind![5]

Collins published *Odes on several Descriptive and Allegorical subjects* in 1747. Within a few years, however, Collins had succumbed to alcohol abuse and mental illness. He died in the care of his sister in 1759.

Collins' contemporary Thomas Gray (1716–1771) was his partner in the eighteenth-century canon. A quiet, scholarly man, Gray only published a handful of poems during his lifetime. His most famous work, *Elegy written in a Country Churchyard*, begun in 1742, was eventually published in 1751, and became an instant bestseller. The quiet reflective themes led some to classify Gray as one of the 'Graveyard School' of poets, along with Oliver Goldsmith, William Cowper, and Christopher Smart. Of these, both Cowper and Smart suffered at times from mental disturbances.

William Cowper (1731–1800) was an unlikely candidate for the poet of the age immediately prior to that of Byron and Wordsworth, but this is what he was. Jane Austen made Cowper favourites of her characters Marianne Dashwood (*Sense and Sensibility*, 1811) and Fanny Price (*Mansfield Park*, 1814). Marianne and Fanny are both sensitive and literary souls; Marianne makes a point of being open and frank, and Fanny is portrayed as simple and naïve. Both, then, are suitable readers of Cowper.

Strangely, for a strong moral influence, Cowper, like his predecessor Collins, suffered intermittently from mental illness and suicidal thoughts. Some of his delusions related to religion; Cowper was strongly involved with a series of religious people of more-or-less Puritan, and certainly Dissenting, kinds. This was one of the ways in which he was subsequently seen as a forerunner of later poets, and certainly as a harbinger of the 'religious revival' of the early nineteenth century. It was almost certainly this aspect which was partly responsible for his popularity with strongly religious people such as Christopher Edward Lefroy.

Anne Lefroy's own juvenile verse was very much a product of this earlier generation. It has the regular beat and rhyming scheme of Pope. It was, as Samuel wrote, produced with apparent ease and facility. Anne adopted stock subjects such as a summons to a more moral life, to her circle of siblings and cousins. There is also the celebration of rural life over the empty attractions of the city, surely redundant in the isolation at Wootton.

Facile as such versifying can appear to the modern reader, it is important to realise that it represented a form of self-expression for Anne Brydges. Assisting her parents to bring up her surviving siblings, Anne demonstrated through her verse that she was not entirely defined by domestic duties. Her personality was not fully subsumed by her family, in the manner customary for young women.

It would seem that Christopher Edward Lefroy arranged his mother's poems broadly chronologically. The order in which they appear is as follows:

1. 'On seeing some school-boys playing in the Green-court, Canterbury'
2. 'Letter to I.B. Esq., Wootton Court'
3. 'To Miss D. and I.B., 1775'

4. 'Letter to her brothers Egerton and John Brydges when at school at Canterbury, written about the Year 1776'
5. 'Enigma'
6. 'To Miss Catharine Hammond'
7. 'Lines sent to the Duchess of Bolton, to excuse the Author from acting the Part of Alicia in *Jane Shore*, which the Duchess had requested her to undertake in a Play performed at Hackwood, about the year 1787, Lady Catherine [sic] Barry acted Jane Shore.'
8. 'To Henry Rice, sent with some bride cake, Drawn through the Ring, 1797, at which Time he was attending his sick Father'
9. 'Put into a Tooth Pick Case, given to H[enry] R[ice], when he left Ashe to go to Cambridge, 1796'
10. 'To her son, C[hristopher] E[dward] L[efroy] when with Richard Clarke, Esq. in the I[sle] of W[ight] dated Ashe, February 15, 1802'
11. 'A True Story versified, the Physician and Jack-Daw, or Christian Courtesy exemplified'
12. 'To C.E.L. on his Birth-Day'

(Christopher Edward Lefroy followed these poems of his mother's with several of his own.)

The first six poems fall broadly into the category of early works. Several were addressed to her siblings, although it is confusing to try to establish who was who. Number 2 ('Letter to I.B. Esq., Wootton Court') is presumably addressed to a male (females were never 'esquire'), yet Anne's surviving brother John (two infant Johns had already died) was only 10 years old in 1774, the year of the poem. He seems a little young to be lectured on relations between the sexes.

1. 'On seeing some school-boys playing in the Green-court, Canterbury'

Of warriors here a fancied train
With drum and fife advance;
While like their streamers light and vain
Their youthful spirits dance.

Perhaps 'mid this fantastic band
Some future Wolf may tread;

When time has nerv'd the infant hand,
And youth its roses shed.

Yon tiny elf on stilts upborne,
A giant stalks the green;
While, by those props that raise his form,
His youthful folly's seen.

'Tis thus when rais'd by wealth or birth,
To fill a lofty sphere;
The idle coxcomb's want of worth,
More plainly must appear.

The Green Court was part of the King's School in Canterbury, believed to be the oldest continually operating school in the world, having been founded in 597 CE, allegedly by St Augustine of Canterbury together with a monastery on the site.[6] The school's recorded history begins in the sixteenth century, with the dissolution of the monastery, and the re-founding of the school under a Royal Charter in 1541. The name 'King's School,' then, refers to Henry VIII, somewhat ironically as he had been responsible for the abolition of the school's former religious basis.

Anne's brothers attended the King's School. The register indicates their dates of admission:

Brydges, Edward Tymewell 1758
Brydges, John William Head 1775
Brydges, Samuel Egerton 1775.[7]

It is likely that Anne wrote her poem after visiting the school with one or other of her brothers, or in leaving them at, or collecting them from, the school. The Green Court was where the schoolboys undertook sports and games.

It may well have been through her brothers that Anne met the man she was to marry, Isaac Peter George Lefroy, who was registered at The King's School in 1755. Isaac Peter George's brother, Anthony, had been admitted in 1752. Henry Rice, future son-in-law of Anne and George, joined the school in 1784.[8]

In this poem, the observer of the boys has a sense of the mysterious potentiality present in children: what will become of them in later life? The observer is conscious that this potentiality can go either way: the young man may prove to be 'another Wolf[e],' or he may become just another pretentious 'coxcomb', a superficial time-waster.

The reference to General James Wolfe may help to date the poem. Wolfe died in the aftermath of the successful British siege of the French stronghold of Quebec City in 1759. Wolfe's victory was seen as a British triumph, yet Wolfe's own death, at the young age of 32, lent a poignant note. Curiously, as the wife of the rector of Ashe in Hampshire, Anne would later become friends with Katherine Lowther, the woman to whom Wolfe had been engaged prior to his death.

The pathos of Wolfe's death is surely echoed in Anne's poem. A boy may turn out a future war hero, but this is no unmixed blessing either to his family or his nation.

2. 'Letter to I.B. Esq., Wootton Court'

Written about the Year 1774, in Answer to one from Miss Sally Fagg, and I. and D.B. to A.L. in which they called her Letter to them a Sermon.

Tho' I hate making mischief and tell-tales detest,
Yet when once people make of good morals a jest,
I cannot help thinking their elders and betters,
Should strive to correct them by lectures and letters;
And I'll never believe the Grand Council at Court,
Know how of all order these youngsters make sport:
And first for Miss Sally, for all she's so meek,
And spite of that delicate blush on her cheek.
She talks with such glee of young St. Leger's charms;
That I own to my friendship she's given alarms.
Nay more be it spoke, to her utter disgrace,
She frankly confesses she's look'd in his face;
Whereas no young Lady, should ever be found,
To lift up her eyes from their station the ground;
But should by her silence and blushes discover,
She expects in each youth, that she meets with a lover;

And if no such offers, wherever she can,
She should rail at that terrible animal, Man;
But further, this Sally's so saucy and pert,
(I plainly perceive she's commenced errant flirt;)
That advice given in words, as sweet as dew on Mount Hermon,
She calls in her insolent manner a Sermon;
Than which there's no word in the language that bears,
An idea so dull to a fine lady's ears;
For thus I'm convinced should they meet with the word,
Would most ladies explain it where'er it occur'd;
A Sermon! 'tis only of nonsense a heap,
That can serve no good end but to put one to sleep;
Indeed when the preacher is handsome and young,
If we sometimes attend to what falls from his tongue;
'Tis not for the sake of the doctrine he teaches,
But only to see how he looks when he preaches;
And if we seem grave 'tis for grief such a face,
Should want the advantage of scarlet and lace;
'Tis thus they exclaim, and I fear this pert Sally,
If her heart could be seen, with these notions would tally;
To cure which I beg, if your worship has power,
You'll make her for penance sit silent an hour;
And my two saucy sisters, her aids and abettors,
You'll command both on Sunday to send me long letters:
For which if you'll do, your petitioner'll pray,
For your health and your welfare, by night and by day.

In this poem, Anne has responded to criticisms from her siblings and her friend, Sally Fagg, that she has read them 'a sermon' about flirting. We can infer that Anne's moralising was sometimes a little hard for her loved ones to endure without complaint. It would seem as if the younger Brydges girls were staying with Sally at the time, so were at a safe distance from their disapproving older sister.

In this light-hearted finger-wagging, however, Anne shows that her literary taste is right up to the minute. The moral tale for young people was a genre which was growing in popularity, and authors from Mary Collyer and Sarah Fielding in the mid-century, to Maria Edgeworth in following decades, made it a genre particularly associated with women writers.[9] Anne clearly felt responsible for the moral development of her younger sisters, and also their friend Sally.

Sally was probably Sarah, the daughter of baronet Sir William Fagg, possessor of estates in both Kent and Sussex. Sir William inherited the baronetcy in the mid-century, after the death without heir of a cousin. He married Elizabeth le Grand of Canterbury, and had a son (later Sir) John, as well as two daughters, Helen and Sarah.[10]

In February 1777, Sally married Edwyn-Humphrey Sandys, who died only five years later.[11] Was this youth of the elaborate name the original 'St. Leger' of Anne's poem?

Poem 3, 'To Miss D. and I.B. 1775' will be discussed in detail in a later chapter.

Poem 4, 'Letter to her brothers Egerton and John Brydges when at school at Canterbury, written about the Year 1776'

> I protest my dear boys, I've but little to say,
> Yet to write I'm resolv'd, if I study all day;
> Should I tell you the wonders, that Edward has done,
> What marvellous fêtes [*sic*] he's perform'd with his gun;
> You'd scarcely believe me in earnest I fear,
> Yet attend I entreat to the truths I declare,
> This morning (ere Phoebus had dawn'd in the east)
> With spirits elated, he left his soft nest,
> Not a partridge or landrayl he vow'd should go free,
> How his sisters lamented this cruel decree;
> We mourn'd the poor birds thus condemn'd to sad fate,
> But who the survivors complaints shall relate?
> Perhaps the fond pair who together at morn,
> Have travers'd the wood, or skimm'd over the lawn,
> E'er night her dark curtain has drawn o'er the scene,
> For ever divided with blood stain the green:
> But of Ned my relation seems quite at a stand,
> Know then, that two partridges died by his hand,
> And one Rayl felt his prowess and sunk on the land,

47

At five he return'd such a figure of fun,
His hair so dishevel'd, his gaiters undone;
So bloody his hands, and his face was so pale,
He look'd like the man who of Troy told the tale;
I'm convinc'd he was tired; but you lords of creation
Never own you're fatigu'd with this sweet recreation;
Tho' to dance for two hours, is quite killing you swear,
Such a bore as no youth of true spirit can bear;
'Tis so foolish thus after a fiddle to hop,
But these girls I'm convinc'd they would dance till they drop,
'Tis thus you exclaim, but to us you declare,
There's no pleasure so great as attending the fair;
Such practis'd deceivers, so used to beguile,
Tho' you curse us at heart, yet your faces can smile,
May you my dear boys, be more true and sincere,
From all kinds of deceit be your souls ever clear;
May each innocent pleasure still wait on your youth,
May your hearts be the temples of virtue and truth;
What more can I wish you? For honors and wealth,
Their want is supplied by contentment and health;
Those mighty distinctions which worldlings so prize,
Never shone with such lustre I own in my eyes;
Yet wealth when employ'd to alleviate distress,
Makes the widow's heart sing, and the orphans to bless,
Is often the source of more pleasure below,
Than other distinctions have power to bestow;
Be wealth then your portion if thus you will use it,
But far, far be it from you, if e'er you abuse it.

Here Anne has written a poem to amuse her brothers Samuel Egerton and John, while they were at The King's School. As in later years she would write long letters to her sons Christopher Edward and Ben, here she clearly seeks to amuse and distract the homesick boys.

The poem's style is mock-epic, consciously evoking the ancient Homeric epic *The Iliad*, particularly in the line 'He looked like the man who of Troy told the tale.' The butt of the joke here is her brother Edward, with his pursuit of game birds, partridges and landrails (a kind of wading bird) likened to the bloody dramas enacted in ancient epic.

Anne's reference is probably to Aeneas, hero of Roman poet Virgil's *Aeneid*, written in the first century BC. Aeneas has escaped from Troy and tells the tale of its destruction to his hostess in Carthage, Queen Dido, in *Aeneid* Book II. The works of Virgil were schoolboy standards in the late eighteenth century, so this would have been a familiar theme for Anne's brothers.

Perhaps because she has introduced this recollection of Aeneas and Dido – a famous love-tragedy of literature – Anne then brings in a battle-of-the-sexes theme. 'Men claim that dancing fatigues them, but they can hunt for hours without apparently feeling any strain.' The familiar trope of men being deceivers is thus given a less serious setting; deceit about feeling tired is surely of no great moment.

This, in turn, allows Anne to hope that her brothers will remain innocent and honest, implicitly in their dealings with girls and women. Yet again, her poem ends with a reminder that becoming rich is less important than using wisely the wealth that one has.

Poem 5, 'Enigma'

> With Monks, and with Hermits I chiefly reside,
> From Courts and from camps I'm at distance;
> The ladies who ne'er could my presence abide,
> To banish me join their assistance.
>
> I seldom can flatter, tho' oft shew respect,
> To the patriot, the preacher, the peer;
> But sometimes, alas! A sad mark of neglect,
> Or a proof of contempt I appear.
>
> I once, (as an eminent poet records,)
> Was pleas'd with the Nightingale's song;
> Yet such is my taste, I leave ladies and lords,
> And oft wander with thieves all night long.
>
> By the couch of the sick, I am frequently found,
> And I ever attend on the dead;
> With patient affliction I sit on the ground,
> But when talk'd of am instantly fled.

Anne here turns her hand to the classic word puzzle of the eighteenth century, the 'enigma'. The format is a description of an unknown item (often in the first person), which the reader has to identify from the clues within the text.[12] Popular magazines such as the *Gentleman's Magazine* and the *London Magazine* regularly published enigmas, and readers often contributed solutions.

One elaborate enigma which appeared in the *London Magazine* of October 1748 had a triple solution:

> Not like the diamond and gold,
> Which some few happy countries hold,
> In ev'ry clime more common I
> With stones and sand promiscuous lie…
> So chang'd am I, since rais'd from earth,
> That strangers could not guess my birth.
> My frame is delicate and nice,
> But may be alter'd in a trice.
> With gentle usage and fair wearing,
> I last for years without repairing.
> The sciences I much promote,
> And truths discover of great note;
> Astronomy and opticks too
> Would, but for me, have little new…
> My foremost letter set aside,
> Leaves *one* that longs to be a bride;
> And if you can the pretty maid
> Her letter first to drop persuade,
> You'll find, with pleasure after all,
> A meek and harmless *animal*.[13]

Anne's enigma is less complex, and one wonders if it took her siblings very long to work out the solution. Anne gives a clue in her enigma which readers educated in English literature would understand. In Milton's *Paradise Lost*, we read that evening was falling in Eden.

> Now came still Evening on, and Twilight gray
> Had in her sober livery all things clad;
> Silence accompanied, for beast and bird,

They to their grassy couch, these to their nests,
Were slunk, all but the wakeful nightingale;
She all night long her amorous descant sung;
Silence was pleased…[14]

Despite the beauty of the scene, 'silence' in Milton's context has a sinister aspect, as behind the scenes Satan is contemplating the corruption of Eve, and paradise's days are numbered. This dual nature of silence is neatly demonstrated by Anne in her enigma: it can denote respect, or the precise opposite – contempt.

Poem 6, 'To Miss Catharine Hammond'

From rural scenes where peace and quiet dwell,
Where no beaux flatters [*sic*], and where shines no belle,
Where books and work our harmless hours employ,
And a calm ramble is our highest joy;
What can my friend expect? I strive in vain,
No lively thought can all my efforts gain:
Yet still one truth these simple lines will prove,
How much my Catharine shares her Anna's love;
When musing o'er the lonely fields I stray,
Or to fair Denton bend my pensive way;
The mirthful scenes that lately charm'd my eyes,
Lively and gay at fancy's call arise;
Again I weave the dance, to music's sound,
Again I gaily trip the giddy round;
Thoughtless and blythe I join the jocund train,
Or smiling listen to soft flattery's strain;
While in my mind these gay ideas rise,
Some melancholy object strikes my eyes;
Or in the vale devotions lowly shrine,
Recalls my thoughts and points to truths sublime,
This world's vain glories fade before my sight,
And my thoughts rise to realms of purer light;
Yet still the chosen few my mind approves,
Whom my fond soul with utmost ardour loves;
Cling round my heart, with them I trace the plains,

Or rise to scenes where endless pleasure reigns;
Amid this band my Catharine's form appears,
Artless and innocent as infant years;
Ah! May no pangs thy gentle breast e'er rend,
Still as thyself sincere be every friend;
Far, far from thee be keen misfortune's dart,
May no sharp sorrows ever touch thy heart!
Oft as returning at the close of day,
By some lone cot, I take my silent way,
Where 'midst the frowns of want, neglect, and pain,
Calm eyed content maintains her peaceful reign,
Where cheerful age enjoys the balmy air,
And some fond mother tends her infant care,
More bright to me these humble forms appear,
Than folly's votaries in their mad career.
Farewell my friend to every virtue dear,
May thy joys brighten with each added year!

Here Anne is imitating the best-known poets of the mid-century, Collins and Gray. Her themes are familiar from their most famous works: the greater value of the humble than the great (a theme of Gray's *Elegy*, 1751); the pleasures of nature rather than the social round (a commonplace of poetry since ancient times).

Anne's poem also celebrates her friendship with Catharine Hammond. The Hammonds were cousins of the Brydges, living at St Alban's Court, Nonnington, some five miles from Wootton.[15] Anne's mother Jemima's sister Charlotte Egerton had married William Hammond of St Alban's Court. They had six children, of whom Catharine-Jemima (probably named after her aunt) was the second youngest.[16]

A letter of Anne's from 1803 indicated that she was still in touch with the Hammonds, friends of her youth.[17] Catharine died unmarried, and a genealogy website suggests that this was in 1804, the same year in which Anne herself was to die.[18] The lives of the two cousins followed very different trajectories. Anne married in 1778, becoming a mother and grandmother, but met a tragic accidental death in the very same year as her cousin and friend Catharine.

Chapter 5

Anne and the Belisarius Affair

'To Miss D. and I.B. 1775'

> While you for gayland's festive dance,
> Adorn your lovely face;
> With pleasure see each charm advance,
> And heighten every grace.
>
> By Marmontel's instructive page,
> I strive *my soul* to dress;
> In charms that may defy old age;
> And brighten in distress.
>
> When Belisarius old and blind,
> To fancy's sight appears;
> Soft pity overflows my mind,
> And fills my eyes with tears.
>
> Taught by his fate, how vain is pow'r,
> How fickle fortune's smile;
> I learn to prize the peaceful hour,
> And scorn ambition's toils.
>
> Surrounded by the pomp of war,
> Had I the hero view'd;
> Those Chiefs attendant on his car,
> His valor had subdued.
>
> Compassion for the sufferer's fate,
> Had o'er my soul prevail'd,

Obscured the Conqueror's glittering state;
And all his glory veil'd.

Despoil'd of honor, riches, pow'r,
Bent with the weight of years;
Helpless and blind in sorrow's hour,
How glorious he appears.

Torn from his brow, in life's first bloom
The warrior's crown may fade;
Or, in the cold and silent tomb
Be wither'd and decay'd.

But round the good man's placid brow,
Unfading wreaths shall twine;
More fresh by time those laurels grow,
Bestow'd by hands Divine.

This poem, addressed apparently to Anne's sisters Deborah and Jemima Brydges ('D. and I.B.', 'I' often being used instead of 'J' as an initial letter) is noteworthy for a number of reasons. It is the most serious and moralising of her extant poems, and it references a runaway bestseller. The poem shows Anne engaging with key cultural debates of mid-eighteenth century Europe, on morality, religion, and the proper role of government.

Anne seeks to contrast social enjoyment with the more serious concerns of life inculcated by 'Marmontel's page'. The work referred to is the 1767 novel *Bélisaire* by Jean-François Marmontel (1723–1799), which dramatised the life of the Byzantine general Belisarius (c. 505–565 CE).

The main sources for the life of Belisarius were the works of Procopius (c. 500–554 CE). Procopius, from Caesarea in ancient Palestine, became legal adviser to Belisarius, early in Justinian's reign (527), and accompanied him on several campaigns. He thus had first-hand knowledge of his subject.

However, Procopius created two very different historical accounts of Justinian and Belisarius. In his *Wars of Justinian*, Procopius told a straight story of largely successful campaigns against the Persians, the Vandals in North Africa, and the Goths in Italy. In his most notorious work, by contrast, the *Secret History*, Procopius took a different approach: describing the events which took place during the reign of Justinian and his consort Theodora, mostly at home in Byzantium, but also across a wide swathe of the empire. The themes of this work are corruption, incompetence, misgovernment, tyranny, violent rivalry between the Blue and Green circus factions, favouritism, and official predation. The results are described as nothing less than empire-wide military, political, and economic disaster.

Anne Lefroy appears to have taken Marmontel's Belisarius as an accurate portrayal, rather than a polemic or satire. She is unlikely to have been familiar with the ancient historian Procopius; he was considered to be a scandalous author, trading in insults about the sexuality of the Empress Theodora, wife of Justinian. This left Marmontel's novel, with its particular political slant, the standard version of Belisarius' life.

By the mid-eighteenth century, the combined and blended story was taken to represent a type of the ingratitude and treachery of corrupt and tyrannical kings towards loyal subjects. This was the approach which Marmontel's novel took.[1] His Belisarius was, like Socrates, persecuted for his truth-telling.

The novel has some strong points; Marmontel's treatment of his subject makes for a compelling historical fiction. The work's great popularity must, to some degree, have been a result of the author's care in setting an authentic ancient scene.

Some individual scenes also have power. The chapter in which Belisarius finds hospitality at the home of a cottager, who turns out to be the Vandals' former king Gelimer – defeated but not dishonoured in former conflict by Belisarius – is effective, and the conclusion to the chapter echoes Voltaire in *Candide* (1759).

> The warlike hero, the great, the good Belisarius! – Now indeed he may think himself happy who digs his garden. With these words the king of the Vandals resumed his spade.[2]

Despite Marmontel's doubts, stated in his preface, which caused him to use Procopius' 'straight', rather than his 'secret' history as a source, Belisarius delivers himself of commentary which recalls the ills depicted in the latter work. The problems of public service receiving poor recompense; the evils of social factions; unjust and chaotic taxation; and the ruinous financial impact of drawn-out war, were shared by the Byzantium of Justinian and the France of Louis XV.

With such ample social and economic material at his disposal on which to make an allegory, some readers at the time questioned why Marmontel insisted on dragging in the matter of religion.

At various points in the novel views are expressed which conflict with standard Christian belief. For example, Belisarius tries to comfort his daughter on the death of her mother Antonina, precipitated by her grief at seeing her husband in a state of blindness:

> She now looks down with pity upon us, and commiserates the lot that detains us in this bad world. That cold, inanimated corpse which lies there devoid of motion, is an emblem of the tranquility her soul enjoys. Thus then you behold how vain and transitory are all the calamities of life; a breath of wind comes, and all is vanished. The empire and the splendor of its court have faded away from the eyes of your mother; and now in the bosom of her God, she beholds this world as a little speck in the immensity of space.[3]

This account, like Antonina's soul, was clearly hovering above that contested airspace between the Stoic and Christian realms (or, if we are to be completely honest, it was on the Stoic side of the DMZ). It proved to be some religious aspects of Chapter XV of the novel which caused it, ultimately, to fall foul of the authorities of the Sorbonne. Marmontel had his Belisarius make reflections of a broadly 'natural religion' kind, but he went too far in suggesting that surely virtuous pagans would find a place in heaven.

He even went to specify which particular pagans should be top of the list: the 'good emperors', Titus, Trajan and the Antonines.

> How much more glorious and refulgent will be the court of Him, who is at last to receive my soul! It will be filled with the Titus's, the Trajan's, and the Antoninus's, those delights of mankind. It is in their company, and that of the virtuous of all ages and of all countries, that the poor blind Belisarius will glow with purest fire before the throne of a good and equitable God.[4]

In sketching Belisarius' view of religion – 'The good man walks with God' – Marmontel had added a footnote consisting of a quote from Seneca: *Nulla sine Deo mens bona est ... Inter bonos viros ac Deum amicitia est, conciliante virtute*.[5]

Appeal to the Stoic Seneca on matters of religious orthodoxy was not likely to conciliate hardline Catholic views. Further, Marmontel's generous heaven undoubtedly seemed a step on the road to Pelagianism, that originally British heresy which denied, or qualified, Original Sin (in claiming, for example, that infants, even if unbaptised, had eternal life): 'the hardiest and most natural heresy in the Christian world'.[6]

Not only that, but Marmontel's chosen virtuous pagans had, to a man, been persecutors of the Christian religion. To take things one step further still, Marmontel justified his stance in a footnote which also denigrated Justinian, not only by implication through Belisarius' criticisms, but *in propria* authorial *persona*:

> It has been decided by the fathers that God will work a miracle, rather than let him perish everlastingly who has faithfully followed the laws of nature. But Justinian, it is well known, was a bigot, and of a persecuting spirit [fanatique & persecuteur' [sc. of pagans].[7]

Criticism of Justinian was one thing, but to appropriate the precious victim status of 'persecuted' for pagans away from Christians was a bridge too far.

Finally, in November, an official censure of *Bélisaire* appeared, but by this time the novel was famous throughout Europe. Marmontel had taken the precaution of sending early copies to crowned heads from Russia to Sweden (he had even sought to dedicate it to his own monarch, an offer which was politely declined).[8]

The novel found particular favour in Protestant countries (although the virtuous-pagan problem had its own afterlife in Holland and Germany, where it dragged on for another decade[9]). The *Gentleman's Magazine* Amsterdam correspondent wrote in 1770:

> Three editions of M. Marmontel's Belisarius have been published here at almost the same time. This admirable work, one of the best that has appeared this century, is

so well known, that the mention of it is sufficient. The Author has here displayed all the charms of his genius, and all the generosity of his mind. To complete his glory, nothing was wanting but persecutions; and persecutions he has had.[10]

An early English translator gives a clue to the work's popularity in England:

Belisarius ... is the friend of civil and religious liberty ... the sentiments, that animate every chapter, almost make a Briton envy a writer, who was born and lives under the monarchy of France; a writer who has had the genius and the courage to think with freedom, even in Paris, where we understand, that the book has been suppressed, and its author sent to the Bastille to do penance for his merit, and the excellence of his talents.[11]

In fact, if this preface was actually written, as dated, in March 1767, the novel had not, as we have seen, by that time been suppressed. Nor was Marmontel imprisoned because of *Bélisaire*, although he had previously served a short sentence after taking responsibility for a satire in fact written by a friend.[12]

The novel's English vogue, in fact, apart from its (not negligible) literary merit, was due to the widespread national sense of being the home of religious liberty, and a corresponding sense of superiority to the benighted and bigoted French. However much religious sentiments might differ within England itself – and at this very time there were varying currents with respect to the extent of Church of England authority – the reading public, however dimly, recognised its inheritance of freedom of belief, expressed most significantly by Locke. This meant that Marmontel's earliest English readers could, indeed, look with amusement and a keen sense of superiority on the situation in Paris.

Anne Lefroy's poem about Belisarius emphasises his virtue, which was of course Marmontel's key theme as well. From a strict Anglican perspective, however, pagan virtue was very much part of the Pelagianism which is directly combated by Article IX of the Thirty-Nine Articles.

Original Sin standeth not in the following of Adam, (as the Pelagians do vainly talk;) but it is the fault and corruption of the Nature of every man, that naturally is ingendered of the offspring of Adam; whereby man is very far gone from original righteousness, and is of his own nature inclined to evil, so that the flesh lusteth always contrary to the spirit; and therefore in every person born into this world, it deserveth God's wrath and damnation…

Good works done by non-Christians are condemned in Article XIII; so much for virtuous pagans.

Works done before the grace of Christ, and the Inspiration of the Spirit, are not pleasant to God, forasmuch as they spring not of faith in Jesus Christ…

However, Anne's poem ends with a vision of Belisarius somehow blessed by God. She clearly saw no doctrinal problem in suggesting that a virtuous pagan would find Divine favour.

It is even likely that Anne's own personal belief system included elements of the dreaded Pelagianism. Several of Anne's young siblings had died as infants. One corollary of Article IX is to emphasise that even young children were, as humans, replete with Original Sin. But Pelagius and his followers in the early fifth century CE apparently denied that infants were infected by Original Sin.

Augustine made it his life's work to combat this view, and to insist that divine grace was necessary for humans to avoid sin. It was his influence which prevailed in doctrinal terms, resulting (inter alia) eventually in the Calvinistic tone of the Thirty-Nine Articles, drafted during the conflict of the sixteenth century.[13] Roman Catholic and Church of England agreed, in principle, on the total depravity of humanity through Original Sin, the necessity of divine grace for both human goodness and salvation, and the insufficiency of good works.

By Anne Brydges Lefroy's time, a comfortable semi-Pelagianism, or latitudinarianism, was common enough within the English church to mean that virtuous pagans could be celebrated as role-models. In addition to celebrating pagan virtue, there was the issue of whether ordinary Protestants actually believed in, or indeed even understood, the 'total depravity' doctrine. Anne was a loving and maternally disposed person, and it seems inconceivable that she would have thought of her young deceased siblings as having been anything but pure and innocent beings; yet Anglican orthodoxy, interpreted strictly, would have seen them as no different from sinning adults.

That Anne's personal belief system rejected the Calvinist harshness explicit in the Thirty-Nine Articles is confirmed by the account later written by her son, Christopher Edward, in his 1826 novel, *Outalissi: a tale of Dutch Guiana*. The hero, Edward Bentinck, is 'a young officer in the Dutch service', and it is clear that the author is recalling his own mother and her religious teachings:

> No young man ever entered life under stronger or more cheerful, grateful, and affectionate impressions of the truth of Christianity than Edward Bentinck. His mother, though a member of the Dutch church, and familiar with the Calvinistic view of revelation which characterises that establishment, was a woman of such superior understanding and fervent charity, that she never could assent to all the repulsive peculiarities in the opinions of its great founder, which either acquired grace, consistency, and attraction from her mode of explaining them, or she confessed at once were beyond her comprehension ... every one is as free to accept the restorative provision as he would have been to stand or fall had he been born in paradise ... if the effects [of Adam and Eve's sin] are partial, it will be simply because men *are free* agents, and will not always follow the light when they see it and know it, but continue in darkness because their deeds are evil. Every man's own bosom tells him that his moral character with his maker must depend upon the inobliquity and disinterestedness of his efforts to obey the will of God...[14]

Anne Brydges Lefroy's engagement with the key religious and ideological controversies of her day is shown by her poem on the theme of Belisarius. Her own religious views were tolerant, expansive, and focused on the importance of virtuous conduct. Marmontel's novel, with its own theme of virtue, struck a chord throughout Europe, echoing even in remote Wootton.

Chapter 6

Marrying George Lefroy

The man whom Anne Brydges was to marry, Isaac Peter George Lefroy, had been born in 1745 at Leghorn (Livorno) on the Tuscan coast of Italy. His father, Anthony Lefroy, born in Canterbury in 1703, had travelled to Italy as a young man to work in the merchant house of Langlois and Sons at Livorno.

Livorno had been a base for English naval operations since the sixteenth century, supporting a considerable English presence. In 1738, Anthony married Elizabeth Langlois (aged 18), and they had a daughter, Phoebe, and two sons, Anthony (b. 1742) and Isaac Peter George, hereafter known as George or the Reverend George.

The boys were sent to England in 1752 to live under the care of their paternal grandmother in Canterbury, and as we have seen, both were enrolled at The King's School, Canterbury, in the mid-1750s.[1] At this point, it is necessary to step back and look at the Lefroy family, a group intensely proud of their family history, and what it must have meant for Anne to have married into this successful, cosmopolitan clan.

The Lefroy family was of Huguenot origin. Subsequent family members believed a semi-mythological version of their ancestors' departure from Flanders, to England in the sixteenth century. This account was that Anthony Lefroy came to England in about 1569, following the persecution of Protestants by Ferdinand Álvarez de Toledo, the Duke of Alva, sent by King Philip II of Spain to his Flemish territories. Alva prosecuted leaders of both political and religious unrest in the Spanish Netherlands, but many ordinary Protestants were also driven to flee.

One of Anne and George Lefroy's grandchildren, scientist and soldier John (later General Sir John) Henry Lefroy (1817–1890), researched his family history in the mid-nineteenth century, and published his account in 1868.[2] Sir John found no evidence to substantiate the family belief in Anthony Lefroy's having left Flanders as early as 1569. He did, however, conclude that Anthony Lefroy left mainland Europe, in all probability, within the following two decades.[3]

Sir John, clearly, was still keen to make a case for the Lefroys as Protestant heroes of the early resistance to Alva. His concluded that the otherwise strange figure of the shapeless cap on the Lefroy coat of arms, and the motto *Mutare sperno* ('I scorn to change'), were evidence that his ancestors had been among the rebel group of Protestant men of the upper and middle classes, under Spanish occupation, who had called themselves the *Gueusans* or 'Beggars'. Sir John drew upon an earlier family document, compiled in part by 'Mrs B. Lefroy' (Jane Austen's niece Anna Austen) in about 1840:

> Of the red cap or hood in our arms, and the motto, *Mutare sperno*, the family belief is that both were assumed when our ancestor Anthoine Loffroy left the Netherlands in the time of the Duke of Alva's persecutions; that the *cap* was intended to represent his adoption of Huguenot principles, and the motto his inflexible adherence to that which he considered the cause of Religion and Liberty.[4]

Anthoine Loffroy joined the Walloon community in Canterbury, Kent. He died in 1612; his wife, also of Huguenot origin, must have died before 1623 when, Sir John found, more coherent records began.[5] The Walloon refugees greatly promoted the fabric industries in Kent; they worked in silk, wool, linen and paper manufacture. They were said to have introduced the linen trade at Maidstone as early as 1568.[6]

Anthoine's son Isaeie may have been a silk dyer. His son was James Lefroy and his grandson Israel Lefroy, both of whom are testified in real estate documents from the later seventeenth century.[7] Israel's son Thomas Lefroy (who died in 1723, aged 43) had married Phoebe Thompson, whose mother was another Phoebe – Phoebe Hammond, of St Albans Court, Norrington.[8]

The Lefroys, then, as well as the Brydges, were related to the St Albans Hammonds. Anne's brother Samuel, in his inimitable way, shed light on the Hammond family:

> St Albans Court is about five miles distant from Wootton,
> and there was a continual intercourse between us, not always
> perhaps entirely cordial; for my mother's sister [Charlotte
> Hammond née Egerton] was an imperious, impatient, envious
> woman, and her husband very weak and shy. The Hammond
> blood was full of provincial prejudices, and thought the race of
> Aucher and Digges greater than the lustre of all the Egertons…[9]

Sir John, to his credit, comments that Samuel here shows a striking
degree of self-blindness, as Samuel's own family pride, not to say
arrogance, was second to none.[10]

Thomas Lefroy and Phoebe had nine children, of whom only two
survived: Anthony and Lucy.[11] Anthony was apprenticed to a London
merchant, Mark Weyland. Sir John made a comparison between the
young Anthony's adventure and comparable journeys undertaken in the
mid-nineteenth century.

> In 1728 [Anthony] went out to Leghorn [Livorno], as in
> these days a young man goes out to Canton or some other
> distant place, to make his fortune.[12]

Anthony Lefroy certainly made his fortune. He married Elizabeth
Langlois, the daughter of his business partner; her brothers, Christopher,
John, Benjamin and Peter Langlois, were also successful in their careers.
Benjamin Langlois was the businessman we met in Chapter 1. He was a
prominent diplomat and public servant, Secretary to the British embassy
at Vienna in 1763, and a trusted assistant to Lord Stormont as Secretary
of State in 1789.[13] Peter Langlois achieved the rank of general in the
military service of the Austrian Empire: Sir John Lefroy focuses at
length on Peter's career.[14]

Among other ventures, Anthony was involved in the trading of
Carrara marble in Livorno.[15] The geographical proximity of Livorno to
the Carrara quarries had meant that for generations the material had
been traded in the port. During the eighteenth century, British traders
replaced the Dutch and North African Jewish merchants who had
dominated the marble trade. The marble merchants formed an oligarchic
bloc which could, and did, influence policies governing local tax and
price-regulation regimes.

It was also a social oligarchy, perhaps illustrated best through the fascinating and various list of the eighteenth-century Anglophone occupants of the Old English Cemetery at Livorno, the oldest Protestant cemetery in Italy. These range from Tobias Smollett (1721–1771), author of the immortal *Humphry Clinker* and *Roderick Random* (a novel which will reappear in a later chapter); William Robert Broughton (1762–1821), Royal Navy officer and surveyor; and Louisa Pitt (c. 1755-1791), lover of William Beckford, author of Gothic novel *Vathek* (1786). Smollett was probably in Livorno because his friend Ann Curry was married to George Renner, a marble trader.[16]

Marble had its peculiarities as a traded resource. Obviously, it was a heavy material which was expensive to transport; indeed, its weight meant that it was often used as ballast. The costs involved in trading marble were therefore considerable, particularly during times of war. However, it was also a commodity highly valued throughout Europe, for decorative and commemorative sculpture.

The London firm of Wallinger and Fletcher supplied marble for generations throughout the eighteenth century. While their standing meant that they could have approached the Carrara quarries directly, instead they generally used Anthony Lefroy as their Livorno agent.[17] In turn, Anthony bought most of his marble from George Renner, for re-sale to Wallinger.

Anthony's business interests clearly allowed him the leisure and the funds, and brought him the necessary contacts, to allow him to follow his passion, which was the preservation and collection of ancient artefacts. His business ventures involved travel to Damascus, Persia and the Levant (one account, in Latin, refers to *commercium nobile in plures Asiaticas Regiones*, 'distinguished business transactions in numerous Asian countries').[18] Anthony was elected to the Etrusca Accademia in 1753. The Accademia Etrusca di Cortona, founded in 1727 by a group of antiquarians, still exists. Its museum and library contain world-class collections.[19]

In Leghorn, Anthony Lefroy's own collection was so impressive as to be known as the *Museum Lefroyanum*, the Lefroy Museum, with its own numismatic catalogue. In a 1763 letter to his brother-in-law Lord Bute, Edward Wortley-Montague (son of the more famous British Ambassador to the Ottoman Empire), described the collection as follows:

> I leave at Leghorn to be sent to your Lordship by the first ship, catalogues of the Greek and Latin gold, silver and copper

medals [i.e. coins] which comprise the cabinet of Mr Lefroy of this place. I shall not take upon me to tell your lordship how compleat and magnificent a cabinet this is, nor how many of the most rare medals there are in it, much less point out those which are not to be found anywhere, I mean in no other cabinet. You are so well acquainted with these matters that I shall only say that ye gold and silver ones are perfectly preserv'd.[20]

Anthony, it appears, instructed buyers to obtain items for him; the Latin catalogue of his collection conveys his anxiety about imbuing his agents with the same love of antiquities which drove him:

It was the privilege of that great merchant [Anthony Lefroy] to be able to give instructions to the captains of merchantmen and to their officers in every part of Europe, but it was no light task to instruct them, first in the thing itself – to instil a love of ancient coins into uncultured minds, and what is a rare thing to find, to obtain their ready attention.[21]

Anthony's friendship with the Venuti brothers, leading figures in the Accademia, is described in the catalogue.

The collection, which as well as over 6,500 coins, included paintings and sculptures, was so significant that in time, it clearly represented something of a burden. One dealer called in to advise him, a Mr Dalton, had suggested that the collection was 'too fine for any private person'.[22]

Anthony appeared to be at a loss to know what should be done with it. He planned to donate several items to All Souls College, and some indeed were placed there, including a remarkable marble tripod, in the form of three maidens standing on three lions, excavated at Corinth. Anthony donated this item in 1771.[23]

A guidebook from 1789 describes the tripod in place at All Souls.

The curious Tripod, of which an engraving is here given, stands in the Vestibule to the Library of All Souls' College, Oxford, with the following inscription:

Aram Tripodem
Olim Matri Deum

In Templo S. Corinthi
Consecratum
D.D.
Custodi, et Coll. Omn. Anim.
Anton. Lefroy Arm.
MDCCLXXI.

This means: 'The Honourable Anthony Lefroy, in 1771, gave and dedicated [this] altar tripod, once sacred to the mother of the gods in the temple [of S… see below] at Corinth, to be preserved at the College of All Souls.

The author cites a discussion by Anthony Lefroy's friend from the Accademia, Preposto Venuti. The tripod was unusual, indeed Venuti argued unique, both in consisting of marble, and in having the pedestal hollowed out in three sections to create feet. Things take a conversational tone with rhetorical questions about the girls' identity and significance:

> The only certain symbols are the lions, which everyone knows to be consecrated by the ancients to Cybele the grandmother of the Gods. But who are these three girls, under whose feet are the lions, and on whose heads the crater of the Tripod is supported? It seems to the learned Critic [Venuti] that they are the handmaids of Juno, the patroness of *marriage* [italics in original], and he therefore concludes this Tripod to be dedicated either to Cybele, or Juno.[24]

The tripod stood obscurely at All Souls for many decades. At the end of the nineteenth century, it attracted some scholarly attention. Percy Gardner (1846–1937), then Lincoln Professor of Classical Archaeology and Art, discussed the tripod in an article in the *Journal of Hellenic Studies* (1896), and led a discussion at the second meeting in London of the Society for the Promotion of Hellenic Studies in February 1897.

Gardner thought parts of the Latin inscription 'curious'. He was unsure what the 'S' before 'Corinthi' might have referred to. He also thought that Anthony Lefroy probably had little reason to assume that the tripod came from Corinth. The only reason was, Gardner estimated, that Lefroy and the Accademia scholars had read the passage in ancient travel writer Pausanias recording the existence, at one time, of a temple to Cybele on the Acropolis Hill at Corinth.[25]

By Gardner's time, the Lefroy tripod was no longer considered unique. Gardner, having noticed that the Lefroy tripod maidens appeared to hold the lions' tails in their right hands, compared a tripod from Olympia, with similar girls and lions, but in a far more fragmentary state.[26] He thought that the tripod might have been used in the service of other gods or goddesses, apart from Cybele.

Stylistic features led Gardner to date the Lefroy tripod to the fifth century BC. He concluded:

> It is the only extant well-preserved example of a kind of utensil, probably quite common in ancient Greece, and of a fixed pattern, which was used for sacred purposes in the various shrines of Greece; most likely … for holding the holy water used for the purification of those who came into the presence of the gods.[27]

In 1911, All Souls College lent the Lefroy tripod to the Ashmolean Museum, also in Oxford, where it remains to this day.[28] It has recently formed part of an exhibition on ancient Greek religion. Clearly, Anthony Lefroy's collection of ancient artefacts is still making a significant contribution to modern understandings of ancient culture.

A number of Anthony's letters deal with his anguish at the loss of a number of his ancient coins, which had been entrusted to a dealer named Hyam to transport to England. It appeared that several coins did not reappear at the end of the journey. Anthony was convinced that fraud was involved.[29]

In addition to this loss, despite a number of legacies from relatives, Anthony found himself in financial difficulties. He was declared bankrupt in 1762. The bankruptcy documentation includes paperwork in which George Renner, unable to obtain payment from Anthony for marble, in turn queries Wallinger's invoice for 1,700 pezze (about £380, many thousands of pounds in today's money).[30]

Finally, to add to family concerns, Anthony's daughter Phoebe (1740–1777) was also causing her family a great deal of anxiety during the 1760s. Distant cousins Elizabeth Hammond and Oliver St John had already converted to Roman Catholicism, and in her twenties, Phoebe decided to do the same.

Livorno's status as an important trading centre made it something of a focus for Protestant conversion. Elizabeth Ann Seton (1774–1821), who was the first native-born American to achieve canonisation (in 1975), became a Catholic while living in Livorno among the business partners of her late husband William Seton (d. 1803). William Seton was buried in the Old English Cemetery in Livorno.

The case of young Phoebe Lefroy was particularly frustrating to a family which, as we have seen, on both the Lefroy and Langlois sides, regarded itself as heirs to a tradition of staunch Protestantism. Even worse than simply converting, however, it appeared that Phoebe's first wish was to become a nun.

With the assistance of a servant, Phoebe dressed in a man's clothing and ran away to Florence, where she was accepted into the convent of Santa Agata. It may be that there was some kind of conversion mania happening among the daughters of the Livorno English traders: in 1763, all three daughters of Mrs Gravier, a silk merchant, declared their wish to convert, and the eldest, Anna, left home to do so. The oligarchy swung into action, and eventually Anna Gravier was returned to her mother.[31]

To Phoebe Lefroy's adventure, the reaction of her mother Elizabeth Langlois Lefroy was stern. She wrote to brother Benjamin Langlois:

> By a few lines I wrote in Mr L[efroy's] letter lately wrote to Kitt [Christopher Langlois] you must have known the whim that has got in Phoebe's head, to prevent which she is to leave the Convent in a few days and go in the country with Mrs Hammond; her father and myself shall never consent to her being a nun of any order, much more so a Capuchin, the poorest, strictest, and severest order they have, and should it happen I should be the most miserable of all mothers ... I tell you all this only by way of informing you of the steps we have taken, to avoid such misery to that poor unfortunate wretch, as I know in spite of her behaviour you yourself would not wish her such a chastisement...[32]

In the event, in 1767, Phoebe married an Italian nobleman, the Count Carlo del Medico, and had several children. The Del Medicos were among the leading families involved in the Carrara marble quarries, so the marriage was probably arranged through a business connection. By this time, however, Anthony Lefroy was bankrupt, and so the connection was of no long-term use to him.[33] Phoebe lost touch with her brothers Anthony and George, and the next generation of cousins had no contact with each other.[34]

Isaac Peter George was generally known as George (or IGPL in abbreviated form). He attended Christ Church, Oxford, and attained a fellowship of All Souls College through a family privilege involving the Hammond and Digges connection.[35] He took orders in September 1772, and in September 1777 was presented to the living of Compton, near Godalming in Surrey. A family tradition has indicated that the living had been purchased, for the sake of transmission to George Lefroy by Jemima Brydges, mother of Anne.[36] This was a common practice in the eighteenth century; the Austen family also benefited from the purchase, by wealthier family members, of relevant livings which could be held in friendly hands until they could be accessed by less well-off clergy in the family. A benefactor of Jane's father, the Reverend George Austen, purchased the livings of Ashe and Deane in Hampshire, to be available if and when an Austen clergyman should require a ready job.[37] As it turned out, Ashe was eventually the parish where George and Anne Lefroy would spend most of their married life.

In July 1778, George Lefroy was appointed domestic chaplain to Amelia D'Arcy, Baroness Conyers and Marchioness of Carmarthen (1754–1784), an interesting and tragic young woman. Sir John Lefroy approvingly quoted the sonorous and impressive appointment documentation:

> KNOW YE that I the said AMELIA BARONESS CONYERS, for and on account of the great Probity of Life, Integrity of Morals, and proficiency in sacred learning of GEORGE LEFROY, Clerk, Master of Arts, and Fellow of All Souls' College, in the University of Oxford, have nominated, appointed, taken, and admitted, and by these Presents do nominate, take, and admit him the said GEORGE LEFROY into the number of my Domestick Chaplains, to serve me in the performance of Divine Offices within my House or Chapel...[38]

In 1773, at 19, Amelia had married Francis Osborne, Marquis of Carmarthen, and they had three children. In November 1778, doubtless disregarding any hints from her newly appointed personal chaplain, the 24-year-old Amelia embarked on a reckless love affair with 22-year-old John 'Mad Jack' Byron (1756–1791), officer in the Foot Guards, and generally loose cannon. As the formal documentation of subsequent divorce proceedings put it:

> The said Marchioness of Carmarthen, and John Byron, Esq., from the time of their first acquaintance, as aforesaid, until Sunday, the thirteenth of December, 1778, (the day on which the Marchioness of Carmarthen eloped from her house with Mr Byron) carried on a criminal and adulterous conversation together, and had the carnal knowledge of each other, and committed the foul crime of adultery…[39]

Mad Jack's late-night visits to the Marchioness, leaving rumpled and stained bedclothes, inevitably became known to a cast of servants – Sarah Harrison, Jane Totty the 18-year-old nursemaid, Rose Lador, William Shadbolt and William Rose the footmen. Jack was not at all discreet in his comings and goings, being heard to whistle or sing as he went up or down the stairs, and a range of witnesses provided depositions which formed evidence in the divorce proceedings which the wronged husband, the Marquis of Carmarthen, commenced early in 1779. The events became a textbook case of divorce following upon adultery.[40]

Choosing her passion for Mad Jack over her husband, children, and exalted social position, Amelia left her home to live a wandering life with him. In 1783, Amelia gave birth to Mad Jack's daughter, Augusta, before dying in January 1784, aged only 29. Gossips such as Mrs Delany, confidante of the great, took pleasure in reports that the dying Amelia had expressed remorse about her life choices:

> Heard that Lady Conyers is dying; they say she is a sincere penitent.[41]

Little Augusta was passed around from one relative to another, while Mad Jack went on to marry, as his second wife, the heiress Catherine Gordon, of Gight in Aberdeenshire, and to father George Gordon, later Lord Byron the poet, in 1788. Mad Jack himself died, at only 35, in 1791. The subsequent, fraught and contested relationship between Augusta and her half-brother, Byron, became perhaps Amelia D'Arcy Osborne Byron's most significant legacy.

History was to repeat itself when, in 1812, Lady Caroline Lamb, at 27, was prepared to leave her husband, William Lamb, and two children, to live with Lord Byron.[42] In this later case, it was the younger Byron who was unwilling; but it is striking that the Byron magnetism operated over two generations on married noblewomen.

The Reverend George Lefroy thus played a walk-on and inadvertent role in a chain of key scandals of the long eighteenth century. He may have reflected that this experience formed one of that class of historical cases in which a moral counsellor is perceived to have had little, or even a negative, influence on his young charge. To the classically educated, the cases of Aristotle as the tutor of Alexander the Great, and of Seneca as the guardian of the young Roman emperor Nero, will have occurred.

Naturally enough, the mid-Victorian account of Sir John Lefroy makes no mention of the tragi-comic sequels to George Lefroy's second clerical appointment. Nor, more surprisingly, does the 2007 account by descendant Helen Lefroy and Gavin Turner, which blandly states only that the chaplainship was 'a position which probably caused [George] some anxiety'.[43] The reason for that anxiety is here, for the first time, explained. The Carmarthen case – like the Castlehaven tragedy in the Egerton family history – was at once a failure of noble ideals in a great family, and a personal disaster for the individuals involved.

Against the background of the imploding Carmarthen household in London, George and Anne were married just after Christmas, on 28 December 1778, at Wootton.[44] The groom was 33 and the bride 31 years old.

Benjamin Langlois had purchased the incumbency of Ashe, in Hampshire, and this was where George and Anne would eventually wish to settle. In the meantime, however, the incumbent, Dr Richard Russell, showed no sign of relinquishing the living which he had held since 1729.[45] Russell was the maternal grandfather of writer Mary Russell Mitford (1787–1855), author of *Our Village* (1824–1832) and numerous other works. Russell was distantly related to the dukes of Bedford, also Russells; his daughter Mary (1750–1830) married Dr George Mitford, and the author Mary was their only surviving child. This Hampshire connection would later lead Mary Russell Mitford to make some unflattering remarks about Jane Austen as a fellow Hampshire local.[46]

It is likely that Dr Russell's inevitable demise was awaited with some impatience by the newly married Lefroys. In the meantime, they stayed for some time in London, in Sackville Street. Here a visitor described Anne in delightful terms:

> [She was] one of the happiest beings I ever saw. She laughed almost the whole time, but it did not seem a mockery of joy but genuine mirth I assure you.[47]

By December 1779 the couple seem to have been settled in Basingstoke, for here their first child, Jemima Lucy (always known as Lucy, no doubt because of the numerous Jemimas already in the Brydges clan) was born. She was christened on 9 December.[48]

George's father Anthony Lefroy had died at Livorno, in July 1779.[49] George and his brother Anthony were both executors and beneficiaries, after a life interest for their mother Elizabeth. The estate was complex, with assets in England, France and Italy. There was also the legacy of the antiquities collection.

Elizabeth was prevailed on by her sons and brothers to return to England. A servant was sent from England to assist and accompany her. Elizabeth decided to make the hazardous journey by land, because of the volume of the possessions she wished to bring. A former colleague of Anthony's, Henry Fonnereau (also part of the British bloc at Livorno), advised her to follow a route through Florence, Bologna, Trieste, Innsbruck, Augsburg, Mannheim, Frankfurt, Cologne, Aix-la-Chapelle, Brussels, and Ostende.[50] As Elizabeth explained: 'It is the shortest way by Germany.'[51]

Elizabeth added that she was bringing her husband's beloved coin collection with her ('I have taken all the medals') but would be leaving bulkier items to be packed and sent later ('As to the packing up the books to be sent, idols etc., whenever it will be prudent to do it, it shall be done by Michele'). 'Idols' must have meant figurines and statues; Michele was a trusted servant of years' standing.[52]

George Lefroy had taken a house for his mother near Basingstoke, and she arrived safely at the end of 1781. Unfortunately, she only enjoyed her new life and proximity to George and Anne for a short while; she died in November 1782, while visiting her brother Benjamin Langlois in London.[53]

The 1780s were a season of deaths and births for the family. Edward Brydges, Anne's father, had died at Wootton in November 1780.[54] On 12 January 1782, Anne gave birth to a son, John Henry George, and the next year to a daughter, Julia Elizabeth, who lived only a few weeks.[55] Another son, Anthony Brydges, was born around this time.[56]

It was also a season of epidemic. Smallpox broke out in 1781, and George Lefroy was involved in parish meetings at which strategies were discussed for coping with the illness.[57] Smallpox was the single most lethal disease in eighteenth-century Britain, particularly in rural areas.[58] Of the 1781 outbreak, an 1839 report recalled:

> In 1781, a year of very extensive and fatal smallpox, 646 patients were treated in the building in Cold-Bath-Fields [London]; and of them 257 died, being at the rate of 40 out of every 100.

By contrast, after vaccination was developed and had been widely practised for some decades:

> In 1838, out of 694 cases, the deaths were 188, being at the rate of only 27 in the 100.

The improvement was attributed to the tendency of vaccination to induce a virtuous cycle:

> Where it fails to prevent small-pox, [vaccination] so modifies and alters the human constitution as to permit the small-pox to run its course with a mildness and safety unknown in 1781.[59]

For the rest of her life, Anne would be a vaccination campaigner (covered in detail in a later chapter).

The seemingly immortal Dr Russell finally died in January 1783, in his eightieth year.[60] George, Anne and their young children could finally move into the Rectory at Ashe, the home where they would spend the rest of their lives.

Ashe is a village west of Basingstoke. The redbrick rectory still stands in gracious solidity and comfort. No doubt the Lefroys brought some items from the collection of Anthony Lefroy, lending a touch of Europe. From the glare of Carrara marble in the market at Livorno, to the quiet views of the Hampshire countryside, George Lefroy had made a considerable journey. Anne's own journey from wild Wootton had been shorter, but still far enough in mental space: from the eldest of a brood of siblings to the hostess in her own drawing-room. Her brother Samuel recalled pleasant memories of this time:

> In [George and Anne's home] I spent many of the happier days of my life; and, when I first married in 1786, hired a small parsonage-house in the parish adjoining to [the Lefroys'], where I lived two years.

Samuel added:

> [George's] house was always full of company, and he delighted to make every one happy.[61]

George and Anne, as a couple, seem to have been truly blessed: well matched, equally fond of going out and entertaining at home, and equipped to bring happiness to others. It was a tribute to them that they inspired such praise from the moody, bitter and self-absorbed Samuel Egerton Brydges.

In 1789 a terrible event affected the extended Brydges clan. Anne's sister Deborah had, in 1780, married George Lefroy's college friend Henry Maxwell (1748–1818), a great favourite with all the Lefroy family. Nine years later, she was writing at her desk at their Harley Street home when a fire broke out. As reported in the *Gentleman's Magazine:*

> ...the poker fell out of the fire and set her clothes in a blaze before she perceived it; she first attempted to wrap herself up in the carpet, but that was nailed down to the floor. She then ran upstairs to her bedchamber, and although pursued instantly by one servant who was on the staircase at the moment, and followed almost instantly by the other servants and Mr Maxwell, their endeavours to extinguish the flames by folding her up in the curtains of the bed and their own coats were ineffectual. The bed wainscot and the

window shutters were set on fire, and one of the servants suffered considerably in his zeal to save his mistress. She was dressed, at the time of the accident in a round calico gown, with an apron of fine muslin very full and wide … The beauty, wit and sweet temper of this unfortunate lady rendered her the object of admiration, esteem and love, to all around her.[62]

The widowed Henry Maxwell remained close to George and Anne Lefroy and their children.

Chapter 7

Jane Shore at Hackwood Park I: Miss L – and Captain Whiffle

In her recently updated book about Jane Austen and the theatre, *The Genius of Jane Austen: her Love of Theatre and why she is a Hit in Hollywood,* Paula Byrne has devoted some space to the Earl of Barrymore and his theatre at Wargrave. She has not, however, actually made the connection with Jane Austen through Anne Lefroy, together with her and Barrymore's mutual friend the Duchess of Bolton. This connection will be explained for the first time in this and the following chapter.[1]

In March 2015, an item was offered for sale by London auction house Chiswick Auctions. It was a playbill, a poster advertising a performance of the play *Jane Shore,* by playwright Nicholas Rowe, at the country house Hackwood Park, some miles from Ashe. The performance was to take place at seven o'clock on Thursday 1 February 1787.

In promoting the item for sale, the performance was identified as one known from the surviving poems of Anne Lefroy. Chiswick's publicity writer even speculated as to whether the 11-year-old Jane Austen could have attended the show. The item was thus marketed on the basis of its connection with Jane Austen.[2]

The source for making this connection with Jane Austen is through Anne Lefroy's poems. The only one of Anne's poems which survives from the 1780s, the early years of her marriage, is one in which Anne responds to a request from the Duchess of Bolton that she would take part in this very theatrical production. Anne's son Christopher Edward introduced the poem in his 1812 collection as follows.

'Lines sent to the Duchess of Bolton, to excuse the Author from acting the Part of Alicia in *Jane Shore,* which the Duchess had requested her to undertake in a Play performed at Hackwood, about the Year 1787, Lady Catherine Barry acted Jane Shore.'

ALL to the task unused my faultering tongue,
Would mar the tuneful strains that Rowe has sung.
Can I, a wife, a mother, tread the stage?
Burn with false fire, and glow with mimic rage?
Quit of domestic peace the calm retreat?
As mad Alicia teach my heart to beat?
And while my bosom bleeds for Shore's sad fate,
Spurn the dejected mourner from my gate?
Too well her woes by Catharine express'd,
Compassions sighs would heave my artless breast;
Ah! Spare me then unable to withstand,
When lovely Catharine asks, and you command.[3]

As readers of Jane Austen's *Mansfield Park* (1814) will know, family theatricals were a prominent feature of country-house life in the period. In fact, as we saw in Chapter 1, the practice had been common since at least the early seventeenth century.

Yet, as Jane Austen depicts through her character Fanny Price, there was always a moral and social question mark over the private performance of mass entertainment. Plays written for the popular stage were often full of double-entendre, if not explicitly sexual language and situations; understandably, for sex – as always – sells theatre seats.

Even leaving aside the questionable content of many plays, there was unease about the undertaking itself. This is the objection which is raised, in Austen's *Mansfield Park*, by Edmund Bertram (before he overcomes his scruples and plays along with the woman to whom he is personally attracted, Mary Crawford):

> In a *general* light, private theatricals are open to some objections; but as *we* are circumstanced, I must think it would be highly injudicious, and more than injudicious to attempt anything of the kind. It would shew great want of feeling on my father's account, absent as he is, and in some degree of constant danger...[4]

Edmund feels that it would be a project which would be unworthy of a noble family while their father is absent on business. It would appear trivial and a waste of time and money, and something which they would not have dreamed of undertaking in their father's presence, because he would certainly disapprove. Yet Jane Austen's family performed family theatricals, which has always left critics wondering why her position in *Mansfield Park* was so clearly disapproving of them. Paula Byrne's book was written ostensibly on the basis of this apparent contradiction.[5]

One case in Austen's extended family may give a hint here. Mrs Austen's relatives included the wife of Thomas Twisleton, promoted to Lord Saye and Sele in 1781, who took his own life in 1788. Within months, his children – notably young Thomas, then still only in his teens – put on a series of performances of popular stage works including comedies.[6] It was clearly inappropriate behaviour for the bereaved family of a newly ennobled man, rather than undertaking the responsibilities conveyed by promotion to the peerage.

In the case of Anne Lefroy's response to Lady Bolton, there were additional complicating factors at play. The Paulet or Powlett family, Hampshire neighbours who feature repeatedly in Anne's letters, were an eccentric and various clan. Charles Powlett, the fifth Duke of Bolton (c. 1718–1765), army colonel and Whig politician, became known as the Marquess of Winchester on his accession to the dukedom in 1754. Until succeeding to the dukedom, Powlett was the Member of Parliament for Hampshire.

In 1765, for reasons unknown, he committed suicide.[7] He was succeeded in the dukedom by his brother Lord Harry Powlett (1720–1794) as the sixth duke. It was Harry who was Lord Bolton, then, in 1787, at the time of the Hackwood *Jane Shore*, and Anne's poem.

In about 1752 Harry Powlett had married Mary Nunn, with whom he had a daughter, Mary, born in 1753.[8] His wife died in 1764, and the following year Harry Powlett married Katherine Lowther, sister of Sir James Lowther, first Earl of Lonsdale (1736–1802). Katherine Powlett, née Lowther, was the current Lady Bolton in 1787, and this explains part of the 'Catharine' reference in Anne's poem.[9]

While Harry Powlett, who had spent most of his career in the Royal Navy, reaching the rank of admiral, was considered a rather bumbling and laughable figure in the House of Lords, his second wife was from a highly ambitious and high-achieving family. Katherine's brother James Lowther had got himself elected for the borough of Cumberland when he was still under legal age.[10] James married, for largely political reasons, Lady Mary Stuart, the daughter of the Earl of Bute and Lady Wortley

Montagu: they had no children. His domineering manner and aggressive approach made him numerous enemies, through a long and unhappy political career.[11] Was his sister Katherine of a similar, or a contrasting personality?

What we do know is that Katherine had a tragic romance in her past, prior to marrying Admiral Harry Powlett. She had been engaged to James Wolfe (1727–1759), British war hero and later general, prior to his departure for war in America. Details are scanty. However, it is clear that Wolfe, in between campaigning, wounds, and intriguing for promotion (that perennial occupation of both Royal Navy and Army personnel in the long eighteenth century), had a history of entanglements and break-ups. He was engaged to Elizabeth Lawson in the period 1747–1750, having a serious falling-out with his family; then this fell through and he reconciled with his parents. Subsequently a Dublin widow of a fellow officer would be lampooned as Wolfe's 'Irish Venus'.[12]

In 1758 Wolfe served under Major General Jeffrey Amherst in operations against the French in North America. After some successes, the operations were suspended in the late summer, and Wolfe returned to England. He was soon appointed to a command for a projected campaign in Canada. In the winter of 1758–59, between assembling a team of his own friends as subordinate officers, Wolfe took the waters at Bath. Here he appears to have become engaged to Katherine Lowther, a former acquaintance. Modern biographers suggest that Wolfe's parents were keen for him to settle down, insisting on an engagement.[13]

Wolfe sailed in February 1759, arriving at Halifax, Nova Scotia, in April (indicating the length of an Atlantic crossing in the spring). Various problems and delays hampered the campaign; the French were well prepared. The difficulties presented for amphibious operations were considerable. In early September, Wolfe's tactical genius was shown by his conception of bringing his troops up a steep section of the cliff some two miles from the city of Quebec. The French commander, Montcalm, was panicked into a hasty encounter in the open, in which his troops were decisively beaten by Wolfe's battle line. Wolfe himself, however, was fatally shot, and died from a series of illnesses and complications.

The operation had a double impact at home in England. Horace Walpole wrote: 'What a scene! An army in the night dragging itself up a precipice by stumps of trees to assault a town and attack an enemy strongly entrenched and double in numbers!'[14] The double aspect of the astonishing victory on the one hand, and on the other, the young commander's death in the very hour of triumph, made for an instant legend.

It also lent an aura to his bereaved fiancée. Katherine Lowther acquired iconic status herself, of a kind not often bestowed on a woman. An 'Ode to Miss L—, on the Death of General Wolfe,' published in the *Gentleman's Magazine* (the nearest thing the eighteenth century had to the internet) for November 1759, paid tribute to her:

> You, gentle maid, above the rest, his fate untimely mourn…[15]

Lady Wortley Montagu, mother-in-law of Katherine's brother, considered Katherine to be the 'greatest sufferer' by Wolfe's death.[16]

Katherine was also to feature in a projected elegy to be written by leading poet William Shenstone. The bookseller and publisher Robert Dodsley thought that an appropriate scene might be Katherine's bedroom:

> The scene, might be laid in [Katherine's] chamber … on the rejoicing night for the taking of Quebec.

Katherine's friends would conceal from her the death of Wolfe, and Wolfe's ghost would appear, inform her of his death, and console her. In the event, Shenstone never undertook the project.[17]

Some accounts indicate that Katherine, either during their brief engagement or afterwards, commissioned a portrait of Wolfe by leading painter Thomas Gainsborough. This work was put up for sale by Bonhams in 2014.[18]

Other artefacts which testify to the relationship include a miniature of Katherine by leading artist Richard Cosway, which Wolfe took with him to Canada. In his will, he wrote that on his death, the miniature was to be set in jewels, 'to the amount of five hundred guineas', and returned to her. This was an extraordinary amount of money to stipulate. For comparison, as we have seen, a labourer in the mid-eighteenth century might earn between 13 and 20 guineas in a year, if in work for the whole period. Relevantly, Wolfe's estate proved unequal to fulfilling the legacies, worth over £7,000, which he had made in his will.[19] The other item Wolfe took was a copy of Thomas Gray's poem *Elegy Written in a Country Churchyard*, also a gift from Katherine.[20]

It appears that there was no love lost between Katherine and Wolfe's mother Henrietta, and the death of Wolfe did not effect a reconciliation.[21] There is one piece of information which, if true, would go towards explaining three otherwise surprising elements of the established historical record: (a) the apparent insistence of Wolfe's parents on his engagement, after their displeasure about his earlier engagement to Elizabeth Lawson; (b) the implacable hostility of Mrs Wolfe towards Katherine after Wolfe's death; and (c) the almost inconceivable amount of money which Wolfe wished Katherine to have in the event of his death.

This snippet is to be found in one of those less-than-reliable resources: the family-history website. That the information presented in these sites is often wrong, and usually self-serving (being posted by descendants, or would-be descendants, of the individuals listed), should not obscure the fact that it is sometimes correct in part, if only rarely substantiated by documentary evidence. Indeed, the fact that such items are often posted by people entirely without general historical knowledge can support, to a limited degree, their status as independent sources.

One such website, ancestry.com.au, alleges that a child was born to Katherine in 1759, fathered by Wolfe. This person is recorded as Sarah Timmings (1759–1834), who later is said to have married Joseph Nash and had nine children.[22] The anonymous poster of this information apparently did not know the date of Katherine's death, which is well attested as 1809 elsewhere on the internet; so, by virtue of historical ignorance, this piece of data falls into the category, cited above, of possibly independent information.

On a different such site, genealogy.com, a writer, 'Natasha', in 2001 recounted a family story, as follows:

> We are told that [Katherine] placed her fatherless child with
> the Timmins family to be raised.[23]

No responses to Natasha have to date (April 2018) appeared on the site. Yet the existence of this Sarah Timmins or Timmings and Joseph Nash is confirmed by the parish record of their marriage on 6 November 1784 at St Thomas' church, Dudley, Worcestershire.[24]

A very confused account of the Lowther, Wolfe and Powlett connections appeared in *The Athenaeum* magazine for January–June 1809, ostensibly in a notice of Katherine's death. Public confusion about a family associated with the peerage is surprising. The wide circulation and regular updating of standard works on the peerage meant that the basic facts about births, deaths, and marriages in great families were available to any journalist prepared to undertake the minimum amount of research.

We recall that Jane Austen, in *Persuasion*, 1818, makes 'the Baronetage' the favourite (or only) reading matter of Sir Walter Elliot. Collins' *Peerage*, just one among these reference works, had first appeared in 1709, while Anne's brother Samuel Egerton Brydges was to release the sixth edition in 1812. There was a practical reason for the wide dissemination of this information: it reduced the scope for pretenders (of whom there were always many) to find support for their claims to noble titles and rich estates.

The extremely garbled nature of the *Athenaeum* version, therefore, suggests that there may have been something unusual going on. The account appears in 'Domestic Occurrences,' for London and Middlesex, which summarised remarkable events including deaths of notable people:

> The Duchess of Bolton (p. 357) was the youngest sister of the late Earl of Lonsdale. Her elder sister, Miss Lowther, who died at Richmond only a few years ago, had been admired, when young, by the celebrated and lamented General Wolfe, to whom her hand was engaged in 1759, when that hero fell, in the moment of victory, before Quebec. Miss Lowther manifested the deepest distress at his fate; and though she possessed many personal attractions, in addition to a very large fortune, she remained unmarried during her whole life. The beautiful copy of verses, hung by an unknown hand on the tomb of Wolfe, in Westminster-Abbey, beginning,
>
> 'Could not Lowther, weeping maid!'
>
> was written in allusion to that fact. Her younger sister was married to Lord Harry Powlett, then captain in the British navy, but whose exploits, in that service, did not entitle him to rank with our naval heroes. Lord Harry was at the siege of Carthagena, in S. America, in 1743, where Smollett has consigned his memory to posterity, though not in the most brilliant or flattering colours. He is the *Captain Whiffle*,

of Roderick Random. By the death of his elder brother he succeeded early in the present reign to the dukedom of Bolton, which became extinct some years ago in his person. He left only two daughters, the eldest of whom, Lady Catherine Powlett, a very beautiful and accomplished person, married the present Earl of Darlington. The Duchess of Bolton, her mother, survived her, and has left the greater part of her fortune, which was considerable, to the Hon. Frederic Vane, Lord Darlington's second son.[25]

The author is not identified; the editor of the magazine was John Aikin (1747–1822), brother of poet Anna Laetitia Barbauld. There are several inaccuracies, the most glaring being the internal inconsistency between the duchess being the youngest sister of James Lowther, Earl of Lonsdale, and 'her younger sister' being married to Harry Powlett. Collins' edition of 1784 gives the order of the Lowther children as follows:

1. James, now Earl of Lonsdale [tradition demanded that the male heir be listed as first issue, even if actually younger than his sisters; James was born in 1736].
2. Robert.
3. Margaret, married March 19, 1757, to Henry Vane, the present Earl of Darlington, and has issue.
4. Catherine, married April 8, 1765, to Lord Harry Powlet [sic], now Duke of Bolton, and has issue.
5. Barbara, unmarried.[26]

For readers not familiar with Smollett's novel, it is worth noting that Captain Whiffle is presented as a highly camp and overdressed homoerotic figure; there is clearly an intention to highlight some less usual form of masculinity in Lord Harry, and possibly even gay affairs. Smollett had depicted Captain Whiffle as maintaining a shipboard relationship with his personal surgeon, Mr Simper:

> He also prohibited any person whatever, except Simper and his own servants, from coming into the great cabin without first sending in to obtain leave. These singular regulations did not prepossess the ship's company in his favour: but,

on the contrary, gave scandal an opportunity to be very busy with his character, and accuse him of maintaining a correspondence with his surgeon not fit to be named.[27]

Roderick Random had first appeared in 1748, so when Katherine married Harry in April of 1765, he was probably already well known as the original of Captain Whiffle. A widowed Captain Whiffle may not have been regarded as a particularly desirable catch, but possibly Katherine Lowther was not in a position to refuse an offer. Neither party to the marriage will have anticipated Charles Powlett's suicide in the following July, which suddenly made Harry, as heir to the dukedom, a much more attractive prospect.

The *Athenaeum* writer, more interested in Smollett's putative caricature of Lord Harry, seems unaware that it was the duchess, not another Lowther sister, who had been engaged to Wolfe. It is extraordinary that the identity of Katherine, Duchess of Bolton, the woman who had become a national celebrity overnight in 1759, could have become so muddled by the time of her death, five decades on. Could it be that her status as national 'maid' had become a family and public embarrassment, and no family member was prepared to go on the public record to seek correction of a misleading account? Katherine's brother James, the Earl of Lonsdale, had died in 1802.

It is possible that a faint tradition that Wolfe and Katherine were 'intimate' before his departure for Quebec persisted into the nineteenth century. The only evidence I have for this surmise, admittedly, is a curious novel which was published in 1899: *French and English: The Story of the Struggle for America*, by Evelyn Everett-Green (1856–1932). Now forgotten, Everett-Green was one of the most widely read children's authors of the later nineteenth century.[28] Her mother, Mary Anne Everett Green (1818–1895), most unusually, combined motherhood with a paid career as an archivist and researcher of Great Britain's State records.[29]

The very purple passages in which Everett-Green describes the (imagined) final weeks before Wolfe's departure seem to deliver some coy Victorian hints to the effect that their relationship involved sex.

> '[At Bath, in late 1758] Wolfe was happiest at home with his mother and friend, and with bright Kate Lowther, with whom he soon became wonderfully intimate…' (Kindle loc. 3031)

'Their eyes met. In hers he read unbounded admiration and faith. It thrilled him strangely. It brought a look of new purpose into his face...' (Kindle loc. 3052)

'Wolfe and Kate were left alone together. He got possession of her other hand. She was standing before him still, a beautiful bloom upon her face, her eyes shining like stars...' (Kindle loc. 3062)

'[Kate] You will storm that great fortress [Quebec] which men call impregnable – you will storm it and you will vanquish it...' (Kindle loc. 3081)

'[Wolfe] Afterwards thoughts of war and strife must have their place; but for once let love be lord of our lives...' (Kindle loc. 3086)

Not just 'intimate', but 'wonderfully intimate'; 'purpose'; 'left alone together'; 'possession'; 'bloom'; these are words which were associated then, as now, with sexual charge. The *Oxford English Dictionary Online* lists 'intimate' used of sexual intimacy first in a newspaper of 1889.[30] 'Possession' was a much older usage, first cited in a reading from 1693, and indeed the *Oxford English Dictionary Online* lists it as *obs.*, with the last recorded example from 1890.[31]

The choice of these terms indicates that Everett-Green was intending to depict a relationship between Wolfe and Katherine with a sexual aspect. This may be because she knew of a long-standing, if generally unspoken, tradition about that relationship. (Dodsley's suggestion about Shenstone setting his elegy in Katherine's 'chamber' might also have been a clue in this direction.) If Everett-Green followed the careful historical practice which her mother had pioneered, perhaps indeed we are dealing with suggestions of historical fact, rather than with pure invention. On the other hand, it may simply have been that – as noted earlier in the chapter – sex has always sold, when it comes to the creative arts, including as part of works marketed to teens and tweens. (We recall the sexual innuendo which pervaded Milton's *Comus*, played at its first performance by leading actors of 15 and under.)

Was it Captain Whiffle or the former Miss L– who was the guiding spirit behind the Hackwood performance? It would seem that there was already, well before the performance of *Jane Shore*, a tradition at Hackwood of putting on public shows. In 1769, several magazines reported on a masked ball and 'illuminations' at the great house.

> *Thursday*, June 1. The duke of Bolton gave a grand ball at Hackwood-park, where the company began to assemble between seven and eight, and by ten o'clock the rooms were very full of masks....The dresses in general were extremely magnificent. The duchess of Bolton was in the habit of a Tartarian princess, embroidered with diamonds ... Mrs Garrick made a very fine figure in the Venetian carnival habit ... Lady Mary Lowther [daughter of the Duke], in the character of an old woman, afforded infinite humour. The duke of Bolton wore a domino.[32]

(The classic 'domino' costume was a loose robe, with a cape and wide sleeves, presumably intended to look vaguely medieval.[33]) It is interesting that the wife of David Garrick (1717–1779), greatest actor and producer of the eighteenth century, was in attendance: Eva Marie Veigel (1724–1822) was a prominent performer in her own right. Garrick himself, over the summer of 1769, was preparing to put on the Shakespeare Jubilee at Stratford-upon-Avon in September, a major event which helped to set the reputation of Shakespeare as the national poet; he may not have had the time to attend himself.

It is with all this in the background that we now return to Anne Lefroy's poem in 1787. Some Austen scholars have alluded to this poem and its background, notably David Selwyn in *Jane Austen and Leisure* (1999 and 2004), but to date no writer has addressed the issues in detail. Selwyn noted that Anne was politely declining her friend Katherine's invitation to take part in the Hackwood performance of *Jane Shore.*[34] Yet there is far more going on here than a formulaic aversion to family theatricals. Not only, as noted above, were family theatricals a crux of moral and social anxiety, but the particular play had political, sexual and emotional significance. The next chapter will examine both the play and the highly eccentric Hackwood cast.

Chapter 8

Jane Shore at Hackwood Park II: Featuring Hellgate and Billingsgate

Jane Shore (c. 1445–c.1527), after all, was England's most celebrated participant in royal sex outside marriage. She was the most famous of the many lovers of King Edward IV (1442–1483). Married for family and financial reasons to a businessman, Jane applied in 1476 to have the marriage annulled as her husband was impotent. Jane soon began her relationship with the king, which continued until his death. Jane's other lovers included Thomas Grey, Marquess of Dorset, and William Hastings, Baron Hastings.

The play by Nicholas Rowe (1674–1718), first performed in 1714, is set after Edward's death, during the protectorate of Richard Duke of Gloucester (afterwards King Richard III). Jane was accused of intriguing with former allies such as Edward's widow Elizabeth Woodville. Rowe's play deliberately recalls Shakespeare's *Richard III* in its depiction of Richard, its choice of characters, and its language.

Jane Shore was the best known of Rowe's numerous works, and because of the ever-popular subject (sex, yet again, sells), was repeatedly revived during the eighteenth century. The play also had a political context which was subsequently exploited by broadly Whig sympathisers.[1] A painting (c. 1793) by William Blake, from his earlier, more conventional phase, shows *The Penance of Jane Shore*, in which Richard has forced Jane to walk in shame through the streets of London.[2]

The character which Anne had been invited to play was that of Alicia. An invention by Rowe, this was Jane Shore's sometime friend, who suspects an affair between Jane and her lover Hastings. Richard and Catesby describe Hastings as in thrall to Alicia:

> *Glos.* And yet this tough, impracticable, heart,
> Is govern'd by a dainty-finger'd girl;
> Such flaws are found in the most worthy natures;

A laughing, toying, wheedling, whimpering she,
Shall make him amble on a gossip's message,
And take the distaff with a hand as patient
As e'er did Hercules.
Sir Richard Ratcliffe. The fair Alicia
Of noble birth and exquisite of feature,
Has held him long a vassal to her beauty.

(Act I, Scene 1)

On one level, then, being asked to play Alicia was a compliment to Anne's liveliness and beauty, despite her being about 40 years old at the time. Alicia and Jane swear undying friendship for one another.

Alic. If I not hold her nearer to my soul,
Than every other joy the world can give,
Let poverty, deformity, and shame,
Distraction and despair, seize me on earth,
Let not my faithless ghost have peace hereafter,
Nor taste the bliss of your celestial fellowship.

(Act I, Scene 2)

Alicia goes on to accuse Hastings of betraying her with Jane (Act II, Scene 1). Hastings actually tries to rape Jane. Alicia, driven by jealousy of Hastings' affection for Jane, responds by informing on both Hastings and Jane via a letter to Richard in which she accuses Hastings of promoting the interests of Edward IV's sons as rivals to Richard. She soliloquises:

Alic. O Jealousy! Thou bane of pleasing friendship,
How does thy rancour poison all our softness,
And turn our gentle natures into bitterness!
See, where she comes! Once my heart's dearest blessing,
Now my chang'd eyes are blasted with her beauty,
Loath that known face, and sicken to behold her.

(Act III, Scene 1)

Jane herself, in a confrontation with Richard, defends Edward's children. Richard is furious:

Glos. Go, some of you, and turn this strumpet forth!
Spurn her into the street; there let her perish
And rot upon a dunghill. Through the city
See it proclaim'd, that none, on pain of death,
Presume to give her comfort, food, or harbour;
Who ministers the smallest comfort, dies.

(Act IV, Scene 1)

Richard accuses Hastings of conspiring with Elizabeth Woodville, and orders him to be executed. In comes Alicia, and confesses that she betrayed her lover Hastings:

Alic. Raving and mad I flew to my revenge,
And writ I know not what – told the protector,
That Shore's detested wife, by wiles, had won thee
To plot against his greatness. He believ'd it
(Oh, dire event of my pernicious counsel!)
And, while I meant destruction on her head,
H' has turn'd it all on thine.

(Act IV, Scene 2)

Hastings goes to his execution, forgiving Alicia but warning her to treat Jane kindly. Act V opens with an eyewitness account of Jane walking the streets, and Scene 2 brings us directly to see her, arriving at Alicia's door.

Alic. What wretch art thou, whose misery and baseness
Hangs on my door; whose hateful whine of woe
Breaks in upon my sorrows, and distracts
My jarring senses with thy beggar's cry?
Jane. A very beggar, and a wretch indeed,
One driv'n by strong calamity to seek
For succours here; one perishing for want
Whose hunger has not tasted food these three days;
And humbly asks, for charity's dear sake,
A draught of water and a little bread.
Alic. And dost thou come to me, to me, for bread,
I know thee not – Go, hunt for it abroad –
Where wanton hands upon the earth have scatter'd it,

89

> Or cast it on the waters – mark the eagle,
> And hungry vulture, where they wind the prey,
> Watch where the ravens of the valley feed,
> And seek thy food with them – I know thee not.

Nicholas Rowe was not William Shakespeare, but this is a very powerful scene. Rowe has Alicia recall not only Shakespeare's newly minted King Harry rejecting his old friend Falstaff ('I know thee not, old man': *Henry IV Part 2,* Act V Scene 5), but several Biblical verses.

'Cast thy bread upon the waters: for thou shalt find it after many days' (Ecclesiastes 11:1) is an injunction to have faith about the outcome of events, by definition unknown in advance; here, of course, it is ironically used by Alicia. She also gestures to another well-known Bible story:

> And the word of the Lord came unto [Elijah], saying Get thee hence; and turn thee eastward, and hide thyself by the brook Cherith, that is before Jordan. And it shall be, that thou shalt drink of the brook; and I have commanded the ravens to feed thee there. So he went and did according unto the word of the Lord: for he went and dwelt by the brook Cherith, that is before Jordan. And the ravens brought him bread and flesh in the morning, and bread and flesh in the evening; and he drank of the brook.
> (1 Kings 17:1–6, King James Authorised Version)

Not only is Alicia demonstrating the utmost cruelty to the friend to whom she has sworn loyalty, she is parodying the word of the Lord. As a quasi-divine allocation of deserts, Alicia shortly afterwards begins to manifest signs of mental illness, hallucinating Hastings' headless body, and running off stage. Jane, for her part, is helped by and reunited with her wronged husband Shore, prior to her finally peaceful death.

Scholars have speculated that Rowe's depiction of the love-hate relationship between Alicia and Jane was a reference to the court friendships which Queen Anne cultivated with particular women such as Sarah Churchill and Abigail Masham.[3] These women were routinely lampooned in the popular press for seeking personal and political gain through their royal relationships. Similarly, Rowe's Alicia seeks to manipulate Hastings and Richard for her own personal and political ends.[4]

Another possible inspiration for Alicia could have been the writer Delarivier Manley, whose writing about political scandals led briefly to her imprisonment in 1709. The scholar Jones DeRitter has read the play as highlighting the risks to politically active women from expressing themselves in writing.[5] If we follow DeRitter's account, this allows us to better appreciate Anne's boldness of approach in expressing her objections to playing Alicia in that very medium – writing.

Anne's objections were related to the very nature of the role in Rowe's play. Once we consider the various aspects of Rowe's Alicia, we can re-read Anne's poem as expressing something rather different from the polite and conventional refusal of 'a wife, a mother' to take part in the morally ambiguous practice of acting. The rhetorical questions – '[Can I] as mad Alicia teach my heart to beat? … Spurn the dejected mourner from my gate?' – begin to look more like an expression of reproach, that she, the wife of a minister of the church, should be thought appropriate to appear in a role which combined treachery, irreligion, and the worst kind of disloyalty to another woman.

Perhaps the cause of more hurt, the person inviting Anne to play the role of the treacherous friend was her 'friend' Katherine, who had already allocated the sympathetic heroine role of Jane Shore to another actress. In addition, if Anne was familiar with any account which indicated that Katherine had borne a child prior to her marriage (whether communicated by Katherine herself or by other channels), she might have felt it unfair that she was being asked to attract the odium attaching to Alicia, while Katherine, through her bumbling husband's elevation to the peerage, had been absolved of any guilt for past offences against social mores. To borrow a phrase from Jane Austen, in contrasting Mr Darcy and Mr Wickham: 'One has got all the goodness, and the other all the appearance of it.'[6]

The playbill which advertised the Hackwood show reads as follows:

HACKWOOD PLAY,
On Thursday, the 1st of February, 1787.
JANE SHORE:
Lord Hastings, by Lord BARRYMORE
Duke of Gloster, by Mr BLOOMFIELD
Belmour, by Mr BROOKE
Catsby [sic], by Mr INGALL

Ratcliff, by Mr TASKER
And Dumont, by Mr POWLETT
Alicia, by Mrs LANGTON
And Jane Shore, by Lady Caroline BARRY.

To which will be added a musical entertainment call'd
HOB in the WELL.
Hob, by Lord BARRYMORE
Sir Thomas Testy, by Mr TASKER
Dick, by Mr BROOKE
Old Hob, by Mr SMITH
And Friendly, by Mr INGALL
Betty, by Mrs BERRESFORD
Hob's Mother, by Mrs SMITH
And Flora, by Mrs SARGENT.
To begin at seven o'Clock.[7]

The leading actor, taking the part of Hastings, was Richard Barry, seventh Earl of Barrymore (1769–1793). He was 17 years old. We can see that Christopher Edward Lefroy misremembered the facts in recording that 'Lady Catherine Barry' played Jane Shore: it was Richard's sister Caroline, not Catherine, and she was 19 at the time.

The Barry siblings were a girl and three boys: Caroline (b. 1768); Richard (b. 1769); Henry (b. 1770); and Augustus (b. 1773). Their father, the sixth Earl of Barrymore, died of fever shortly after the birth of Augustus. Richard showed signs of great intelligence, and was sent by his widowed mother to live and study with the Reverend Tickell, at Wargrave in Berkshire.[8]

The Barrys' mother died in 1782, and their maternal grandmother, the Countess of Harrington, provided some care for them. She was keen for the boys to 'uphold their rank', and so provided young Richard with £1,000 pocket money on his going to Eton, aged 14, in 1784.[9] The earl's subsequent notorious extravagance perhaps began here. The Countess of Harrington herself died shortly afterwards, and the last relative who might have exerted some good influence on the young Barrys was gone.

Richard spent two years at Eton (1784–1786), acquiring a taste for boxing, both as a spectator and a participant. He and his friends also attended the second spring meeting at Newmarket in 1785, and, as a 16-year-old novice punter, he won a thousand guineas on Rockingham to win at seven to four. A passion for the turf was begun.[10]

How the earl made the acquaintance of Katherine, Lady Bolton is not known, but it may have been through racing. The Boltons had no sons, so there was no direct connection through Eton. Nor is it clear whether Lady Bolton's interest in the young earl was maternal, or similar to Mrs Bennet's from *Pride and Prejudice* (seeking a husband for her daughters), or of a 'cougar' style sexual nature. While we are not sure of Katherine Lowther Powlett's birth year, she was probably about 20 in 1759, the year of her engagement to Wolfe, so she must have been in her late forties in the later 1780s. With Captain Whiffle for a husband, she may have been tempted to seek young male attention, and her friendship with the teenage earl was apparently very close.

The earl's biographer, his friend and protégé John Williams, also known as Anthony Pasquin, tells a revealing anecdote about the relationship between Richard and Lady Bolton. They communicated in a secret language, which she taught to him:

> [The earl] taught me a particular language, which he assured me had been invented by the Duchess of Bolton, who instructed him; its singularity was effected by a singular arrangement of one vowel and one consonant, and by this means it was wholly unintelligible to any person not knowing the secret: many persons have thought us talking nonsense, when we were really exchanging ideas often at the expence of those around us.[11]

It is likely that the earl and the duchess were using some variant of pig-Latin, although it would be surprising if the duchess had to teach this to a boy who had attended a public school. Pasquin may also be hinting that the duchess also instructed the earl in matters other than linguistic.

Lady Bolton also encouraged the young earl's already strong addiction to horse-racing. Pasquin writes:

> Lord Barrymore's *entre* upon the turf was in the year 1787, when he accompanied the Duchess of Bolton; and the first racer he bought was a filly called *Yarico*, from

the late Colonel O'Kelley; with this filly he made his first match at Newmarket, against a horse of Mr Davis's, called *Copernicus*, this match his Lordship won: – he engaged in the hazardous, but pleasurable pursuits of the turf, with that ardour and spirit to which the natural turn of his great mind impelled him upon all occasions.[12]

The Earl of Barrymore bought numerous racehorses, and of course had to employ a number of staff to maintain his stable. It was acknowledged that he showed remarkable knowledge about horses and, even at this young age, his expertise was called upon in allocating handicap weights.[13]

The two passions of the earl's young life, it turned out, were racing and the stage. Both were combined in his first venture into show business: becoming part-owner of the Royal Circus in St George's Fields, London. The circus was conceived as a rival venue to Astley's, the well-known circus attended by Jane Austen in 1796, and by several characters in her novels (notably Harriet Smith with the John Knightleys in *Emma*).[14] Barrymore's friend Delphini produced a pageant displaying wild animals such as big cats, and the performance concluded with a genuine stag hunt. Despite novelties like this, the Royal Circus did not prosper as a business venture.[15]

At around this time, and possibly through horseracing connections, the earl and his siblings became friendly with the Prince of Wales, later the Prince Regent, and eventually King George IV (1762–1830). The prince was not lacking in wit, and is said to have bestowed the following nicknames on the Barry set. Richard was 'Hellgate' because of his wild living. Henry was 'Cripplegate', as he, like Byron, had a club foot. Augustus, later to become a clergyman, was 'Newgate', as it was said to be the only prison with which he was not personally familiar. For her part, Caroline was 'Billingsgate', because of her use of bad language.[16]

It was no doubt the Hackwood production of *Jane Shore*, in February 1787, which reinforced the earl's love of the stage. As the playbill indicates, following the main play was a shorter piece, a 'farce', as was often the practice in professional theatres. At Hackwood, the afterpiece was *Hob in the Well,* with the earl taking for himself the plum comedy role of Hob, the yokel hero of the piece.

This playlet, or mini-opera as there were numerous songs included, was more commonly known by the name of its heroine, *Flora*, or sometimes by both names: *Flora, or Hob in the Well*. It is under this double name that it appears in an edition of works by Colley Cibber (1671–1757), although it was not, in fact, by Cibber.[17]

The plot, such as it is, was originally a sub-plot of a five-act comedy by Thomas Doggett, *The Country Wake* (1696).[18] It morphed into its own afterpiece, solely driven by the comic strength of the character of Hob, a sturdy West-Country type, who survives being thrown into a well by the mildly villainous Sir Thomas Testy. This version was *Hob; or the Country-wake* (1720), a comic afterpiece. A further development was made by John Hippisley, fresh from creating Peachum in *The Beggar's Opera*, who worked up the whole into *Flora; or, Hob in the well* (London, 1729).[19] *Flora* retains a special significance in the USA, as it was performed in Charleston, South Carolina, in 1735, the first public performance of an opera on the American mainland.[20]

The threadbare plot begins with Flora, the young niece and ward of Sir Thomas Testy, revealing her plight to her maid Betty, another comic classic role. Flora sings:

> How wretched are we orphans made,
> By dying parents' wills betray'd
> To guardians powers, who oft invade
> Our freedom, to our cost?
> Like captives they their wards confine,
> Pretending care; but with design
> To prostitute them for their coin
> To who'e'er bids the most.

Note that 'coin' was clearly intended to rhyme with 'confine' and 'design', a fact which we know from other poetic sources from the eighteenth century.[21] Betty responds that for her part, she was ditched by her lover because of his new passion – 'another more darling mistress called *Claret'*.

> *Flo.* And how do you find yourself now?
> *Bet.* As most folks are, after the loss of an old lover.
> *Flo.* How's that?
> *Bet.* Ready for a new one.[22]

Boom-boom! Flora confides that she is in love with Mr Friendly, and he with her, but her uncle's guardianship prevents their meeting.

> *Bet.* Why, run a risque, Madam.
> *Flo.* What risque?
> *Bet.* Run away with him.
> *Flo.* Psha! How is that possible! When my uncle locks me up as if I were his only bottle of brandy?
> *Bet.* You know, Madam, I have sometimes the keys of both in my keeping – and if you please to uncork your conscience, I'll undertake, in eight and forty hours, Mr *Friendly* shall have at least half a dozen go-downs of you.[23]

Risqué indeed. The double-entendres abound. We meet Friendly and his contriving servant, from internal evidence named Richard (hence the 'Dick' in the Hackwood cast list). Friendly convinces the young yokel Hob to carry a letter to Flora.

> *Friendly.* Well, *Hob*, canst thou carry this letter to Sir *Thomas Testy*'s house for me?
> *Hob.* Yes, zir, yes.
> *Fri.* Do so, and give it to Madam *Flora*; but take care nobody sees you deliver it.
> *Hob.* Yes, Zir – but must I carry it to-night? 'tis main dark.[24]

Despite his prolix misgivings, Hob takes the letter, but is intercepted by Sir Thomas Testy, who beats him, grabs the letter and reads it, learning of Friendly and Flora's plans to elope. Testy, in a rage, gets his servants to dump Hob into a well.

> *Hob.*…Pray vorbear, and don't murder an innocent man.
> Sings: I never till now was conzarned in strife,
> Have mercy, Sir Thomas, and spare poor Hob's life,
> And give me my vreedom, as I had before –
> I'll be a good boy, and I'll do so no more.
> Indeed I won't –
> *Sir Tho.* In with him I say –

Hob. O Lord! Maister Jonathan [Sir Thomas' servant],
I vorewarn you, don't be conzarned in this: consider what
you do.
Sir Tho. Oons! In with him.
Hob. You are all principals, there are no 'complishes
[accomplices] in murder. Help! Murder!
They put him down, and Exeunt.[25]

Hob is soon rescued from the well, by his parents, the innkeeper Old Hob
and his wife, passing by. There is more comic business when Mrs Hob,
getting what she thinks will be water as she winds up the bucket, sees
Hob instead:

> Lud, lud, 'tis main heavy – Heyday – I believe old Nick's in
> the bottom of the bucket, for my part. [*Hob* cries out] Oh, a
> ghost; a ghost!
> [*Hob* appears in the bucket, and she lets the rope go, and he
> sinks again]

Hob, in fact, is indestructible, a force of nature. A village festivity (the
'country wake') gives Friendly the opportunity to pose as a ballad-
singer and approach Flora in disguise, as well as to sing some songs.
Hob reappears in his normal role of innkeeper's boy, offering 'red Port,
or white Port, or such sort of stuff' or 'Zack' (sack, a sweet wine) to
Friendly and his servant. Hob's catchword is 'Ch'am coming, ch'am
coming,' (I'm coming), as he is summoned in all directions at once.

He then takes on the role of MC for the country dancers:

> Set to now, *William* -ah, rarely done! In *Mary*; ah, dainty
> *Mary!* Turn her about, *John* – now, now! A murrain
> [plague] – You're quite out. Look, *Ralph* should ha' cast off;
> and while *John* had turned *Mary* about, *Tomas* should ha'
> led up *Nan*, and *Joan* met *Ralph* at the bottom agen; mean-
> while, *John* should have sided with *Mary*, and then *Mary*
> should back to back with *Ralph*, and then *Tomas* had come
> in again, in his own place; and so all had been right. Come,
> begin again.[26]

Next Hob then gets into a fight with one Roger, put up to the task by Sir Thomas, 'breaks his head', and all is well. Meanwhile, Friendly and Flora have disappeared together, and the furious Sir Thomas challenges Friendly's servant Dick:

> *Sir Tho.* 'Sdeath, sir, what business have you to hinder me?
> *Serv.* Sir, I have no business at present, but to hinder you.
> *Sir Tho.* But pray, Sir, how comes it to be your business?
> *Serv.* Because, Sir, it is my business to do my master's business; and I have some modest reason to believe, that he and the parson are now doing your niece's business.
> *Sir Tho.* The devil! Murder! Where are they, villain?
> *Serv.* Pray, Sir, compose yourself, for they are here.
> Enter Friendly, Flora, and Betty.[27]

Sir Thomas refuses his blessing to the couple, and exits in a rage. All the friends celebrate the wedding, including Hob, and the company sings the final verse:

> Now from envy free – all friends loyally
> Supplicate with me our guardian divinity
> To bless the king and queen, and royal progeny.
> Send us peace, trade's increase, health and prosperity.
> May Cupid's darts strike sure – but be the cause the cure;
> In virtuous deeds delight – Happy all unite
> In friendship and love.
> [A dance, and Exeunt.][28]

Slight and hackneyed as its plot is, *Hob in the well* represents a major undertaking for a group of amateur players. There are a great many songs interspersed with the dialogue, which will have required a band of professional or semi-professional musicians. In addition, the stage business required a wall (for Flora to escape over) and a visibly functioning 'well' (for Hob to be thrown into and emerge from), so construction was called for. There had to be a functioning tavern with a bar, as well as a dance floor. There are scenes set at night as well as by day.

Most clearly, the role of Hob is a demanding one. Hob is all things to all people, and the scene in which he runs the tavern and the country dance is a virtuoso piece, demanding all the young earl's stagecraft. Clearly, he loved to be the centre of attention, possibly a natural outcome of having been orphaned at a young age.

It was perhaps this stage experience at Hackwood which led the earl to his most notorious extravagance: the creation, during the following year 1788, of his very own theatre at Wargrave, where he had gone as a young boy to be educated by the Reverend Tickell. He seems to have regarded Wargrave village as his home, and was well known, with his brothers, for carrying out practical jokes in the area, such as swapping inn signs overnight, so that the publican of the 'Rose and Crown' would find that his premises had been re-named 'The King's Head'.[29] Possibly to appease irritated locals, he also put on cricket games and village festivities.

The earl commissioned a small opera-house to be built opposite his home at Wargrave. It was to be built under the direction of a Mr Cox of the Theatre Royal, Covent Garden. Stage machinery was a special feature. The costume department, provided by leading costume professionals, cost £2,000. The overall cost of the theatre was estimated at £60,000 (several thousand times the yearly income of a working man at the time).[30] Audiences included the great (such as the Prince of Wales) as well as the locals.

An early performance at the Wargrave Theatre took place nearly two years after the Hackwood performance, on 25 January 1789. The earl starred in the character part of Brass, in Vanbrugh's *The Confederacy* (1705), and also as Sebastian in *The Midnight Hour*, a farce by the French writer Antoine-Jean Dumaniant, translated by Mrs Inchbald and acted at Covent Garden in the same year as at Wargrave, 1789.[31] The earl's acting strength apparently lay in comedy, as his Brass 'caused much amusement, and won applause'.[32]

The earl would also amuse himself by slipping out after a Wargrave performance, and mixing with the patrons emerging from the theatre. If he heard any comments about an actor, he passed these onto the relevant people at supper, 'exaggerated with all his powers of wit and raillery'.[33]

In 1788, the year after the Hackwood *Jane Shore,* Lady Caroline Barry, while on a visit to Paris, married Louis Pierre François Malcolm Drummond, the Comte de Melfort. The titles of John Drummond, former Earl of Melfort, who followed James II into exile in 1688, were forfeited in 1695, but Louis XIV of France granted titles to the Melfort clan (not recognised in England). The couple returned to England, and the comte entered into his brother-in-law the earl's activities. However, the marriage between him and Lady Caroline was annulled 'for some reason', as her brother's Victorian biographer John Robert Robinson blandly states.[34]

In fact, there were very few reasons for which an annulment could be granted; fraud – because of an assumed identity by one or both parties, or by one or both parties having been under legal age; or incompetence – one or both parties having been unable to give informed consent (e.g. because not of sound mind). Lady Caroline, having married in July 1788, was under the legal age of 21 (she was born in 1768), so this may have been the, or a, ground for annulment.[35] As Lady Caroline was an orphan as well as under age, a lack of parental consent might also have been claimed as a reason for annulment.[36]

There was, however, also a ground for seeking annulment in the allegation of the husband's impotence, although this was very, almost vanishingly, rare: of 262 nullification and separation cases in the London Consistory Court from 1670 to 1857, only seven involved allegations of impotence.[37] Their rarity, however, was compensated for by the high level of public interest they generated, and published transcripts became popular.[38]

On the other hand, identities of the parties were often disguised by the use of initials (e.g. A v D).[39] While we do not know the precise reason for Lady Caroline's marriage to the comte being annulled, it is possible that impotence was a factor, although as noted above, if one or both parties sought a formal separation, her age at marriage could have been cited. It would clearly depend on which party sought the action; by the late eighteenth century, most litigants were men, but in the 1800s a majority of women brought the suits.[40]

Not content with having one theatre at Wargrave, the earl managed to acquire a London site, in Savile Row, and open it as a theatre in 1790. The first play was *The Beaux' Stratagem* (George Farquhar, 1707).[41] The earl also required additional accommodation for the guests he invited to attend his theatre, as they regularly returned to his town residence in Piccadilly to eat and stay.[42]

Before long, the expenses of horseracing, two theatres, a large staff including theatre professionals, and gambling, began to cause problems for the Barrymore household. The earl stood for the Commons seat of

Reading, 'with a view to evading his creditors', as the official History of Parliament sardonically relates.[43] He courted the electors with a magnificent banquet at the Crown Hotel, of which the standout feature was a turtle weighing 150 lb, but was unsuccessful.[44] However, he did secure the seat of Heytesbury shortly afterwards, apparently as a favour from William A'Court (1747–1817), the hereditary holder.[45] There is no record of his parliamentary activity, only of his perpetual absence from Parliamentary duties.

Barrymore may, however, have been aware of how far he had always failed in the duties of his rank. His biographer, Robinson, tells an anecdote which may indicate self-awareness of the extent to which the earl had fallen short of living up to his talents. At the Reading Free Debate Society, it is recorded that the earl addressed the gathering on the topic of 'whether the continuance of the Slave Trade was consistent with the sound policy of a Free Nation'. All aspects were canvassed, concluding with a summary of the degrading effects of the slave trade and the cruelty of its persistence. Its effect on the listeners was,

> to make the most reflective of them deplore that so great a gift of logical and eloquent oratory should hitherto have been sacrificed at the shrine of '*Folly*', instead of in the service of the Nation.[46]

Meanwhile, Cox the theatre designer had never been paid in full, and in 1792 commenced legal action to recover the £449 he considered owing to him. The judge, Lord Kenyon, in finding for the plaintiff, had this to say about the destructive effect of private theatricals, both in general and in the particular case of Lord Barrymore. Lord Kenyon's comment about 'designing men' should perhaps, in Earl Barrymore's case, have included designing women as well, since it appears that Lady Bolton had been a key influence.

> He lamented this young nobleman had, during his minority, been surrounded by designing men, who, instead of storing his mind with useful literature, had, he was afraid, depraved his taste and perverted his disposition. With respect to the tendency of private theatricals, [Lord Kenyon] doubted extremely whether they ever inculcated one virtuous

sentiment; he had known instances when they had had a contrary effect, as they usually vitiated and debauched the morals of both sexes, the performers seldom retiring from the entertainment but every *Romeo* knew the estimate of his *Juliet*'s virtue![47]

In October 1792, the auctioneer James Christie (1730–1803), founder of the great auction house, sold at the premises the materials of the earl's theatre: machinery, bricks, Portland stone, flooring, doors, and other items. Shortly afterwards, the earl's racing stud was sold.[48]

It was in these straits that Barrymore took on a captain's commission in the Berkshire militia.[49] His military duties did not appear to interfere very much with his membership of social circles such as the 'Bacchanalian Society', or with amusing himself by acting, in real life, the role of 'Hob' – directing the activities of a local pub, even down to cooking a chicken and vegetables and serving supper to the assembled patrons.[50]

In March 1793, Barrymore sought permission from his colonel, Earl Craven (a distant connection of the Austens and Lloyds) to accompany a troop directed to escort a group of French prisoners to Dover. On the way, the earl played his accustomed role of Hob in the pub at Folkestone, where the group had halted for refreshment.

Once under way again, the earl took the reins of his carriage. With the jolting of the gig, a loaded gun which had been left on a seat fell, discharged, and the bullet entered the earl's face under the eye. Despite urgent assistance, the earl was dead within forty minutes.

> So ended Richard Barry, seventh Earl of Barrymore, Viscount Buttevant, Baron Barry of Olethan, Ibaune, and Barryscourt, descended from a noble line of ancestors, whose name and fortunes he had dimmed and marred.[51]

A career of expense, of racing and theatricals, begun under the wing of Katherine Lowther Powlett, Duchess of Bolton, on the occasion turned down by Anne Lefroy, had ended with a negligent discharge and accidental death; just when the earl was, finally, undertaking a service to his country – 'giving back', as we say nowadays, for the gifts with which nature had provided him. He was not yet 24 years old.

Chapter 9

Samuel's Claim
(A Genealogical Digression)

When biographers reflected on Samuel Egerton Brydges' life, they wondered that such an intelligent man could have been so obsessed with his baseless claim for a noble title.

Sir Walter Scott's son-in-law, John Gibson Lockhart, wrote of Samuel in reviewing his *Autobiography* in 1834:

> Sir Egerton may be compared to a man who has a good pair of eyes of his own, and now and then condescends to make good use of them; but who, from some fantastic caprice, has so long indulged in the habit of looking at all the world, his own image included, through an artificially tinted lens, that he is never at his ease when the unfortunate toy is in his pocket.
>
> There are, in a word, two circumstances which have poisoned this accomplished man's existence: first, the failure of his family to satisfy the House of Peers ... that they had made out a legal claim to the honours of the old barony of Chandos; and secondly, his own failure in achieving for himself a first-rate name as an English author...[1]

Lockhart notes that, despite his voluminous output of reminiscences (*Recollections,* published in Geneva in 1825, and *Autobiographical Memoir* from Paris, 1826, as well as the two-volume *Autobiography* under review), Samuel managed to conceal from the reader the main events of his long life. These were as follows. Brought up at Wootton, he attended Maidstone School (1771–75), the King's School at Canterbury (1775–80), and Queen's College Cambridge (October 1780 – Christmas

1782). He left Cambridge without taking a degree. Samuel then toyed with the law, entering the Middle Temple, London, in 1782, and was called to the bar in 1787, but never practised.[2] He married Elizabeth Byrche in 1786, moving to Hampshire to be near the Lefroys. In 1785, Samuel's first volume of poetry, *Sonnets and Other Poems* appeared, to limited reaction; this caused him to suffer years of depression.

Other works followed, including the novel *Arthur Fitz-Albini* (1798). Jane Austen, even now at not quite 23 a shrewd book reviewer, wrote of it:

> We have got 'Fitz-Albini'; my father has bought it against my private wishes, for it does not quite satisfy my feelings that we should purchase the only one of Egerton's works of which his family are ashamed. That these scruples, however, do not at all interfere with my reading it, you will easily believe. We have neither of us yet finished the first volume. My father is disappointed – I am not, for I expected nothing better. Never did any book carry more internal evidence of its author. Every sentiment is completely Egerton's. There is very little story, and what there is told in a strange, unconnected way.[3]

The novel apparently gave considerable offence to Samuel's country neighbours, who recognised caricatures of themselves. Samuel, in an authorial footnote, insisted that he had been restrained in replacing his original manuscript depictions of neighbours with banks of asterisks, to suggest that there was more offensive material which he could, should he be inclined, have included. One neighbour is described as follows:

> Mr B—, the son of ***********[more than six lines of asterisks follow, to indicate a lengthy excision] He hates the company of all, over whom he cannot preside; and, with an affectation of humility, is more proud and envious than any body I know. But his pride, instead of being manly, and his envy, instead of being bold, display themselves in sneers, in peevishness, in oblique scandal, and dark insinuations. [To which is added a footnote:]

The author, in the former edition, mutilated this character, which, as it stood in the MS was in his conception the best drawn in the book, lest there should be an individual foolish enough to take it to himself. He is informed that his forbearance has been ineffectual. A greater clamour, and more bitter resentment, could not have pursued him if the most offensive page had never been cancelled. But, for the present, he scorns the ample retaliation he has in his hands; and therefore suffers the asterisks still to stand. Feb 25, 1799.[4]

In indicating that Samuel's family was ashamed of the work, Jane is probably meaning that Anne, and/or the Reverend George, had indicated that they found it embarrassing. *Fitz-Albini* must have received some favourable comment on its first appearance, however, because even the paranoid Samuel was able to acknowledge this in his preface to the second edition of the novel (1799):

To appear a second time before the publick, who have given so favourable a reception to the former edition of this Novel, without some acknowledgements of gratitude for the praise bestowed upon it, would seem like a want of that sensibility, of which, the few who know the author, will never accuse him. His earliest ambition was literary fame; but solitude, indolence, hopes, perhaps too sanguine, prematurely and violently chilled, and some very complicated ill-usage, certainly little merited, had for a while torpified, if not enfeebled, his mind...[5]

Samuel seems to have been aware of the kind of criticism of his novel – the lack of a story-line – to which Jane Austen referred. He adds:

The author was perfectly aware, that the paucity of incidents would be deemed by many a great deficiency. But, as he always valued sentiment and reflection above perplexity of plot, which, when once unravelled, ceases to interest, he has chosen to follow his own ideas of excellence.[6]

It is even possible that Anne had passed on to Samuel a hint from Jane about her views about the first edition.

He was also perpetually in debt and unable to manage his estates, despite having inherited properties from his parents and wives. His first wife Elizabeth died in July 1796 aged only 30, after bearing Samuel two sons and three daughters. Not quite two months later, Samuel married Mary Robinson, with whom he had five sons and five daughters.[7]

In 1792 Samuel had retired to Denton Court near his birthplace of Wootton, devoting himself to literature and the study of antiquities and genealogy. Even before this, in 1789, he had begun to be obsessed with his own ancestry, and had persuaded his elder brother, the Reverend Edward Tymewell Brydges (1749–1807) to make a claim for the extinct barony of Chandos.

As it happened, this case had a connection with Jane Austen's family. The Dukes of Chandos were connections of the Leighs of Adlestrop, Austen's mother's cousins. James Brydges, the third Duke of Chandos (1731–1789) was the brother of Caroline Brydges (1730–1804) who married James Leigh (1724–1774), one of the Leigh cousins of Mrs Austen. The Duke of Chandos had no surviving son; and he brought up his sister Caroline's son, James Henry Leigh (1765–1823), of Adlestrop, and later of Stoneleigh Abbey. James Henry Leigh no doubt expected to inherit the fortune, and probably the title, of his uncle, but this was not to be. (He did, in 1813, succeed to the estate of Stoneleigh Abbey, and his son Chandos Leigh, named in hope after his great-uncle, was eventually, in 1839, to attain the revived title of Baron Chandos.[8])

The Duke of Chandos died in 1789 leaving only daughters, the elder being Lady Anne Elizabeth Brydges (1779–1836).[9] She may have been a model for Austen's Lady Anne de Bourgh, in *Pride and Prejudice*: a marital prize not for her own merits, but as the heiress of an important and wealthy man. Her mother, the duchess, suffered from mental health issues, and in 1791 was decreed by a court decision to be insane; her two daughters were placed in the care of guardians (the younger daughter was called Georgiana, in another echo of *Pride and Prejudice*).[10]

The lack of a male heir to the Dukedom of Chandos undoubtedly encouraged pretenders. One was Anne's brother, Samuel Egerton Brydges. In October 1789, a month after the duke's death, the Reverend Edward Tymewell Brydges (prompted by Samuel) presented a petition to King George III, claiming the 'dignity of Baron Chandos of Sudeley', as a lineal male descendant of the sixteenth-century Anthony Bridges, third son of John Bridges, the first Baron Chandos (d. 1557).[11]

The Privileges Committee of the House of Lords first heard the claim in December 1790; verbal testimony was heard in February 1791. Jemima Brydges, the mother of Anne and Samuel, gave evidence that she had heard her husband say he was of the Chandos family, and the Reverend George Lefroy gave similar testimony.[12] Indeed, Jemima Brydges apparently bankrolled Samuel's claim from its beginning in 1789, to its conclusion in 1803. The cost of employing researchers and agents, and reimbursing witnesses for their expenses, will have been considerable.[13]

The outline of Samuel's claim (it was just a fig-leaf that his brother Edward was the claimant; the energy behind the project was all, as Jane Austen said, 'completely Egerton's') is given below. It is to be noted that where it appears obscure, it probably was. Key elements of the evidence remained confused and confusing all along, despite the efforts of several participants to elucidate them.

First, it is important to be clear about Samuel's motivation in undertaking a lengthy, expensive claim. He was desperate to have noble ancestry in his male line, not only among his maternal ancestors. That his mother, Jemima, was a member of the famous Egerton family was insufficient for his self-esteem.

> I am one of these very few, whose own mother was an Egerton. The lustre of the Bridgewater family cannot be doubted by any one who is an English genealogist...[But] all that strikes me is this, – that a distinguished female descent will not do, unless there is an honourable male stock to graft it upon.[14]

Samuel also made his motivation clear in the preface to *Fitz-Albini*. He believed that ancient titles supported great traditions and culture, promoting social harmony rather than the reverse.

> Convinced as the author is, that what to shallow understandings appear unphilosophic remnants of feudal prejudice, have the deepest foundation in wisdom, and tend to soften, instead of aggravating, that inequality of ranks,

which, constituted as we are, must exist among human beings, he feels deeply interested in recalling and enforcing these old-fashioned opinions.[15]

Most observers found nothing dishonourable about Samuel's and Anne's father's ancestry. Yet Samuel was determined to make a connection, through his father Edward Bridges, with the first Baron Chandos, Sir John Bridges.

History was clear that Sir John Bridges, who died in 1557, left five sons: Edmund, Charles, Anthony, Henry, and Richard. Edmund succeeded to the title Baron Chandos, but as he died in 1676 without male heirs, the title passed to Sir James Bridges, great-grandson of Sir John's second son Charles Bridges. It was James' great-grandson, also James, who was the third and last duke, dying (as outlined above) without male issue in September 1789.[16] If there were definitely no surviving male descendants from Edmund or Charles, then a male heir of the body of Sir John's third son Anthony would be entitled to the barony.[17]

On this basis, Samuel endeavoured to prove his descent from Anthony Bridges. Few facts are known about Anthony (born before 1532; living in 1584; death date unknown[18]), but he did appear to have been married, to a woman of the surname Fortescue, and to have had at least two children, Robert and Katherine. It is not clear if Robert and Katherine were his only children (there may have been a third child, Elizabeth, later married to Thomas Braine[19]). Katherine was married to Sir John Astley of Maidstone, Kent; he died in 1639, and she in 1648, without issue.[20] Literally nothing was known for certain about Robert Bridges apart from his name, yet it was as the descendant of Robert that Samuel made his case.

Samuel constructed his claim on the basis that his older brother Edward Tymewell Brydges was:

1. Son and heir of Edward Bridges of Wootton, who was
2. The brother and heir of John Bridges of Wootton, who was
3. The son and heir of John Bridges, also of Wootton, who was
4. The son and heir of John Bridges of Canterbury, who was
5. The only surviving son and heir of Edward Bridges, of Ospringe, who was

6. The son and heir of Robert Bridges of Maidstone, who was
7. The only son and heir of Anthony Bridges, the third son of John, the first lord Chandos.[21]

Following some initial, probably cursory study, Samuel's claims were put before the House of Lords Privileges Committee by the Attorney-General in April 1790. The report contained the claim, made by Samuel, that Robert Bridges had two children, Edward and Ann, who were twins, and were baptised on 25 March 1603. It further stated that this Edward Bridges married a Catherine Sharpe at Feversham, Kent, in June 1627.[22]

Difficulties with scheduling and witness appearances meant that the Lords Committee did not consider the matter until 21 December 1790, and a package of evidence was tabled on 17 February 1791. Key pieces of evidence included a copy of the parish register of All Saints, Maidstone, featuring the baptism of Edward and Ann, son and daughter of Robert Bridges, on 25 March 1603. Another piece of evidence was the will of Sir John Astley, containing a bequest to Ann, or Agnes, described as the niece of his wife Katherine (née Bridges).[23]

Hearings were heard in 1791, 1795, and eventually in 1802/03. Ann's existence was attested by a genuine document (Sir John Astley's will). The baptism record of Edward and Ann, however, appeared to have been written more recently than the surrounding records.[24] In addition, the identity of Edward Bridges was a matter of confusion.

If a putative Edward Bridges, nephew of Lady Katherine Astley, had been alive at the time of her death in 1648, he would have been expected to have made a claim on her estate. Lady Katherine died intestate and without issue, and administration of her estate was granted to another relative, John Bridges, after a legal contest with his cousin Frances, Countess Dowager of Essex, a granddaughter of Edmund Bridges.[25] Yet if Samuel's putative ancestor Edward Bridges was alive in 1648, surely he also, as another interested cousin, would have thrown his hat into the ring. As there was no record of an Edward Bridges appearing at that juncture, the Attorney-General in the 1802 hearings, Spencer Perceval (later prime minister, and assassinated in 1812), declared:

> The conclusion is that Edward could not have been living, or that there was no Edward at all.[26]

There was a real Edward Bridges who had married Katherine Sharpe, but there was nothing to connect this man to the Chandos line.

Personally, Samuel had not convinced the Lords committee that he was a reliable witness. The Attorney-General noted:

> His evidence is very extraordinary and contradictory.[27]

A number of agents employed, at various stages, by Samuel also provided contradictory and confusing accounts. A Mr Townsend, who had worked on the case on Samuel's behalf, seemed to be muddying the waters when asked about the Maidstone parish registers: he could not recall anything extraordinary about them, even though other observers, as noted above, had thought that the entry on the baptism of Edward and Ann Bridges was a recent interpolation.[28]

It also appeared that there had been occasions during the 1790s when Samuel had been left unsupervised in a room full of records. A William Cullen, clerk of the Canterbury Registrar's office, was cross-examined.

> 'Mr Brydges might have been in the office by himself?'
> 'Mr Brydges might certainly have been alone; and I might have been called out during part of the time. When Mr Brydges has made search, it has been usually only for an hour, and I have been usually attending him…'[29]

A further witness was called: leading local historian of the county of Kent, Edward Hasted (1732–1812), who at around this time had been imprisoned because of debt and was living in poverty. Hasted's exhaustive *History and Topographical Survey of the County of Kent* had been published in four folio volumes between 1778 and 1799.[30] Samuel's attempt to establish his claim in the House of Lords was one thing; it was another to attempt to influence, or rewrite, history. Yet he also appears to have also done this, as part of the claim process. He had managed to convince Edward Hasted to include in his history, Samuel's claim of descent from the Dukes of Chandos.

Readers of Hasted's *History* find the following information in the pages about Wootton:

> The TITLE of *Baron Chandos* is *now claimed* by the Rev Mr Brydges, of Wootton-court, the eldest son of Edward

Brydges, esq. as being the direct descendant of Anthony, third son of John Brydges, *created lord Chandos, baron of Sudley,* by queen Mary, and his claim to it has been for some time pending in the house of lords.[31]

The Lords queried the source of this information, when Hasted appeared before the Committee on 29 April 1803:

[Hasted answered] that he had received it from the present claimant, Mr Edward Tymewell Brydges.[32]

But Hasted had, it appeared, seen no documents which would support the information. Hasted added, naïvely:

The pedigrees … I took from their own mouths, believing that gentlemen of respectability would tell me the truth.[33]

Under questioning, Hasted said that he had known the claimant's late father, Edward Bridges (d. 1780), and had conversed with him numerous times. Old Mr Bridges had never said anything about a link with the Dukes of Chandos.[34]

The facts of the Bridges/Brydges family seem to be the following. Samuel was:

1. The son of Edward Bridges of Wootton (d. 1780), who was the son of
2. John Bridges, the son of
3. John Bridges, the son of
4. Edward Bridges of Ospringe, Kent, who was married in 1627 to Katherine Sharpe of Feversham.[35]

It was this Edward Bridges (number 4 in this list) whom Samuel wished to identify as the putative Edward, son of Robert Bridges. But in fact, there was no verified link to any putative children or grandchildren of Anthony Bridges.[36] The Kent Bridges were in trade: Samuel's great-grandfather John Bridges (number 3 in the list) was a grocer at Canterbury, as attested in his will (1699). Samuel mentioned this will, although before the Committee in 1794 he denied having searched for it, and had his agent also deny it.[37] The life of John Bridges (grocer) was a 'quiet and productive' one, and did not deserve to have been despised and rewritten by descendants who had benefited financially from his hard work.[38]

The most gross fabrication appeared to have been in the Maidstone parish register. To recap the necessity of this stratagem: the existence of an Ann or Agnes Bridges, niece of Lady Katherine Astley and therefore understood to be daughter of Robert Bridges, was separately attested in Sir John Astley's will. However, no nephew Edward Bridges, as son of Robert Bridges, was known to history. It was perhaps more plausible to make use of Ann's conjectured birth year of 1603, and create for her a twin brother, than to invent an entirely new brother with a random birth year: so this is what Samuel or his agents probably did.

However, a double baptism entry took up more space than a single one. George Frederick Beltz (1774–1841), a professional genealogist, wrote in his 1834 account of the case:

> It was therefore absolutely necessary to make an erasure somewhere, and found to be most convenient to expunge two entries terminating the year 1603 (which entries, with two other entries of baptism still remaining, and celebrated on the same day, had been inclosed within a bracket,) in order to acquire the necessary space, and at the same time, preserve the original bracket, and the numbers 116 and 117 in the margin, which had evidently once referred to the two erased baptisms, and which were, after the interpolation, intended to refer appropriately to the baptism of two individuals, viz. Edward and Anne Bridges.[39]

The erasure also took out the minister's certifying signature at the end of the year, which actually made more space than needed. To fill in the resulting gap, these words were added: *'Finis istius anni'* (The end of that year).

These words did not appear in the register at the end of any other year.[40] Even by the primitive standards of forensic assessment of 1803, this appeared very suspicious.[41]

It also appeared that some other pieces of evidence had been faked by Samuel or his agents, including a document which purported to give evidence about the existence of a number of other Astley relatives.[42] There were also questions about the identity, age, and marriage status of Ann or Agnes, Lady Katherine Astley's niece.[43] These served only to muddy the waters, adding no weight to the key matters of whether Edward Bridges had actually existed, was a son of Robert Bridges, or was an ancestor of Samuel.

Clearly, both Anne Brydges Lefroy and Samuel had been brought up with a belief in the Chandos claim. There is some evidence that Anne was, in her way, just as invested in the claim as her brother was, but it is unlikely that she knew how little evidence there was to support it. The siblings seem to have adopted the spelling of their name 'Brydges' in the belief that it was more authentic, historically, than 'Bridges,' as well as suggesting a connection with the Chandos house. As Beltz put it in a sarcastic footnote:

> This gentleman [Samuel] and his elder brother, the claimant, affected, about this time [in the 1780s], doubtless not without a view to their immediate object, to write their surname 'Brydges,' in imitation of the practice in the ducal family for some generations back. But their father, who died in 1780, signed his name 'Bridges' to his will and codicil.[44]

The name Anthony was regularly used in both Lefroy and Brydges families. We have seen that one of Anne and George's sons, Anthony, had died, on 27 of January 1800. Every following year Anne kept the day as one of mourning, declining invitations from friends who were unaware of the date's significance for her. She writes to Christopher Edward in January 1803:

> There is to be a Ball at Kempshot on Thursday next to which the Rices & your Cousin are to go but it is the 27th of Jan:ry of course I shall not be there…[45]

In May 1803 Anne even induced her sister-in-law Mary, Samuel's second wife, to call *her* newborn son Anthony, although probably Samuel had no objection (his previously born son had Anthony as a middle name).

> Your Aunt Mary was brought to bed of a fine boy on
> Thursday morning by my desire he is to be named Anthony,
> may he be as good as my angel was![46]

The reason, it would appear, was that Anne was convinced that Anthony
Bridges, third son of the first Baron Chandos, was indeed the ancestor of
herself and Samuel. She became quite distressed when Sir Nash Grose,
a judge in the Isle of Wight, seemed to have a mistaken idea about
Anthony Bridges. She wrote especially to Christopher Edward's boss,
Richard Clarke, to get him to correct the misunderstanding:

> I find by a letter from [Christopher] Edward just received,
> that Sir Nash Grose supposes my Brother to claim the
> Barony from a *Brother*, & not a *Son* of Anthony who was
> the third Son of Lord Chandos I was so much pleased with
> the conversation I had with him the morning we spent at
> the Priory that I am hurt Sir Nash should suppose that any
> family could pursue so unfounded a Claim as ours must be,
> if his idea was correct will you allow me therefore so far to
> presume upon your friendship as to beg of you to explain
> to Sir Nash that it is from the *Son* and not the *Brother of
> Anthony*, that we are descended?[47]

This was ironic, considering that if Anne had really been aware that the
entire existence of the son of Anthony – Robert Bridges – was shrouded
in mystery, she must have known the very slender, or indeed non-
existent basis for the claim. Anne later regretted attempting to persuade
Mr Clarke to intervene, writing to Christopher Edward:

> I was not mistaken as to what Sir N.G. said but upon reflection
> I think you had better burn my note to Mr Clarke & take no
> further notice of the conversation I have always approved of
> Madame [de] Genlis maxim never to combat prejudice with
> reason & I know not how I came to depart from this rule in
> the present instance.[48]

During the period in which the claim was being heard for the final time,
in 1802/03, Anne's letters indicate anxiety about proceedings:

'Your Uncles claim was to have been heard yesterday & Lord Bolton was so good as to go to town to attend the Hearing... so that I trust we shall see your Uncle in possession of his right e'er long.'[49]

'Your Uncles claim has been once heard & is to come on again tomorrow I hope they will have it decided this Sessions Lord Bolton is most kind & friendly we are all greatly obliged to him.'[50]

'Your Uncles claim goes on very prosperously.'[51]

'I trust all difficulties with regard to your Uncles claim are over & that next year we shall congratulate him as Lord Chandos...'[52]

This optimism proved to have been misguided. On 16 June 1803, the Lords concluded,

> That the petitioner ... hath not made out his claim to the title and dignity of baron Chandos of Sudeley.[53]

This was putting it mildly. The outcome was not, contrary to the surprising statement in a review of Anne Lefroy's *Letters* which appeared in *JASNA News* in 2008, a case of,

> ...the sluggish incompetence of the courts later skewered by Charles Dickens.[54]

In fact, it was the only fair outcome on the basis of the little and suspect evidence which Samuel had managed to produce. As for family friend Lord Bolton, who had been so 'kind & friendly', he abstained when it came to the vote.[55]

On 15 June 1803, Anne wrote regretfully:

> The papers have probably informed you, that your Uncles claim is decided against us...whatever was the cause we must bear the effect with fortitude & remember the time will come when truth & justice shall universally prevail, *we know* we have a right to the rank we have been claiming *that* no decision of the House of Lords can take from us...

As we would expect from her, however, Anne quickly counted her blessings:

> Whilst you & your Brothers & Sister are well & happy I will not grieve at the loss of a title.[56]

Samuel, however, continued to grieve, complain, and generally assert his rights. Bizarrely, he even took to calling himself *per legem terrae Baron Chandos of Sudeley* (by the law of the land, Baron Chandos of Sudeley).[57] His self-serving autobiography, in two long volumes, dwelt at length upon his grievances.

George Frederick Beltz, who decided in 1834, after thirty years of Samuel's long-winded and persistent complaints about the failure of his case, to publish an independent and authoritative account, summarised:

> The few remaining spectators … could not fail to observe that – instead of meeting the points at issue by a full and satisfactory narrative of the case, with the requisite citation of convincing proofs, and a logical discussion of their several bearings upon the question – the ingenious baronet [Samuel was by then Sir Samuel] has been content to leave its main features in obscurity; preferring innuendo, satire and invective, to the weapons of greater efficacy which would doubtless have been within reach of his powerful talent, had his premises been founded in truth.[58]

The Chandos Peerage case was a surprising instance of how an intelligent and talented person could allow his life to be consumed by a futile quest for an aristocratic identity. It was, however, far from an isolated occurrence. The Leigh Peerage case (1828–29), which was also to involve members of Jane Austen's extended Leigh family, confirmed the hypnotic attraction of a title in an age when, paradoxically, political and social influence was beginning to spread well outside traditional aristocratic models.

And what happened about the Dukedom of Chandos? As things turned out, it had been settled all along; the Brydges and the Leighs had never stood a chance. We recall that in *Pride and Prejudice*, Lady Catherine de Bourgh considers that the marriage of Lady Anne and Darcy had practically been arranged when they were children. Lady Anne Brydges, heiress of the late Duke of Chandos, was married in 1796, when she was aged 16 and her bridegroom 20 (that is to say, both were under legal age). It was said that the marriage had been first arranged when the groom was only 10 years old.[59] Her husband inherited her wealth and a direct claim to her late father's dukedom. This lucky man was Richard Temple-Nugent-Grenville (1776–1839).

In 1799, by royal licence, he added Brydges and Chandos to his family name, adding insult to injury for Samuel Egerton Brydges. Now known as Richard Temple-Nugent-Brydges-Chandos-Grenville (surely some kind of record for multiple barrels), in 1822 he was raised to the peerage as Marquess of Chandos and Duke of Buckingham and Chandos.

He was fat, hugely unpopular, and in June 1804 opposed Wilberforce's bill for the abolition of the slave trade.[60] Let the official history of Parliament (always refreshingly frank) sum up:

> The dukedom with which [Temple-Nugent] was rewarded [for political favours] did not satisfy his immense ambition and he continued to press his claims for high office. His greed, his inflated conception of his own ability and importance and the unattractiveness of his personal character made him an increasingly odious and contemptible figure in serious political circles, where many would have endorsed the comment of Mrs Arbuthnot that he was 'utterly without talent or the respect of one human being'.[61]

Could this man, seen as a usurper of the rights and inheritances of Brydges and of Leighs, be the reason for Jane Austen's well-known dislike of the Christian name Richard, otherwise hard to explain? It may simply have been that Jane and Cassandra had a standing joke about their father's old student, Richard Buller. Most recently, Margaret Doody has tackled this perennial puzzle, without reaching a conclusion.

If Temple-Nugent-Grenville was the ultimate source of the 'Richard' joke, the dates would fit. Jane Austen's earliest known 'Richard' witticism dates from 1796, some months after Richard Temple-Nugent-Grenville's premature marriage (the relevant letter is dated 15/16 September 1796; the marriage had taken place in April 1796).[62] If, as suggested, the arrangement had been in place for some ten years prior to the marriage, there was ample opportunity for it to have become a known irritant in the Brydges, Leigh and Austen families.[63]

Part Three

Through a Glass, Darkly

Chapter 10

Ashe: Home, Family, Neighbours

In 1888, the then rector of Ashe, Rev. Francis Walter Thoyts, produced a slim history of his parish of Ashe.[1] Thoyts had a special affection for the parish, where he had been rector since his institution on 21 March 1873.[2] The officiating Bishop of Winchester was Samuel Wilberforce (son of the anti-slavery campaigner William), best known as 'Soapy Sam', and as the opponent of Thomas Huxley in the famous debate of 1860 at the British Association on the subject of evolution (Darwin's *On the Origin of Species by Means of Natural Selection* had appeared in November 1859). Wilberforce died only months after instituting Thoyts as the rector of Ashe.

In his little book, Thoyts comes across as a little fussy, but fundamentally interested in the people who had preceded him in the parish of Ashe. The work consists mainly of lists of people: the rectors, going back to Sir Henry Beaufiz in 1309; the churchwardens; the parish clerks; and, perhaps most surprisingly, a selection from registers of births, marriages, and burials of the ordinary people of Ashe, from the early seventeenth century.[3]

The parish name in the Domesday Book (1086) was Esse, which is said to mean 'water'. Thoyts records several variant names through history: Essche, Ayssche, Asshe.[4] There may, or may not, have been a monastic house in the area during the Middle Ages, perhaps indicated by placenames such as 'Pilgrims' and 'Beggars' Clump'.[5]

Thoyts found it difficult to be clear about many events in Ashe's past. One documented event was that William of Wykeham (1320–1404), Hampshire man, Bishop of Winchester and Chancellor of England, in 1366 bought the Manor of Ashe from Sir Edmund de Stonor.[6] Thoyts allowed himself to conjecture that William – supervisor of grand building projects – might have had a hand in the construction of the church of the

Memorial stone to Anne and George in Ashe Church. (Stuart Wilson 2018)

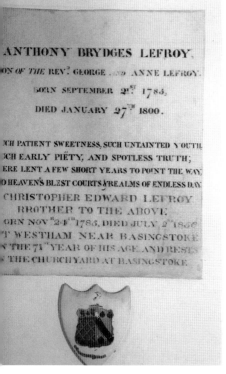

ANTHONY BRYDGES LEFROY,

ON OF THE REV? GEORGE AND ANNE LEFROY.

BORN SEPTEMBER 21ST 1783,

DIED JANUARY 27TH 1800.

ICH PATIENT SWEETNESS, SUCH UNTAINTED YOUTH
ICH EARLY PIETY, AND SPOTLESS TRUTH;
ERE LENT A FEW SHORT YEARS TO POINT THE WAY
O HEAVEN'S BLEST COURTS & REALMS OF ENDLESS DAY

CHRISTOPHER EDWARD LEFROY
BROTHER TO THE ABOVE
ORN NOV 24TH 1785, DIED JULY 2D 1856
T WESTHAM NEAR BASINGSTOKE
N THE 71ST YEAR OF HIS AGE AND RESTS
THE CHURCHYARD AT BASINGSTOKE

Memorial stone to Anthony Lefroy and Christopher Edward Lefroy in Ashe Church. (Stuart Wilson 2018)

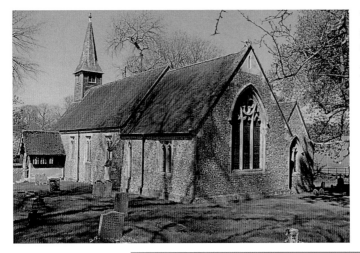

'Holy Trinity and St Andrew's Church,' Ashe. (Stuart Wilson 2018)

Rectory, Ashe. (Stuart Wilson 2018)

Denton Court, home of Samuel Egerton Brydges. (Stuart Wilson 2018)

'Billingsgate Eloquence' (Caroline Barry). (© The Trustees of the British Museum)

Shops along High Street, Canterbury. (Stuart Wilson 2018)

Westgate, Canterbury. (Stuart Wilson 2018)

Reception quarters, Carisbrooke Castle, Isle of Wight. (Stuart Wilson 2018)

Eastgate Hospital, High Street, Canterbury. (Stuart Wilson 2018)

Playbill advertising performance of
Jane Shore, Hackwood Park, 1787.
(Courtesy of Chiswick Auctions)

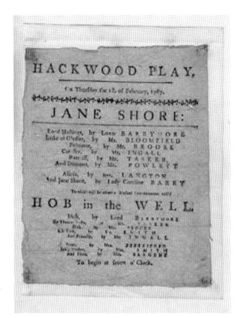

'Les Trois Magots' (Lord Barrymore
and his brothers). (© The Trustees of
the British Museum)

Norman porch, The King's School, Canterbury. (Stuart Wilson 2018)

Gatehouse, Carisbrooke Castle, Isle of Wight. (Stuart Wilson 2018)

Key to Ashe Church. (Stuart Wilson 2018)

Site of former All Saints Church, High Street, Canterbury (supposedly opposite old Lefroy house). (Stuart Wilson 2018)

Entries in The King's School register, including that of Isaac Peter George Lefroy. (Courtesy of Peter Henderson, Archivist, and The King's School)

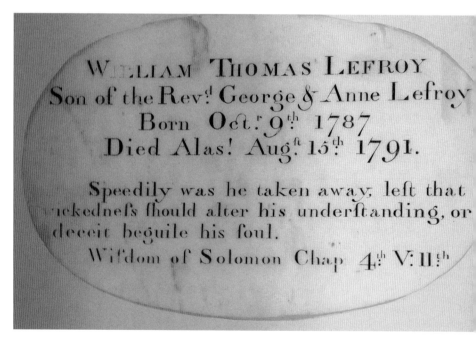

Memorial stone to William Lefroy in Ashe Church. (Stuart Wilson 2018)

Holy Trinity and St Andrew at little Ashe. Thoyts ventured to suppose that the Norman piscina (a shallow basin used for washing communion utensils) had been created, or used, by the great William himself:

> I love to think that, if ever William of Wykeham celebrated the Holy Communion in the church, supposed to be of his building, he used that piscina.[7]

Another, less happy, event seemed to have taken place in the fourteenth century. The church was the setting for some kind of major conflict, involving bloodshed.

> On the 28th July, 1332, John de Stratford, Bishop of Winchester, absolved Richard de Haveringe, layman, who was present at a conflict which had recently taken place around (*circa*) the church of Asshe, on which occasion, it is said, the church was polluted by the shedding of blood...

The following year, the church itself was exorcised.

> On the 19th June, 1333, Richard de Chaddesle, chancellor and vicar general, granted permission to Brother Benedict, Bishop of Cardica, to purge in the prescribed form, with holy water (*aqua exorzizata*) the church of Asshe, not consecrated, polluted by the shedding of blood, so that divine service may not be suspended.[8]

For the most part, however, the history of Ashe had proceeded much as the history of every other parish in England. There were disputes about inheritance, land ownership, and livestock; rich parishioners sometimes made bequests of ongoing charity; and people were born, were married, and died.

In 1733, Ann, daughter of rector Dr Russell and his wife Elizabeth, was buried at Ashe 'under the east window of the church in the churchyard'.[9] On Christmas Eve 1748, another daughter, Frances, was born to Dr Russell and (presumably) his second wife Mary. A third daughter, Mary, followed in 1750.[10]

Frances died in 1772, aged 24, and was 'buried on the north side of her brother's grave, as near as could be to the said chancel'.[11] It must have been a sad duty for Dr Russell to conduct the burial services for his children.

Not only parishioners were buried. Russell must have recorded this, reported by Thoyts:

> A poor man who was found dead in the lane leading to the Warren House, on the 23rd October [1778], was buried 25th October, the coroner having sat upon the body yesterday. His name supposed to be John Johnstone, by a certificate found in his pocket, and brought to me after his burial.[12]

Dr Russell himself was buried there in 1783, his age recorded here as 88.[13]

His daughter Mary had married George Midford or Mitford, of Alresford. They must have come back to Ashe for certain family events, including tragic ones. In 1786 we find the burial of Francis Russell, 'the son of George Midford [*sic*] of Alresford, and Mary his wife, daughter of Dr Richard Russell, late rector of this parish.'[14] A second Francis was buried in 1789.[15] As is shown by her precocious juvenilia, Mary Russell Mitford was in some ways a classically spoiled 'only child', but these events remind us that she was not the only child of her parents; rather, she was their only surviving child, a subtle but important difference.[16]

The new rector, George, and Anne Lefroy and their family begin to appear in the parish records. In 1785 we find the christening of Christopher Edward. 1787 saw the christening of William Thomas Lefroy, and 1791 saw that of Benjamin (Ben) Lefroy.[17]

Anne was probably 40 years old at William's birth, and 44 at Benjamin's. We may find this surprising, but apparently it was not considered particularly unusual at the time for second or later pregnancies, although it probably would have been for first pregnancies. A genealogical expert wrote in 1834:

> Although instances of pregnancy [of women in their forties] are not infrequent in women who have been in the habit of child-bearing; yet it is most extraordinary that a woman should *begin* to bear children at that advanced age.[18]

In August of 1791, just months after Ben's birth, tragically, young William died.[19] He was commemorated in a monument in Ashe church, which reads:

> William Thomas Lefroy, son of the Revd George & Anne Lefroy. Born Oct. 9th 1787, died alas! Aug. 15th 1791. Speedily was he taken away, lest that wickedness should alter his understanding, or deceit beguile his soul. Wisdom of Solomon Chap. 4th V: 11th.[20]

In 1795 the family nurse was buried. George recorded:

> Judith Murrell, widow, aged 60, who near sixteen years faithfully discharged the duties of a nurse to all the children of the Revd. George Lefroy.[21]

A third tragic death of one of George and Anne's children took place in 1800. It is recorded baldly by Thoyts:

> Anthony Brydges, son of Rev. George and Anne Lefroy.[22]

Apparently his death resulted from a riding accident two years prior.[23] We learn this from a letter from Benjamin Langlois, with a date of December 1799:

> Poor George Lefroy, (Rev. I.P.G. Lefroy), has had the misfortune to lose his second son about a month ago, a very promising youth of about sixteen [*sic*]. His complaint was found to be an extraordinary enlargement of the Heart, for which no account can be given, unless it arose from a bad fall he had from a horse about 2 years ago, when, I understand, they neglected to bleed him. The poor Father and Mother were very much affected, and the more so as this unfortunate Boy suffered most cruelly for some weeks before he died.[24]

Benjamin Langlois' rather cold-blooded account suggests that in addition to the grief occasioned by Anthony's illness and death, George and Anne were tormented by a sense of guilt about a failure to obtain what was the all-purpose eighteenth-century treatment, 'bleeding'.

The monument in Ashe church to Anthony reads:

> Anthony Brydges Lefroy, son of the Revd. George and Anne Lefroy. Born September 21st 1785. Died January 27th 1800.

> Such patient sweetness, such untainted youth,
> Such early piety, and spotless truth;
> Were lent a few short years, to point the way,
> To Heaven's blest courts, & realms of endless day.[25]

This verse may have been written by Anne herself, as it is not known from other sources.

Anne was permanently affected by the deaths of her children Julia, William, and Anthony. As it happens, it is from shortly after the time of Anthony's death that we begin to have Anne's first-person accounts of her daily life, in the form of her letters to Christopher Edward.

Christopher Edward had been sent to study with the Reverend Faithfull at Warfield in Berkshire. Faithfull had attended Merton College and been presented to the living at Warfield in 1793.[26] At 15, Christopher Edward had been sent to the Isle of Wight to work in the law office of Richard Clarke.[27] Clarke (1736–1817) of Newport, Isle of Wight, was an attorney working on local matters of law. He was not married; his unmarried sister Lydia lived with him as his housekeeper (referred to in Anne's letters with the courtesy title of Mrs Clarke).[28]

Ben also went as a young boy to study with the Reverend Faithfull, then was sent to Winchester School at the age of 12, in 1803.[29] The Reverend George and Anne's daughter Lucy was at this time engaged to Henry Rice. Anne found herself, for the first time in many years, often with none of her surviving children present. This clearly brought back the grief of losing those who were deceased.

Because of the frequency of perinatal and infant mortality 200 years ago, we tend to assume that the deaths of children were taken more-or-less for granted. Perhaps this was so, to some degree, although scholars have debated this point. There is also a view that even if parents of the seventeenth century invested less emotion in their children, because of expected mortality, prevailing attitudes seem to have undergone a change by the early eighteenth century.[30] For strong Christians such as Anne, the familiar tenets of the church, such as 'The Lord gave, and the Lord hath taken away – blessed be the name of the Lord' (Job 1:21), and the conviction of meeting again in a future life, offered some consolation.

Yet the grief was still raw. Anne did not hesitate to express it in correspondence with Christopher Edward:

> Friday 29 [May 1801]. This was the first morning in the course of 21 years that I ever arose at home without having my heart cheered by the sight of one at least of my children, & I cannot discribe [*sic*] the melancholy sensations it occasioned, but I must submit with patience to this deprivation, & will endeavour to support my spirits by looking forward to that time, when the pain of separation will be done away forever, & we shall I trust meet to part no more.[31]

After the summer holidays, the next parting was just as painful, and made even her usual social round unpleasant to Anne. In a clear case of psychosomatic symptoms, she even felt unwell.

> My dearest Edward
> Though I was with kind & long loved friends, you cannot easily imagine how my heart sank when I parted from you all last night, I believe it is the first time in nearly 22 yrs, when I have retired to rest without having either your father or one of my children under the same roof, & the reflection was so painful that I could not keep up my spirits … I derived little amusement from the bustle that surrounded me: in the evening we went to the Ball which was very full, & to me very stupid, & I rejoiced when I heard the carriage was waiting at the door…
>
> Wednesday we again went to the [Winchester race] course, & in the evening to the Play, the House is small, & the Performers very indifferent, & I came home tired & unwell.[32]

In these days of instant communication, we may feel a pang of worry if we do not hear from a child within half an hour of texting them.

Dependent on the post, Anne often felt anxious when a letter failed to arrive from Ben or Christopher Edward.

It is clear that the anxiety called forth her deepest fears of, once again, losing a child forever. In this case, she channelled her pain and worry into creating a poem as the main part of her letter. Anne always addressed Christopher by his middle name, Edward. Hester Boham (1757–1834) was the housekeeper to the Lefroys, and clearly Anne discussed her fears with her.[33]

No letter from my Edward yet,
Tho' twelve long days are past,
Say Boham, is't not passing strange
His silence thus should last?

Tomorrow sure a line will bring,
The wish'd tomorrow come
But adds alas! One figure more
To disappointments sum.

Yet Reason tells my anxious heart,
To calm each idle fear,
Where Truth & Virtue live you dwell,
No harm can reach you there.

Each night & morn to visit thee,
On Fancys wings I fly,
Hang o'er thy couch, and watch thy sleep,
With fond maternal eye.

What words a Mother's love can tell?
Around the heartstrings twin'd,
Deep in the soul its roots are fix'd,
Inseparably joined.

Three times my breaking heart has bled,
When from my sight convey'd
My Darlings pressed th'untimely bier
And in the grave were laid.

Yet still for them affection glows,
And bids my soul aspire
To view once more their Angel forms,
Amidst the Heavenly Choir.

Tho' Faith and Hope their aid combine,
To sooth my sorrowing breast,
Yet oft the silent tear will fall
And rob my nights of rest.

The blessings that I still possess
My God in mercy spare,
For them all gracious Power vouchsafe
To hear a Mothers Prayer.

From vice from folly guard their youth
Nor let their footsteps stray
From where Religions chearing light
Illumes the trav'lers way.

So shall my eyes in peace be clos'd
My soul in hope shall rest
Nor death when'er the stroke shall come
Strike terror to my breast.[34]

Clearly thinking that Christopher Edward might find this embarrassing, Anne adds:

My dearest Edward
I trust to your partiality for not finding fault with the above lines they have nothing but truth to recommend them & Poets you know always write best upon fiction but I am a Mother & not a Poetess…[35]

Despite protesting that she was 'not a Poetess', Anne must have found some relief in creating verses which expressed her deepest love and fear. These verses also provide a contrast to the legendary cheerfulness for which she was known. Anne, in fact, had no hesitation in expressing unhappy emotions to her beloved son.

Anne may have also had some anxiety about the man who was about to marry her daughter Lucy. Henry Rice (1776–1860) entered Christ's College, Cambridge, in 1796, and resided until 1800, but did not graduate.[36] Nonetheless, he was the curate of Ashe and Deane 1801–05.[37]

The Lefroys apparently knew him from before his Cambridge days, when he already seems to have been a favoured suitor for Lucy, then still in her teens. Two of Anne's poems, from 1796 and 1797, are addressed to young Rice (as Anne called him):

> Put into a Tooth Pick Case, given to H[enry] R[ice] When he left Ashe to go to Cambridge, 1796.

> WHEN jests and when laughter enliven the hour,
> When drown'd in the bowl, reason loses her power;
> Of far distant friends this memento shall tell,
> Of the tears which they shed when they bid thee farewell,
> To awaken each virtue that lives in thy heart,
> And warn thee from folly and vice to depart;
> And thus when old time sheds his snow o'er thy head,
> From thy cheeks when youth's roses for ever are fled;
> May hope's steady ray gild thy life's calm decline,
> And her wreath round thy temples bright honor entwine.

It is possible that here Anne expressed a foreboding that charming Henry Rice would at Cambridge be tempted into 'vices', notably drinking and gambling. According to family tradition, Rice later had a destructive gambling habit, whether or not this was the case in these early days.[38]

The other poem addressed to Henry is in terms of approval of his attendance on his father in an illness. Henry's father was also Henry Rice, of Bramling near Canterbury. It is therefore possible that the Rice-Lefroy-Brydges acquaintanceship had dated back to Kent days. Henry senior was a captain in the East India Company:[39]

> To Henry Rice, with some bride cake, Drawn through the Ring, February 5 1797, at which Time he was attending his sick Father.

GO magick composition and impart,
Thy happiest influence to dear Harry's heart;
When sorrowing from a Father's couch he goes,
And broken slumbers cannot sooth his woes;
Bid fairy scenes of future bliss appear,
And hopes gay visions his sad spirits cheer;
Tell him his kind attentions; (e'en tho' vain,
Their lenient power to heal a parent's pain;)
O'er his own life their precious balms shall shed,
And draw down Heaven's best blessings on his head;
And when o'er youthful days as years advance;
His memory throws a retrospective glance;
As messengers of peace these hours shall rise,
And speak, with angel voice, his title to the skies.

The custom of drawing wedding cake through the (wedding) ring was, according to Hazel Jones, 'a messy business'.[40] The procedure had something to do, apparently, with predicting the future for friends and relatives of the marrying couple.

Folklorist and antiquarian John Brand (1744–1806) described the custom at length in his very popular work *Observations on Popular Antiquities of Great Britain* (1777):

> The connection between the bride-cake and wedding is strongly marked in the following custom, still retained in Yorkshire, where the former is cut into little square pieces, thrown over the bridegroom's and bride's head, and then put through the ring…
>
> In the North, slices of the bride-cake are put through the wedding ring: they are afterwards laid under pillows, at night, to cause young persons to dream of their lovers…. The pieces of the cake must be drawn nine times through the wedding ring.[41]

A novel from 1815 has this to say:

> 'Well, I dare say you will have a large piece of wedding-cake, for you seem to be great favourites.'

'Oh,' said Fanny, 'Lord R's mind will never find amusement in drawing wedding-cake through a ring; he cannot be so frivolous.'

'Why, my dear little villager,' said Miss V, 'every body in London thinks of it, all dream upon it, and you don't know what an importance it gives you, to have a bit of a Countess's wedding-cake; and I beg you will both send me a very legitimate piece that has been nine times through the ring.'[42]

The cake must have been extremely solid in consistency (of 'magick composition', in Anne's poetic phrase), to be able to be both cut into tiny squares, and to retain its structure after nine passes through a small ring. That wedding guests sometimes dispensed with the proceeding is clear from Mary Russell Mitford's 1816 account of:

our entirely forgetting to draw any cake through the ring, so that our fate still rests in abeyance.[43]

Anne was no doubt forwarding the 'ringed' wedding cake to Rice as a reference to his future marriage with Lucy, reinforced by her expression 'fairy scenes of future bliss'.

After some delays, the marriage between Lucy and Rice indeed took place on 20 July 1801. Anne wrote to Christopher Edward:

Ceremony: your Sister behaved with great calmness God grant she may be happy she shall sign her new name for the first time to this letter…

Lucy Rice (as she now was) did add a few lines, but not before brother, George junior, had inserted this witticism:

The bride behaved very penitently & everybody thought her case very hard. J.H. George Lefroy.

Anne concluded the letter with a hasty but happy postscript:

Ben: is just come in & quite well.[44]

Following the wedding, Rice and Lucy took a honeymoon trip to Wales of four to six weeks, during which time the Reverends James Austen and George Lefroy, between them, will have covered Rice's curate duties at Deane.[45]

It was her family's company which Anne loved most, but some neighbours were more congenial than others. Anne complained:

> I heartily wish Hackwood was within 2 instead of 9 miles, as I have no Neighbours whose society I more covet than that of the inhabitants of Hackwood Park.[46]

By 1801, there was a different Lord and Lady Bolton at Hackwood from the couple described in Chapter 7, Harry 'Captain Whiffle' Powlett and the former Miss Lowther. Lord Harry had died in 1794, leaving the Dowager Duchess, who lived until 1809.[47] The couple had two daughters, but no sons. Harry's brother, Charles, the fifth Duke of Bolton, had, in the case of default of Harry's male issue, entailed most of his properties onto his own illegitimate ('natural', in the euphemism of the time) daughter Jean (or Jane) Mary Browne-Powlett.

In 1778 Jean Mary had married Thomas Orde, who upon Jean's uncle's death in 1794 succeeded to the considerable estates, including Hackwood. Orde assumed the additional name of Powlett, and in 1797 was raised to the peerage as Baron Bolton of Bolton Castle in Yorkshire. In 1800 the Lord Lieutenancy of Hampshire fell vacant, and Orde-Powlett applied. He duly became Lord Lieutenant of Hampshire as well as Governor of the Isle of Wight.[48]

The new duke, Thomas Orde-Powlett, was apparently an agreeable man. Anne's brother Samuel Egerton Brydges, in his revision of *Collins' Peerage* which appeared in 1812, had this to say:

> His Lordship was a man of very powerful talents, great industry in business, extensive political knowledge, and many amiable moral qualities. He had a zeal in the cause of those, whose interests he embraced, which placed him high in the ranks of benevolence. He had the eloquence of a strong, an acute and discriminative understanding, which, though it may not have all the attractions of brilliant flashes

of the fancy, or melting appeals to the heart, must always excite the admiration of cultivated minds.[49]

As always with Samuel, the praise was faint, and stinted with qualification. For her part, Jane Austen reported a peculiarity of Lord Bolton's, being his fondness for his pigs:

> My father is glad to hear so good an account of Edward [Austen Knight]'s pigs, and desires he may be told, as encouragement to his taste for them, that Lord Bolton is particularly curious in *his* pigs, has had pigstyes of a most elegant construction built for them, and visits them every morning as soon as he rises.[50]

Anne was sorry when Lord Bolton missed a social event because of illness:

> Lord Bolton was unwell & did not come this we all regretted as he adds more than anyone to the pleasure of a party.[51]

Because of his frequent visits to Carisbrooke Castle on the Isle of Wight, of which he was the Governor, it sometimes happened that Lord Bolton was able to update the Lefroys with news of Christopher Edward. This, of course, gave great pleasure to Anne:

> 'I called at Hackwood in the morning & [saw] Lord Bolton who said you was quite well…'[52]
>
> 'We dined at Hackwood last Thursday I find the family talk of coming to Carisbrooke very soon this I know you will rejoice in & tho' we shall miss their absence from this Neighbourhood I will not regret it as you will be the gainer.'[53]

We are left wondering about the personality of Lady Bolton, whose society was so pleasant to Anne Lefroy. As the illegitimate daughter of a peer, perhaps she had had no particularly easy or luxurious path, although in marrying Thomas Orde – of solidly middle- to upper-class background, having attended Eton and Cambridge – she must have achieved at least a comfortable life.[54] Presumably she had been brought up in the knowledge that she was heir to her father's estates, yet his suicide in 1765 must have been a shock to her as to every other observer. Jane Austen sheds no light here; she simply reports that, at a ball in November 1800:

> Lady Portsmouth had got a different dress on, & Lady Bolton is much improved by a wig.[55]

Perhaps Jean Mary, aware of her own fortuitous route to the peerage, was modest and unassuming about rank. (Certainly, we read of no faux pas like her predecessor's proposal to cast Anne as Alicia in *Jane Shore*.) We do know from Anne's account that one of Lady Bolton's servants was considered rather as a friend, perhaps indicating a relative absence of snobbishness in Lady Bolton:

> Poor Lady Bolton is in great trouble at present as her old Housekeeper Mrs Carter who was more of a friend than a Servant died on Monday last we were to have dined at Hackwood that day but were of course put off on account of this event…[56]

Other important neighbours were the Portals. The Portal family, like the Lefroys and Langlois of Huguenot origin, were local land and business owners. They owned the paper mills at Laverstoke, and also Ashe Park.[57] James Portal had inherited the property in 1763, and let it out to tenants.[58] Jane Austen wrote to Cassandra in 1796:

> We had a visit yesterday morning from Mr Benjamin Portal, whose eyes are as handsome as ever.[59]

In London in June 1799, apparently Jane still found Benjamin Portal (1768–1812), an Oxford friend of her brother James, quite attractive:

> Benjamin Portal is here. How charming that is! – I do not exactly know why, but the phrase followed so naturally that I could not help putting it down.[60]

One long-term tenant was James Holder (1747– c. 1804).[61] The Holders are also known from Jane Austen's letters.

A mysterious and eccentric neighbour was the Earl of Portsmouth of Hurstbourne Park. This was John Charles Wallop, third earl (1767–1853), of limited mental capacity. His estates and property were managed by trustees. In 1799 he was married to Grace Norton (1752–1813), who to some extent controlled his violent and antisocial behaviour. After her death in 1813 he was married for a second time to the daughter of John Hanson, Lord Byron's man of business. The marriage was in name only; the new countess had several children with a lover. During the 1820s another inquiry *de lunatico inquirendo* took place, which concluded that the earl had, in fact, been insane since 1809. The second marriage was annulled. The earl, however, survived until 1853.[62]

Was the full extent of the bizarre nature of the household at Hurstbourne widely known among their neighbours? It is not entirely clear from Anne's letters, although there are some hints in that direction. In October 1801, Anne writes to Christopher Edward:

> This morning the King Queen Prince Adolphus & the Princesses passed by about 10 o'Clock after having slept at Andover I thought the King looked thin & ill was it not very strange that Lord Portsmouth did not offer them his house instead of letting them sleep at an Inn?[63]

Here Anne may have simply been expressing a doubt, or she may have been making a rather heartless joke about the nightmare quality of both the Hurstbourne household, and the intermittent incapacity of King George III himself.

However, the Portsmouths were involved to some extent with local society. Anne reports to Christopher Edward that on 3 November 1801, 'Lord & Lady Portsmouth the Portals & Mr Holder dined here.' She gives no further commentary, but this is not unusual.[64] In August 1802, Anne writes:

> Friday In the morning I drove Mr & Miss Vincent to Hurstborne Park Lord & Lady P were gone to town but we found Mrs & Miss Gordon at home…[65]

The Portsmouths also hosted their neighbours at balls. Jane Austen reports in the letter already quoted from November 1800, at a ball probably hosted by the Portsmouths:

Lord Portsmouth surpassed the rest in his attentive recollection of you [Cassandra], enquired more into the length of your absence, & concluded by desiring to be 'remembered to you when I wrote next.'[66]

Anne writes about the Portsmouths' ball of the following November (1801):

We came home by Stratfield Saye in order to bring the two Miss Salters that they may go with us to Lord Portsmouths Ball on Thursday next.[67]

Alas, the ball was as eccentric as its hosts:

Thursday Nov:br 19th We went to the Ball at Hurstborne Park it was not half so pleasant as the one last year they danced in the Saloon instead of the Library I believe there were about 100 people in the room & 24 or 25 couple; we did not get home till nearly 6 o'clock your father was afraid of the cold of the Library & did not go Lord P. was either out of health or out of humour & only stood up two Dances there was scarcely anything to eat at Supper & the Gentlemen complained that the wine was very bad & very scarce four panes of glass were broke in the windows of the Saloon by people who were looking in at the dancers who Lord P. will call upon to pay for them I do not know he still tells John whenever he happens to meet him that he will have his guinea … Lord P. talks of going to town to prepare for his wifes lying in. I fancy he will have plenty of time to prepare before such an event takes place –[68]

Lady Portsmouth was at this time in her late forties, hence Anne's joke. Although she herself had given birth to Ben at age 44, as discussed above, it was considered highly unlikely for first pregnancies to occur in the forties.

The Harwoods were another family with whom the Lefroys were close. John Harwood (1747–1813) was the local squire, living at Deane House with his wife Anne. Their three sons, John (b. 1770), Earle (b. 1773) and Charles (b. 1783) feature in both Jane Austen's and Anne's letters.[69]

Earle, who was serving in the Royal Marines, continued to cause worry to his parents and neighbours. In 1797 he married a woman of apparently shady background, then in 1800, while on active service, he apparently shot himself, though not fatally and not on purpose. Jane Austen had told the story, as widely reported in the neighbourhood, to Cassandra:

> About ten days ago, in cocking a pistol in the guard-room at Marcou, he accidentally shot himself through the Thigh. Two young Scotch Surgeons in the Island were polite enough to propose taking off the Thigh at once, but to that he would not consent; & accordingly in his wounded state was put on board a Cutter & conveyed to Haslar Hospital at Gosport; where the bullet was extracted, & where he now is I hope in a fair way of doing well.[70]

The island where Earle was serving was an important strategic asset in the ongoing conflict with France. The Îsles Saint-Marcouf are a pair of uninhabited islands off the Normandy coast, occupied by the Royal Navy as a forward base. For uninhabited islands, they certainly saw a lot of history in this period. In 1795, the crew of the HMS *Shark* mutinied because of the harsh conditions on the base, and went with their ship over to the French.

In 1798, the British, notably the Royal Marines of whom Earle Harwood was one, repelled a French attack, with the French – despite their much superior numbers – suffering a major setback in what was seen as a rehearsal in miniature for any invasion of England.

It was against this background of actual war-fighting that poor Earle Harwood from Deane suffered, in October 1800, his tragi-comic guardroom injury. James Austen accompanied Earle's brother John Harwood to visit Earle and bring back news for their worried parents.[71]

It is this injury which Anne, several months later, describes in a series of reports to Christopher Edward:

> We went to Ashe Park to dinner & met the Bramstons & all the Harwoods Earle was there he is too lame to return to his military duty at present but looks well & is in high spirits... [72]

> Earle Harwood is to leave Deane tomorrow I fear forever as
> the Ship he belongs to is going to the East Indies & he has
> little chance of standing the heat of the climate the wound
> in his hip is not yet healed & he will be lame all his life –[73]

It is likely that the actions around Marcou, as related by Earle Harwood
to family and friends, made quite an impression on Jane Austen. The
commander of the British garrison at Marcou in May 1798, at the period
of the French attack, was Lieutenant Charles Papps Price, of the *Badger*,
a converted Dutch ship. He must have had good intelligence, because he
was forewarned of the French attack in flat-bottomed boats operating out
of Le Havre. Price was thus able to open fire as soon as the French boats
became visible at dawn. The French reported about 900 killed and over
300 wounded; only one British marine was killed, with four wounded.[74]

As we know, Jane Austen was to immortalise Lieutenant Price
in *Mansfield Park* (1814). The victory at Marcou was a significant
microcosm of what, it was hoped, would be the outcome of any attempted
French invasion of the English mainland (as would be widely anticipated
in 1803/04: see Chapter 11). Perhaps this, in addition to whatever reports
Earle Harwood, in his lengthy recuperation, made to visitors and friends,
led eventually to the creation of Royal Marine Lieutenant Price. The
original Lieutenant Charles Papps Price was said to have been a coarse
man, repeatedly passed over for promotion, who apparently spent most
of his time on the islands with a prostitute he had brought over from
Portsmouth.[75]

Brian Southam, in *Jane Austen and the Navy* (2005), suggested that
Earle Harwood's experience might have formed part of the background
to Austen's masterly depiction of Fanny's rough, hard-drinking, coarse
father, but does not appear to have been aware of the connection with the
original Lieutenant Price in the operations around Marcou.[76]

Chapter 11

Mentioning the War

Britain's long-standing conflict with Revolutionary France – a constant background to Jane Austen's and Anne Lefroy's lives and writings – reached home soil in February 1797, when a French invasion force arrived at Fishguard in Wales, under the command of American Colonel William Tate. It was forced into an ignominious retreat after clashes with British militia and sailors, but the episode indicated that the British mainland could not be considered invulnerable in a pan-European conflict.[1] In October of that year, the Austrians signed the Treaty of Campo Formio, which ceded Belgium to France, and recognised French control of the Rhineland and much of Italy.[2]

Increasingly without European allies, Britain continued operations by sea, as we saw in Chapter 10. In March 1801, British naval commander Horatio Nelson won a victory over the Danish fleet at the Battle of Copenhagen. The British action was intended to intimidate the Danes from ceding their fleet to the French. Thanks to skills in both naval tactics and diplomacy, Nelson secured a ceasefire with the Danes, and later in the year negotiations opened with the French.[3]

After much manoeuvring, the Treaty of Amiens was signed in 1802. One of the terms was that Britain recognised the French Republic, while Napoleon's object in signing the Treaty, it gradually became clear, was to exclude Britain politically and commercially from Europe.[4]

Within the year, Britain became convinced that Napoleon had no intention of observing the Treaty terms, particularly in his attempts to exert control over countries such as Switzerland in what have been called 'cold-war encroachments'.[5] In retaliation, Britain refused to observe its own undertaking to evacuate its colony at Malta. Provocations and counter-posturing ensued, and on 17 May 1803, the Royal Navy captured all the French and Dutch merchant ships sailing around

Britain, confiscated their cargoes, and took their crews prisoner. A day later, Britain declared war. In return, France arrested all British males in France and Italy. Historians have debated for decades about whether Britain or Napoleon should be accorded greater responsibility for the failure of the Treaty.[6]

Although her occupations were primarily with family and local matters, such a restless intellect as Anne's was unlikely to have ignored the momentous events taking place in Europe, and at home. The British press was growing in independence; newspapers were becoming increasingly important as vehicles for public opinion.[7] After the Treaty of Amiens broke down, the British Government encouraged anti-Napoleon propaganda in the press.[8] It was in 1803 that English cartoonist James Gillray first depicted a 'lean, sallow, thoughtful, driven "Little Boney".'[9]

The English people were in no doubt that Napoleon intended to invade. In view of his considerable preparations, this is also the view of historians.[10] By the summer of 1805, 100,000 French troops were encamped at Boulogne. Over 2,000 boats capable of transporting 167,000 men from the Channel ports were prepared.[11]

The British responded with massive preparations for the anticipated attack.[12] A Bill was introduced in July 1803 for local conscription of men aged between 17 and 55, but so many volunteers came forward – 300,000 in Britain and 70,000 in Ireland – that the Conscription Bill was dropped as unnecessary.[13] With over 380,000 volunteers (plus 70,000 in Ireland), and a combined military force of over 615,000 by December 1803, Britain was preparing the largest army in its history, although there were well-founded concerns about the readiness of many of its members.[14]

Even before the outbreak of war, and while the Treaty notionally held, hostilities were anticipated. In March 1803, Anne had written to Christopher Edward to ask what his supervisor Mr Clarke thought about the turn of events.

> What does Mr Clarke say about the impending war? I trust
> it will please God to preserve us as he has hitherto done.[15]

On the Isle of Wight, notionally a front-line province, and bored with his work at Mr Clarke's office, 17-year-old Christopher Edward made several overtures about joining the militia, through the spring of 1803. Anne and George were horrified:

> By ... trust alone ... in the protection of a merciful God can this nation be saved your father bids me say that at present he cannot *approve* of your entering into a Volunteer, or any other Corps; that if ever it becomes necessary for *all* the young men to arm, he certainly would not wish you to shrink from the task, but till then he thinks it will only tend to unsettle & take you from your employment without being of any use.[16]

That was in March. Another plea must have come in May:

> I will first answer the most important part of your letter that which regards your going into the Volunteers your father desires me to say he would not upon any account have you do it at present then when all other young men are called upon to come forward he does not mean to wish that you should shrink but that till the absolute necessity arrives he thinks the entering into any Corps a very bad plan...[17]

Clearly requiring support for their position, the Lefroys had consulted family friend Stephen Terry, who was himself a lieutenant in the North Hampshire militia. The objections appeared to be the expense, for young men who could not afford it, and the time-wasting, to which they were prone anyway:

> Stephen Terry with whom your father talked upon the subject on Thursday last said entering into a Volunteer Corps in the Isle of Wight was one of the worst & most ruinous plans a young man could pursue & that if he could prevail his Brother should not do it upon any account so you see we are not singular in our opinion upon the subject but even a Soldier & I believe a very good one advises against it...[18]

Like Christopher, Stephen Terry's younger brother John was in Newport in the Isle of Wight, possibly also studying law.[19] At least Christopher

Edward and John could complain together about their families not understanding them.

There was clearly some religious fatalism at play here, with Anne and George trusting that God would preserve England as He had done to date, but their attitude may also reflect, even if subconsciously, the English cultural opposition to militarism. The problem was felt to be that young men who might have been useful in their normal lives, would be turned by military service into annoying good-for-nothing braggarts.

The poet William Cowper, in *The Task* (1785, a poem to which Jane Austen referred in *Mansfield Park,* 1814) expressed this view most powerfully in his description of a country lad, balloted into the militia, who slowly adopts a military bearing, then finds himself at a loss on his return to the plough. Cowper's account is all the more vivid from being conveyed in simple words, many of only one syllable:

> By slow degrees,
> Unapt to learn, and form'd of stubborn stuff,
> He yet by slow degrees puts off himself,
> Grows conscious of a change, and likes it well;
> He stands erect; his slouch becomes a walk;
> He steps right onward, martial in his air,
> His form, and movement; is as smart above
> As meal and larded locks can make him; wears
> His hat, or his plumed helmet, with a grace;
> And, his three years of heroship expired,
> Returns indignant to the slighted plough.
> He hates the field, in which no fife or drum
> Attends him; drives his cattle to a march;
> And sighs for the smart comrades he has left.
> 'Twere well if his exterior change were all –
> But with his clumsy port the wretch has lost
> His ignorance and harmless manners too.
> To swear, to game, to drink; to shew at home
> By lewdness, idleness, and Sabbath-breach,
> The great proficiency he made abroad;
> To break some maiden's and his mother's heart;
> To be a pest where he was useful once;
> Are his sole aim and all his glory now.[20]

Christopher Edward did, in the end, join the Volunteers, and Anne was very proud of a flattering newspaper report about the Isle of Wight unit, the Regiment of Loyal Newport Volunteers.

> Captain J.W. Allee's company of Riflemen, attached to the Regiment of Loyal Newport Volunteers, fired ball-cartridge, on Monday last, at a figure target, placed 120 yards distant, and in a few minutes after the signal to fire, the board was completely perforated, and literally cut to pieces, for out of 600 ball-cartridges 189 went through the target, every third ball having effect – a firing that would have done credit to the most veteran troops of this or any other Kingdom.[21]

British authorities had only within the last few years adopted widespread use of the rifle. Again, cultural considerations had played a role here, with a sense that the rifle was for civilian hunting use, not military. The change in approach was a direct response to French tactics. Rifle trials were held at Woolwich in early 1800, with shots fired at 300 yards. The Baker rifle, after some modifications, was adopted.[22] Christopher Edward was thus at the cutting edge of military technology for the time.

Anne ensured that he would also have new underwear, for facing the enemy:

> I have sent you some Welsh flannel to make you drawers & an under waistcoat in case you should be called out to oppose the great enemy of the human race – I trust in God however he will never reach our shores – remember when your flannel waistcoats &c are washed to tell the woman never to wring them, but just squeeze the water out of them & hang them up & let them drain till they are quite dry…[23]

Anne clearly realised that a teenage boy needed laundry instructions set out, if at all possible, in words of one syllable.

Subsequently, Christopher Edward even toyed with joining the regular army, a plan from which his parents very firmly dissuaded him. In 1804, Anne heard a report that the Royal Military Academy, then at Marlow in Buckinghamshire, was to be moved to Winchester. She was afraid that Ben, too, would be tempted to adopt the red coat:

> If this is true I suppose Ben: & Johnny [Brydges, Ben's cousin] will now & then see each other but I hope in God Ben: will not take it into his head to wish to become a Soldier.[24]

In the event, the Academy moved to Sandhurst in 1812, where it remains today.[25]

George junior, then at university, had also contracted the Volunteer craze, joining the local Ashe, Deane and Hannington unit. Despite herself, Anne became quite involved:

> The Corps are to meet tonight at Deane & I have been all this morning employed in making Camp colours to mark out the ground.[26]

George soon experienced first-hand the frustrations of working in a military team under incompetent command:

> George is terribly plagued by his Captns dilatoriness & indecision they have got their arms but the uniforms are not yet made...[27]

Some local characters, however, went a little too far with their enthusiasm for a smart uniform.

> Harry St John who is a Lieutnt in Sir H[enry] Mildmay's troop came in his uniform with a very fine embroidered *Sabretash* (I do not know how to spell the word) dangling at his heels – everybody thought it would have been much more proper if he had appeared in his black coat...[28]

The problem here was partly that Henry-Ellis St John was a clergyman, rector of Winchfield, and was appearing to value worldly military rank over his godly status.[29] It is not clear whether Anne knew that St John's commander, Sir Henry St John Mildmay (1764–1808), Hampshire politician and rival of Lord Bolton for local honours, was an associate when in London of society courtesan Harriette Wilson. She tells several anecdotes in which Mildmay is a participant.[30]

Throughout 1803, talk of invasion was everywhere.

> They are so alarmed in Kent about Invasion that your
> Uncle Harrisons Servants have of themselves formed a
> little Corps & exercise every evening your Uncle Egerton
> has raised a Troop & your Uncle Edward will I believe
> command a company of Infantry as he did before... Rice is
> going as Sergeant into John Portals troop.[31]

If even self-absorbed Samuel ('Egerton') roused himself to community service, things must have seemed dire. And if Napoleon actually invaded, he would have Anne to deal with:

> In case of actual invasion I am sure you [Christopher Edward]
> would exert yourself as much as anyone in defence of your
> country your Religion & in short everything that is dear to
> you & God forbid I should prevent your coming forward in
> such a glorious cause – I think I could handle Cartridges if
> not fire a musket myself upon such an occasion...[32]

For its part, French propaganda made fun of this very scenario. An anonymous cartoon from late 1803 shows serried ranks of middle-aged Englishwomen defiantly waving their fans against the oncoming French ships ('Liberté des mers' on their sails), while a redcoat cowers beneath their skirts.[33]

In the previous year, Anne had already made a contribution in the cause against Napoleon: not with a musket, but in the war of ideas. Her brother-in-law Henry Maxwell had proposed an interpretation of the dream of Daniel in the Bible (Daniel 7). In this dream, Daniel reported seeing four beasts, the fourth of which had ten horns, and among these sprouted up a little horn:

> I considered the horns, and behold, there came up among
> them another little horn, before whom there were three of
> the first horns plucked up by the roots: and behold, in this
> horn *were* eyes like the eyes of man, and a mouth speaking
> great things.
>
> (Daniel 7:8, King James Version)

Maxwell convinced Anne that this was a prophecy of Napoleon's recent takeover of France, ancient Burgundy, and ancient Lombardy in Italy, confirmed by the 1801 Treaty of Luneville between France and Austria. Bizarre as it may seem to us to relate Biblical prophecies to current events, there was a sense of apocalypse, that England was passing through a period of particular cosmic significance.

It was certainly the case that Napoleon's military victories in continental Europe had been, among some groups, regarded as almost supernatural. The British consul at Bologna reported in 1797 the awe the French armies inspired:

> [it is impossible to] convey an adequate idea of the impression of terror and astonishment which accompanies the Republic's armies in their conquest of Italy; where they are venerated as a superior order of beings to whom nothing is impossible, and are looked upon in much the same way as the followers of Cortez were by the Mexicans.[34]

Anne outlined the Maxwell interpretation and asked Christopher Edward if he would discuss it with Mr and Mrs Clarke:

> We had a letter from your Uncle Maxwell yesterday in which he desires us to read with attention the 7th Chapter of Daniel to see how remarkably the prophesy of the little horn is now fulfilled – the little horn is by all commentators supposed to be the Infidel power, which was to pluck up by the root three of the ten Kingdoms into which the Roman Empire was divided: by the Treaty of Luneville Buonaparte is put into possession of the only three Kingdoms which retained their names to the present times, viz: those of the Franks and Burgundians in France, & the Lombards in Italy mention this to Mr & Mrs Clarke, & I am sure they will be as much struck as we have been when they read the Chapter; how blind must those be who see not the hand of God in the wonderful events now crowding fast upon each in almost every corner of the Globe![35]

Anne went further. She wrote an article promoting Maxwell's interpretation to the editor of the *Gentleman's Magazine*, and it was published in the October 1802 issue under the heading 'Application of a remarkable Prophecy in Daniel'.

> Oct. 8. Mr URBAN, In these eventful and alarming times, every real Christian seems to be particularly called upon to make publick any conjecture that tends to confirm the truth of Revelation, and to strengthen our trust in that merciful Being, who alone 'ruleth the raging of the sea and the madness of the people.' With this conviction upon my mind, I am anxious (through your means) to communicate to the publick an explanation of the little horn mentioned in Daniel, and which seems never yet to have been satisfactorily applied...
>
> [I] shall leave it to those who are better skilled than myself in the language of Prophecy, to pursue the enquiry; only remarking that, if there is a real foundation for applying the description of the little horn to the usurpation of Bonaparte, great consolation must arise from considering how short the period is, to which his reign seems clearly to be limited.[36]

Accordingly, the final verse from Daniel 7, quoted in Anne's article, conveyed the prospect, sooner or later, of Napoleon's defeat:

> Ver. 26. 'But the judgment shall sit; and they shall take away his dominion, to consume and to destroy it unto the end.'[37]

As Anne's publication of her and Maxwell's thesis indicated, the propaganda war against Napoleon was conducted in part through the medium of allegories and symbols, some Biblical, others classical. An elaborate Gillray cartoon from August 1803 shows Napoleon at dinner in Egypt where the words 'Mene, mene, tekel, upharsin' appear on the wall as written by a divine hand.[38] This too is a reference to the Book of Daniel 5:25–8, in which, at the feast of the King of Babylon, Belshazzar, the divine words appear: 'You have been weighed in the balance, and found wanting.' The image is meant to suggest that divine justice will avenge crimes committed by arrogant conquerors.

Regarding her and Maxwell's Daniel interpretation, Anne did not want her authorship public, writing to Christopher Edward:

> You will not of course mention who put [the article] in but I thought you might like to see it & therefore I told you who put it in.[39]

Against such a background, Christopher Edward also seems to have taken part in the war of ideas. Anne wrote to him in February 1803:

> A thousand thanks for the trouble you took in transcribing so much from the Anti Jacobin it gave me great pleasure to find how highly [Samuel's latest novel] *Le Forester* was spoken of – we are just reading Sir Robert Wilsons account of the [French] expedition to Egypt he fully authenticates the storys of Buonapartes crueltys with regard to the massacre of the Garrison at Jaffa & the poisoning his prisoners What a monster is this idol of the French nation![40]

Christopher Edward himself seems to have ventured into Biblical interpretation, for Anne politely responded to his conjectures in April 1803:

> Thank you for your explanation of the Number of the Beast these are wonderful times & I doubt not but a few years more will explain many prophecies which remain to be accomplished.[41]

The Number of the Beast was the number 666 (or possibly 616), as indicated in the Book of Revelation 13:18. It seems that Christopher was treading a well-worn path, as,

> Innumerable explanations have been given of the cryptogram.[42]

The number is a puzzle: each letter in both Greek and Hebrew also represented a number as well as a sound, so a name could be represented by a figure corresponding to the sum of the letters. Apparently the most likely verbal solution of the numerical cipher was 'Nero Caesar'. It is likely that Christopher interpreted the puzzle as referring to Napoleon, but this is one of many conjectures not supported by scholarly opinion:

> The many ingenious attempts to refer it to such persons as Mohammed, the Pope, Napoleon or M. Luther may be safely dismissed.[43]

Preparations continued into the early months of 1804. Anne did what she could:

> The two Songs too we are much pleased with & I intend to write them out for the band at Basingstoke – I believe there is nothing more useful in exciting & keeping up the spirits of a Nation than popular songs.[44]

Accordingly, Anne also updated a poem by Robert Burns, 'Robert Bruce's address to his Troops at Bannockburn', better known as 'Scots Wha Hae (wi' Wallace bled)'. Burns' version (1793) was an expression of Scottish nationalism, circulated in an environment in which Scottish radicals were suspected by the British Government of sympathy with the French revolution. It was ironic, then, that Burns' poem was thus co-opted by Anne in the cause against France. The tune, 'Hey Tuttie Tatie', is a slow march, and Anne explained that she had heard the local children sing it at Cowes. The table gives Burns' original, and Anne's adaptation, which she intended for the use of the Newport Volunteers. It is not clear whether Anne's version received any performances.

Robert Burns, 'Scots Wha' Hae' (1793)	Anne Lefroy, 'Brave Medina's Sons Awake' (1803)
Scots, wha hae wi' WALLACE bled, Scots, wham Bruce has aften led, Welcome tae your gory bed, Or to victorie.	Brave Medina's Sons awake For your Kings and Country's sake All your dearest rights at stake Rise to Victory!
Now's the day, and now's the hour; See the front of battle lour; See approach proud EDWARD's power, Chains and Slaverie.	Now's the day and now's the hour; See the front of battle lour; See approach proud Gallia's pow'r Chains and Slavery!

Wha will be a traitor-knave?	Who will be a Traitor-knave?
Wha can fill a coward's grave?	Who so base to be a Slave?
Wha sae base as be a Slave?	Who can fill a coward's grave?
Let him turn and flee.	Let him turn and flee!
Wha for SCOTLAND's king and law,	Who for Britains King and Law
Freedom's sword will strongly draw,	Freedoms sword will strongly draw,
FREE-MAN stand, or FREE-MAN fa',	Freemen stand, or Freemen fa',
Let him follow me.	Let him follow me!
By Oppression's woes and pains!	By oppression's woes and pains!
By your Sons in servile chains!	By your sons in servile chains!
We will drain our dearest veins,	We will drain our dearest veins,
But they *shall* be free!	But they shall be free!
Lay the proud Usurpers low!	Lay the proud Usurper low!
Tyrants fall in every foe!	Tyrants fall in ev'ry foe!
LIBERTY's in every blow!	Libertys in ev'ry blow
Let us Do – or Die!	Rise to Victory[45]

Anne died in December 1804, and thus did not live to see the Napoleonic invasion threat evaporate. Through early 1805, Nelson and the French admiral Villeneuve feinted and opposed each other between the Mediterranean, Gibraltar, and Boulogne. In early August 1805, Napoleon was ready to embark his massive army at Boulogne. As late as 23 August he wrote: 'There is still time – I am master of England.'[46]

Nelson, however, was blockading Villeneuve in the harbour at Cadiz. The next day, Napoleon ordered his army to disperse from Boulogne and march east to the Danube. When in October Villeneuve was ordered to emerge from Cadiz to sail for Naples to counter an Anglo-Russian expeditionary force, Nelson and Collingwood pounced, destroying most of Villeneuve's 30-plus ships, with only three left fit for action.[47] At the Battle of Trafalgar, Napoleon's chances of invading Britain were crushed. Faced with his overwhelming defeat by the Royal Navy, Napoleon later denied that he had had any intention of invading England.[48]

Chapter 12

In Sickness and in Health

One of Anne's abiding preoccupations was health. She had lost siblings in infancy, and three of her own children, to illness or misadventure. Having her young surviving sons, Christopher Edward and Ben, at a distance, also increased her anxiety about all aspects of health. In addition, her husband, the Reverend George, appeared to suffer from mysterious but persistent ailments.

It is useful to sketch, in broad terms, the background of medical knowledge and practice as it existed at the beginning of the nineteenth century. One way to do this is to look at the Lyford family, of whom several members were doctors in the area of Ashe and Winchester from the mid-eighteenth century onwards.

John Lyford senior (1740–1829) was a surgeon working in Basingstoke. His younger brother Charles Lyford (1743–1805) was a surgeon in Winchester. The elder John's son, Charles Lyford junior (1778–1859), was the 'Mr Lyford' who regularly makes an appearance in Anne's letters. He was his father's partner and successor in the local practice.

Surgery was a very ancient, but rapidly changing discipline. Since prehistoric times, broken bones had been set, foreign bodies removed, infected matter and tumours cut out, but it took the constant wars of the eighteenth century to bring a more scientific approach. One British pioneer was John Hunter (1728–1793). He began his career as an assistant to his brother in a school of anatomy, later serving with the British army in the 1760s. In dealing with the aftermath of war wounds, Hunter was faced with the limitations of the discipline as it was:

> To perform an operation, is to mutilate a patient we cannot cure; it should therefore be considered an acknowledgement of the imperfection of our art.[1]

Returning to London, Hunter entered a dental practice. He also gave a series of lectures on muscular motion. It was Hunter's intuition that a detailed knowledge of comparative anatomy (including between animals and humans), as well as the causes of diseases, was critical background for the surgeon. In 1785 Hunter's discovery of collateral circulation in deer antlers allowed him to make a successful intervention in a human patient, utilising the same principle.[2]

Hunter continued his research and lecturing as well as his practice, always advising on the relation between form and function, and noting that observation and experiment must precede generalisation. Hunter also studied fossils, and his last paper for the Royal Society proposed that the fossil record suggested the earth was 'thousands of centuries' old. Friends advised him to suppress such a dangerous paper, and it was not rediscovered and published until fifty years later.[3]

While Hunter was practising, lecturing and publishing in London, in Winchester Charles Lyford senior was serving the Royal Hampshire Hospital as Apothecary and Surgeon from 1768 to 1805. Several hospitals had preceded this institution in Winchester, which was completed in 1759 with funds from a bequest from former mayor of Southampton Richard Taunton (d. 1752).

The new hospital, which comprised six wards, was the first to be fitted with underfloor ventilation to encourage the circulation of fresh air. It also had its own well, bringing water filtered through the chalk of the South Downs. Early in this period, the hospital struggled with a smallpox epidemic, worsened by the groups of soldiers and militia stationed in the area. Against this local background, it is possible that fears about outbreaks of disease contributed to Anne and George's unease about Christopher Edward joining the Volunteers in 1803.

It is likely that the Lyfords honed their surgical skills, as Hunter had done, on deceased cadavers. Under the 1751 Murder Act, surgeons were permitted to dissect the bodies of executed murderers. Winchester's Crown Court, where Anne liked to attend from time-to-time, provided a regular supply of executed murderers to the hospital.

The hospital served the whole of Hampshire, and continued to grow. By 1825, during the career of the younger Charles Lyford, the Hospital staff consisted of three physicians, two 'Extraordinary and Consulting' surgeons (one being Lyford), three simple surgeons, an apothecary, the matron and nurses for sixty inpatients and 300 outpatients.[4] The medical staff were also expected to treat the whole community.

John Hunter's first and most distinguished student was the researcher and doctor Edward Jenner (1749–1823). A local doctor, Jenner practised in Gloucestershire, travelling on horseback in all weathers across an area of 400 square miles. A house call during a severe frost in 1786 caused him to suffer hypothermia, of which, like a good medical observer on the Hunter principle, Jenner left a detailed account.[5]

In the eighteenth century, most people in Britain would be exposed sooner or later to smallpox, which killed at least twenty per cent of people affected. Since 1721, when Lady Mary Wortley Montague had introduced it in England after observing it in use in Constantinople, variolation had been practised as a preventative for smallpox. Variolation was the introduction into the skin of matter from smallpox pustules, with the aim of inducing a small but protective infection. It was not particularly reliable, and brought a risk that people in contact with variolated patients would contract the fully virulent strain. Jenner was experienced in variolation, but began to look for safer and less unpleasant alternatives.

It was suspected that rural people in regular contact with cattle, who had often been exposed to the cattle disease cowpox, had better immunity against smallpox. Cowpox is a variant of the disease which has only mild symptoms in humans. Jenner discussed the matter with Hunter and others, consistently with Hunter's strong interest in comparative, cross-species physiology. Jenner performed the first documented inoculation with cowpox matter in 1796, on 8-year-old James Phipps, with cowpox-laden material taken from a dairymaid, Sarah Nelmes.

When Jenner published his results in 1798, including his belief that cowpox inoculation provided lifelong protection against smallpox, reactions were mixed. As today, there was scepticism about his optimistic stance on the basis of a small sample of cases. In addition, some opponents objected on religious grounds to the transfer of animal material into humans.[6] However, the importance of the work meant that by 1801, Jenner's book had been translated into Latin, German, French, Italian, Dutch, and Spanish. Smallpox was a global killer, and this was a significant advance.

It is important to realise that Hunter, Jenner, and Lyford had no idea that the diseases which they were attempting to treat were caused by organisms far smaller than those few which had, to that date, been revealed by microscopes. Smallpox and cowpox are caused by viruses, and before the end of the nineteenth century the existence of these very small pathogens had only been conjectured, never actually confirmed. As we take for granted modern-day knowledge about the underlying causes of disease, we can be the more impressed by the researchers who operated without that background information.

A few years after Jenner's ground-breaking work, Anne Lefroy was in correspondence with him. We have seen that her mother's brother, John, died in his teens from smallpox, and that when she and George were newlyweds in Basingstoke there was a debilitating outbreak. Anne was determined to take advantage of Jenner's discovery to immunise as many people as she could. She writes in March 1802 to Christopher:

> I forgot to mention that I last week received a letter from Dr Jenner who has sent me some vaccine matter & I am going to begin inoculating [*sic*] immediately.[7]

Anne approached her vaccination work thoughtfully, realising that the after-effects of vaccination – a sore, stiff arm – would be most inconvenient for working people. She must have previously received vaccine matter from Jenner, because as early as the summer of 1801, as she was waiting for the wedding of Lucy and Rice to take place, she writes:

> You enquire about the Cowpox I have only left off inoculating till the hot weather or rather till the Harvest is over as it would be inconvenient to the poor people to have a stiff arm for some days in this busy season in the autumn I am to have many patients.[8]

Anne continued her work into the winter, when the risk of outbreak was greatest. At periods when smallpox had broken out in the neighbourhood of Ashe, Anne's vaccination program clearly increased in popularity.

> I am very busy in inoculating for the Cowpox as the Smallpox has broke out in several of the villages round.[9]

The villagers could see that Anne's previous vaccinations had been effective. A virtuous cycle of immunity developed, where people who had previously been vaccinated were now able to help others who were sick.

> I am now again very busy in Cowpox inoculation as the Smallpox is in many of the Villages around us the common people are all now eager to be secured from infection. Mr Bramston [neighbour] inoculated 140 in one day & numbers of those whom I inoculated last year & the year before have been employed in attending their neighbours who have the Small pox & not one has had the least symptom of having taken the infection.[10]

The Bramstons were neighbours at Oakley Hall; Wither Bramston (1753– 1835) had married Mary Chute of The Vine. Throughout February 1803 (a very cold winter) the danger persisted, and Anne and Mr Bramston continued to work. Presumably they had both undergone vaccination, so their personal risk was reduced, but it is impossible not to respect their dedication as front-line volunteer health workers.

> Mr Bramston & myself are as busy as ever on the Cowpox inoculation Mr B in one day inoculated 200 the small pox is very much about us & in many cases fatal.[11]

The previous winter, Anne had ensured that her little grandson, Lucy and Rice's first child, called Henry and nicknamed Harry or Toddy, still a baby, was also vaccinated:

> Little Harry was inoculated for the Cowpox on Friday sen'nite his arm looks as well as possible.[12]

It is not an exaggeration to say that Anne Lefroy and Wither Bramston, between them, probably saved the lives of scores of local people through their vaccination program.

Despite what we might think of as her rather credulous approach to Biblical predictions of Napoleon, Anne brought a more evidence-based attitude to medicine in general. She writes in February 1803, while in the thick of her vaccination schedule:

> I cannot place much faith in the wonderful accounts
> of cures performed by the metallic tractors, or in the
> extraordinary [power] of Galvanism but as this is an age
> of discovery perhaps I may live to be convinced that they
> are true.[13]

Anne herself had seemed to be convinced of the powers of the 'tractors' in the autumn of 1801. The Reverend George Lefroy seemed to be affected by rheumatism. He tried the 'tractors'. These were metal rods, looking like large horseshoe nails, which were drawn over the affected body part, and were claimed to treat inflammation with electromagnetic energy. They were patented in 1796 by Elisha Perkins, an enterprising American who brought his product and its miraculous properties to Britain.[14] The rods were to be drawn in strokes over the affected area. Many people reported relief from a range of complaints.

Among these happy patients were the Reverend George, and several of the Lefroys' servants and acquaintances. George Lefroy had been in such pain that he could not ride or stand for a long period, and the Reverend John Orde – vicar of a neighbouring parish – urged George to take a break from his Sunday duties, and leave the service to him. By the Monday, however, after treatment with the tractors, George was much improved:

> I rode in the morning & after I returned your father went out
> upon my mare & found he could ride without any difficulty
> indeed I trust the complaint is now nearly removed he has
> had the Tractors tryed twice & certainly found benefit from
> them. Fields eye is much better & both Bettys & Priors
> Rheumatism cured I will send you one of Perkins Books
> as perhaps Mr & Mrs Clarke may like to see it Betty had
> this morning a very bad ear ach[e] which the Tractors cured
> entirely in about 20 minutes.[15]

Any cure accomplished by the tractors was entirely the result of a placebo effect. This had effectively been demonstrated the year before by John Haygarth, a Bath physician who, sceptical about the highly popular device, had made replicas in wood instead of metal. Haygarth wrote that both the metal originals and the wooden replicas had exactly the same results, leading him to conclude that:

> the whole effect undoubtedly depends upon the impression which can be made upon the patient's Imagination.[16]

Haygarth wrote up and published his investigation, one of the first documented demonstrations of the placebo effect.

One medical case which clearly puzzled Anne was that of neighbour Mrs Russell, probably a relative of the former Rector of Ashe.[17] Mrs Russell's health issues receive no fewer than ten mentions in Anne's letters, indicating that it was a frequent topic of speculation and gossip. Mrs Russell suffered from 'dropsy', the term for generalised oedema or build-up of excess fluid. This can be caused by a number of underlying conditions, including kidney disease, liver disease, heart failure, or chronic lung disease.[18]

In the early 1800s, however, only the symptom could be identified and treated. Anne writes in the summer of 1801:

> Mrs Russell looks rather better, but I fear she must go thro' the operation of tapping before she has any chance of recovering, & even then it is a very doubtful case.[19]

Texts from the nineteenth century indicate that tapping, or draining, fluid was employed very generally. The features of the liquid drained off gave some clues as to which underlying condition was involved.[20]

Next September Anne writes:

> I went to Basingstoke in the morning & saw poor Mrs Russell; she went thro' the operation of Tapping last Monday, & appears tolerably well, but I am afraid Lyford does not think her safe.[21]

It is unclear whether only excess fluid, or excess weight, was involved, as only a few weeks later Anne writes:

> Poor Mrs Russell seems to me larger than ever, but she does not complain & appears to enjoy society very much.[22]

It was acknowledged that tapping was a procedure which would have to be undergone repeatedly.[23] In January 1803 we read:

> Mrs Russell has been tapped a second time & has gone thro' the operation better than at first she is now in great spirits & [looks] remarkably well.[24]

However, appearances were illusory, for by August:

> Poor Mrs Russell is I fear dying but perfectly sensible & resigned.[25]

In September:

> Mrs Russell still lives but grows weaker every day.[26]

We hear no more of Mrs Russell after September 1803; no doubt whatever underlying condition was causing her oedema was claiming her at last.

One disease with which Anne was preoccupied was measles, probably because it was a disease which primarily affected young people. Trying to prevent Christopher Edward and Ben from contracting measles was a way in which Anne could try to keep them safe in general, a proxy means of care. In November 1803, Anne was very worried about reports of measles at Ben's boarding school in Winchester:

> Last Wednesday I was much alarmed by hearing that the Measles had broke out at Winchester School & that 17 boys were in bed with the complaint ... having no one to consult I followed my own inclinations & fetched [Ben] home immediately not so much to prevent his catching the measles as to take care of him if had already caught it ... he has at present no symptoms of it but that is no proof he will not have it as it is sometimes I understand a fortnight or three weeks in the blood before it appears...[27]

Measles was another disease caused by a virus, and therefore its transmission was not understood. It was, however, as Anne's letter indicates, known to be highly contagious, particularly in settings in which there were large groups of young people in close proximity. Anne was correct in her estimation of the incubation period. The New South Wales Health Department states in its Measles Fact Sheet:

> The time from exposure to becoming sick is usually about 10 days. The rash usually appears around 14 days after exposure.[28]

Anne was exercising caution in removing Ben from school, not only because of the disease itself, but because measles has the potential to bring complications, including secondary infections and even encephalitis (swelling of the brain).[29] Measles itself caused death on a par with, and even, in parts of Britain, exceeding smallpox in this period.[30] Luckily, Ben did not develop any symptoms of measles, and was able to enjoy an early start to his Christmas holidays. Other Winchester students were not so fortunate: two weeks later, Anne reports that by now forty boys had come down with the illness.[31]

For Christopher Edward's part, in the leadup to seeing him at Christmas that year, Anne advised him to take precautions against infection.

> [I] *intreat you* to have a little samphire sewed up in a black silk bag, about an inch & half square, tye i[t] round your neck, & let it hang to the pit of your stomach, before you leave Newport, as the measles are so much at Winchester & indeed everywhere about, that you may perhaps pick them up on your journey, if you do not take this precaution pray do not neglect this advice my dearest child for your own & for Bens & Harrys sake I should be very sorry you should catch the Measles.[32]

While Anne was right to be concerned particularly with protecting toddler Harry from the disease, her advice to Christopher was not based in verified science. Samphire is a coastal plant, traditionally used in sauces, but it also contains useful quantities of vitamins (indeed, it has been touted as a coming 'superfood', in the jargon of our own times).[33] However, in a bag tied around Christopher Edward's neck, the vitamins would not have boosted his immunity. Fortunately, therefore, all the Lefroys and Rices escaped the measles outbreak of autumn–winter 1803.

Anne herself enjoyed remarkably good health, but her regular outings with horse or donkey involved some risk. In the autumn of 1803, amid anxiety about the fate of Samuel's claim, and the continuing invasion scare, Anne broke a bone in her leg:

> The Donky tripped & off I came & snapped the small bone [of the leg] but Lyford most fortunately was passing bye it was therefore soon set & I really suffer very little pain but I suppose I must be contented to lie upon the Sofa for two or three weeks & then be lame for as many months.[34]

The setting of a bone without anaesthetic must have been extremely painful, but Anne's tone is light; in writing to her son, she is not going to complain. In the following weeks, however, she experienced some low spirits: 'I own I feel very low.'[35] For such an active person, enforced idleness was difficult to endure.

> I grow tired of lying upon the same Sofa all day long.[36]

By November, Anne was able to attend the Hackwood ball, and to take little Harry to see George's Volunteer unit drilling.

> Little Harry was quite delighted yesterday to see the Volunteers & hear them Huzzah he tried to Halloo too as loud as any of them.[37]

12-year-old Ben, away at school in Winchester, was clearly worried about his mother's leg. In one of his few surviving letters, preserved because Anne forwarded it to Christopher Edward with hers, we hear his anxious tone:

> I am very glad to hear that you are able to go out and feel more comfortable than you did. I suppose that the bone now is pretty near united.[38]

In a sentence which must have been painful for his mother to read, poor Ben adds:

> My school business here is pretty easy but it is the boys that I dread.[39]

Bone-setting will have involved manipulation and probably the use of some kind of splint to keep the fracture stable while it healed.

In addition to the physical ailments which preoccupied Anne, her letters give indications of psychological conditions. Lucy gave birth to her second child, a daughter named Sarah, in June 1804. (Anne did not like the name, which was no doubt given in honour of Rice's mother: 'I assure you your Neice [*sic*] is much prettier than her name.'[40]) A series of remarks in ensuing letters indicate that Lucy's recovery from the birth took longer than expected. Anne's conversational tone attempts to mask what must have been great anxiety about her only surviving daughter:

> 'Lucy…seems low & not inclined to eat this morning, but I hope & trust she is going on pretty well.'[41]
>
> 'Your Sister was but very indifferent during [Rice's] absence [at Newport], & I am sure would have grown worse & worse till his return she is now able to sit up 2 or 3 hours in her great Chair, & I hope tomorrow will be carried into the Drawing room.'[42]
>
> 'Your Sister I thank God mends tho' slowly yesterday she came up here in the Gig & is to return this morning she is still very weak but can now walk without assistance & is quite free from fever.'[43]
>
> 'Your Sister is much better.'[44]

It would seem that Lucy was suffering from fever and quite possibly from post-natal depression. The pervasive hormonal changes now known to affect post-partum women were not recognised or understood. Even Anne seems to be willing Lucy to recover, rather than consoling her, or appreciating the magnitude of her daughter's illness. While the incidence of post-natal depression has always been relatively high (estimated as affecting one in ten mothers), it has only in very recent times been recognised as a genuine and treatable condition.[45]

There are also hints in Anne's letters that her husband, the Reverend George, suffered from depression as well as a range of vague physical complaints. His health receives over forty references. George mentions his 'depression of spirits' as a chronic problem, in a letter to Christopher Edward which he appended to one of Anne's.[46] Problems include rheumatism (for which, as we have seen, the tractors were effective, perhaps indicating that the ailment was not caused by physical inflammation); gout; a troublesome cough.[47, 48] Anne herself hints that George's preoccupation with his symptoms was something that perhaps should be discouraged:

> I think [visitor Mr Cottrell's] conversation was of great use to your father raised his spirits & took off his thoughts from his own complaints which are now I thank God so much better that I think he is in quite good health as I have known him enjoy for some years.[49]

As with childbirth, it has been known for some decades now that ministers of religion are at some elevated risk of developing depression, in part because of their set-apart status from their parishioners.[50] The role of the parish minister encompassed counsellor, theologian, and community leader, as well as the normal demands of a family. Interestingly, it appears that it was his Sunday responsibilities which sat particularly heavily; we have seen that Mr Orde filled in when George was affected by rheumatism. There are several entries of this kind:

> 'Friday. We were of course alone your father was very tired with doing duty twice tho' I thank God he goes thro' the service with less difficulty than he did some time ago.'[51]
> 'Your father went thro' his duty with less fatigue than usual.'[52]

Anne hopes that a long ride through Compton, Warfield, Stratfield Saye and home, taking over a week, will be good for George:

> I hope & trust the long ride will be of great service to him – his head tho' better is not quite well.[53]

Some months later, Anne describes her relief when George joins her on a visit to her relatives in Canterbury. Clearly, she had been apprehensive about his state upon arrival.

> Your father arrived here on Saturday about 1 / 2 past 8, well & in good spirits & having borne his journey without fatigue I thank God he seems to be wonderfully better than when I left home.[54]

It would seem that George's default state was in some kind of poor health, such that Anne comments when he exceeds that standard. In writing that she will not attend the Kempshot ball, as it is to be on 27 January (the date of their son Anthony's death), she adds that George will probably not attend either:

> tho' he is I thank God pretty well (indeed I think better than usual) yet does not like to be up all night.[55]

A social commitment on the scale of a public ball, on top of his usual duties, is likely to have been overwhelming for George.

It may have been the constant public speaking, and public display, which George found so wearing in carrying out his Sunday 'duty'. In addition to the general pressures of his role, George Lefroy had buried three of his own children, which must have affected him, as it had also affected Anne.

The ambiguous nature of many of George's complaints is indicated by a comment by Anne in January 1804.

> Your fathers gout has been more painful since you went but as they assure me his health will be the better for it I must not repine at what he now suffers.[56]

Gout is an inflammatory condition, usually of a joint or of the feet, which develops because of an excess of uric acid, which forms tiny crystals in the joint. For some reason, it was believed to help prevent other diseases from occurring, and this explains Anne's otherwise apparently rather callous decision not to commiserate with George (she may also have been, as noted above, aware that he dwelt too much on his complaints already).[57]

In addition to the normal round of diseases, Charles Lyford sometimes had to deal with the results of nothing less than battlefield-style trauma. One day in 1802, Anne reacted to the culmination of a tale of distress. The events were related in the *Hampshire Chronicle* in June:

> Mr Iremonger, vicar of Wherwell … read a warrant for the arrest of John Fry, charged with the offence of leading a disorderly life and leaving his wife and family often in

distress. As the warrant was read, Fry struck Iremonger over the left eye with a billhook, a blow so violent that it severed his head. Dr Lyford was sent for immediately, took the fractured pieces from Mr Iremonger's wound and trepanned him…[58]

Trepanning was a procedure by which the skull was opened to release dangerous build-up of fluid. Fry threw down his weapon and surrendered, and was committed to gaol. In all probability, he would have been sentenced to death for a crime such as attempted murder.

Later in the summer, Anne writes:

> Poor Mr R Iremonger has been again trepanned as there was a collection of matter upon the brain which it was absolutely necessary to remove but he is at present going on as well as possible.[59]

Mr Iremonger will have suffered headaches, possibly vision difficulties, and other problems after such an horrific head injury. Estimates for survival rates following trepanning in pre-modern societies have ranged from fifty to ninety per cent.[60] Having already lived some months after the attack, possibly Mr Iremonger survived longer, thanks to Dr Lyford's use of the ancient technique (often performed with saws and drills) of trepanning.

Chapter 13

Animals and Plants

Anne Lefroy loved animals, partly because in them she could see the beautiful plan of a benevolent Creator. Her kind heart also looked with sympathy on the animals which took such an important role in the village life of the time, as workmates and companions, and which often did not receive adequate care.

We saw in Part Two that she seemed to have mixed feelings about the legitimised slaughter of wild birds in which her brothers, like most men of their class, took part. This was one among several cases in which Anne's feelings of sympathy were at odds with the general values of her society.

As animal news was likely to be of interest to both her boys, Anne regularly added animal updates. A Sunday dinner with Earle Harwood and the Holders was interrupted by a farm drama caused by an adventurous cow, which fortunately had a happy ending:

> After dinner William came in, in great distress, to say one of the cows had gone up the stairs into the room over the [Farm] Stable & that they were afraid she would break her neck in coming down … after a long consultation they fixed a rope to her horns & with great difficulty brought her safe to the bottom step & threw her down upon a heap of straw without she be hurt.[1]

Donkeys and horses were in constant use for transport, as regularly as we now inhabit our cars today. Anne was always driving herself or others in a cart or carriage:

> We drove the Donkey to Deane … Miss Carleton & I drove to Kingsclere to see Dame Smith … We drove to Deane in

the morning and found your Sister & Rice quite well … Miss
Carleton & I drove to Deane & returned to dinner … Miss
Carleton drove me so far as Oakly Hall in Mr Lovett's Gig…[2]

Anne 'drove the Crop Horse' to pick up the Miss Salters for a visit.
Clearly she enjoyed driving:

Nothing can go better than Crop does & I flatter myself
I am become a very tolerable Coachman – in the evening
we sat & worked & read till 10 o'Clock but Harriot Salter
was so tired with her dance the night before that she had
great difficulty in keeping her eyes open.[3]

She also rode the donkey on occasion:

I have got a footstep put to the pad Tom rides with, & now
sit very comfortably in the true Gipsy stile.[4]

Probably Anne meant, by 'Gipsy stile', riding the donkey rather than
driving it. She will not have meant riding astride, as it was not until the
twentieth century that women abandoned side-saddle use.[5]

Not every landowner treated donkeys and horses as considerately as
the Lefroys. One ongoing saga in Anne's letters concerned the donkey
belonging to Charles Powlett, the Boltons' slightly untoward relative.
The story of the donkey, which insisted on moving in with the Lefroys,
indicates that Anne could not stand to see animals ill-treated.

Would you believe that tho' Charles Powlett is removed to
a house close by Winchester his Donky has again found his
way to Ashe & I want your father to let him remain here.[6]

In the new year, back came the Powletts' donkey:

Charles Powlett's poor Donky came back here on Friday
last & I have persuaded your Father to let me keep him
at least as long as they can spare him, for they really both
starve & overwork him & I cannot bear he should be so ill
used – my Donky is near having a foal.[7]

In the event Anne bought Charles Powlett's donkey, to use while her own donkey was on 'maternity leave'.

> I have repurchased the poor old Donky from Charles Powlett the one I had is with foal & of course will be unfit for use for some months & I am glad to take poor old Jack out of such bad keep as he has been many months past.[8]

There are hints in the surviving record that Anne was also keenly interested in plants, doubtless, again, as an example of God's beautiful creations. The 2007 volume edited by Helen Lefroy and Gavin Turner includes a colour plate of a painting by Anne of two dragonflies. The caption states: 'A painting by Mrs Lefroy in "British Insects".'[9] The list of cited works describes this: '"British Insects", a collection of water-colours by Mrs Lefroy.'[10] We also recall that Benjamin Langlois' bequests included a:

> triple magnifying glass mounted in mother-of-pearl and set in silver gilt … that it may be useful to her in her botanical amusements.[11]

Benjamin Langlois' attitude to Anne's interest in botany was that it was an 'amusement', rather than serious study. The truth was simply that Anne was interested in all aspects of nature and nurturing. As well as caring for Ben's animals, she looked after his vegetable garden:

> It was so wet that I could not get out, except just as far as Bens Garden which I make a point of visiting every day, I have set a Honysuckle & some Mignionet by the seat, & this rain will I trust ensure their growing, some sweet peas which I put in since you went are already 5 or 6 inches high, the lettuces are growing very strongly, & the mustard & cress have afforded us many plates of very good sallad, I mean in their room to put in some peas that Ben: may be able to gather a plate for himself in the holydays…[12]

Christopher Edward had helped by making a garden bed for Ben:

The little garden you was so good as to make for Ben: I have had weeded dug & put into perfect order that it may [be] ready for any seeds you choose to put into it when you come at Christmas.[13]

All natural phenomena were to be considered as evidence of the Creator's work, and potentially as symbols of His mysterious activity. In the autumn of 1801, against a background of hopes for peace with France, it was observed that the season's apples appeared different from their normal form:

All the common people here are delighted with the prospect of peace they say they knew the times would turn for that all the kernels of the apples are turned a different way from what they usually are the point used to be up to the eye it is now down to the stalk I laughed at this assertion till by cutting several apples we found the observation true.

Anne is careful not to give undue credence to the belief of the common people, but hopes that Christopher Edward and the Clarkes will come up with more empirical data:

I do not believe it is an omen but the fact is I believe established beyond a doubt as far as it relates to the growth of this neighbourhood pray observe whether it is the same in the Isle of Wight & ask Mr & Mrs Clarke if they have made any observations upon this subject —[14]

As with her love of animals, it is evident that part of Anne's interest in plants is due to her reverence for their 'evidence' about the creative work of God.

The Lefroy family all loved outdoor activities. Ben's Easter holidays in 1803 sound idyllic:

Ben: & his cousin Johnny are gone to Polhampton to fish for Minows which is their favourite employment they every morning after they have done their tasks sally forth upon their Donkeys & take a scamper round the country…[15]

Johnny & Ben: spend several hours every day in fishing at Polhampton they have caught a great number of Minows Loaches & Banstickles & yesterday they brought home a very fine Trout…[16]

Anne found herself the manager of Ben's considerable menagerie when he was away at school:

Bens Squirrel is alive & merry his Rabbits too are come so that I have now 3 Rabbits 4 lambs, two Dormice, a Squirrel & a Cat to take care of for him.[17]

The four lambs were a result of this happy event in the spring of 1802:

This morning both Bens ewes produced Twins which will I think be to him a matter of great joy.[18]

The story of the squirrel was a delightful one. It also had a special significance for Anne.

I must tell you an extraordinary event Ben has had a young Squirrel given him which the old white cat suckles with the greatest care & seems to be as fond of it as if it was a litter of her own.[19]

An account of this inter-species cuteness appeared in the *Gentleman's Magazine* for May 1802 under the title 'Squirrel nurtured by a Cat'. Almost certainly, Anne herself contributed this article, which is by-lined 'A Constant Reader'. Anne displays a keen interest in animal behaviour, and there is also a metaphorical sub-text about the demands of motherhood, whether surrogate or not:

If you give the squirrel a nut or an almond, it will leave the cat, and eat the food you present to it, while the cat stands by with great patience, and when the squirrel has finished its repast, will lie down and let it suck till it is tired; it then runs away till it is again in want of food, which is again supplied by its unwearied charitable nurse.

While fond in general of most animals, clearly Anne was not really a cat person:

> I know not how to account for her kindness to an animal, not only of a different sort, but of a species which it is (I apprehend) her nature to destroy, except we allow, that, whilst cats in general are cruel and deceitful, some amongst them are benevolent and generous.

For Anne, the strange yet gratifying phenomenon represented a case of God's mysterious but beautiful creative work:

> If we were to indulge our speculations upon this subject, it would lead us far into the disputed question upon the future life of brutes. I will, therefore, only observe, that, as at present 'we see through a glass darkly,' we must wait with patience till that time shall come when we may hope all the wonders of the creation will be laid open to our astonished view, and we shall exclaim with tenfold energy, 'How excellent are thy works, O Lord! In wisdom hast thou made them all.'[20]

Contrary to Benjamin Langlois' view of Anne's natural observations as an 'amusement', her article shows that for her, it was much more than that. In uniting keen scientific observation with Christian faith, Anne foreshadowed the attitude of the English scientists, most of them men, of the 1830s. Her authorship is confident and assured. That she was proud of her work and wished Christopher Edward to know that it was hers is indicated by her referring him to it.

> Have you looked for the account of Bens Cat & Squirrel in the Gentleman's Magazine of last month if you have not pray do read it.[21]

Meanwhile, the star animal himself seems to have flourished, and Anne provided regular updates. 'Bens Squirrell goes on very well' (she writes again to Christopher Edward), 'comes out of the shed & plays about the garden & does not have any inclination to run away.'[22]

The squirrel and 11-year-old Ben got up to some tricks which caused Anne some uneasiness:

> Bens Squirrel had made itself a nest at the top of one of the fir trees in the Garden but often comes down to visit the Cat in the Gardiners House & eats nuts out of Bens hands or takes them out of his mouth when they lie upon his tongue this however is I think rather a dangerous experiment & I have desired it may not be repeated.[23]

The animal antics continued through the summer:

> I forgot to mention that Ben: has got a Squirrel from Ashe Park almost as tame as the first & the [little] cat plays with it nearly as much.[24]

Alas, the next winter brought sadness to Ben's little farm:

> Ben: was sadly mortified just before he left home he had a litter of young Rabbits & cold weather killed them all.[25]

The squirrel survived the winter:

> Bens Squirrel is alive & well he has got two tame Rabbits they produced a litter of five during the severe weather but they all died.[26]

Ben must have acquired some more rabbits during the year, because in the same letter (dated 24 September) in which he asks anxiously about Anne's leg, and expresses his dread of 'the boys' at school, he is also concerned about his rabbits:

> The mornings now begin to get very cold. Are any of my rabbits dead.[27]

The love of horses and riding was clearly a family trait, exhibited before he could walk by little Henry Rice, Lucy's eldest child. Anne writes delightedly in April 1803:

> Little Harry has just been here I hope & trust that before
> another month is over he will run alone his great delight is
> to be set on a Horse or Donkey…[28]

Big Uncle Ben, all of 12 years old, would give Harry a donkey ride in
front of him:

> Little Harry is so fond of going in the Donky carriage that
> he crys terribly when he is taken out he often gets a ride
> upon the Donky before his Uncle Ben: who doats upon
> him – I quite long for you to see him.[29]

A new animal would be added in the summer of 1804:

> Ben: desires his love & thanks for your message about
> Guinea Pigs he has had one given him by Rice & is promised
> another if it comes he need not trouble you for one but it is
> not yet quite certain.[30]

The Guinea Pigs were shortly confirmed: Rice obtained three for his
young brother-in-law:

> Ben: has just got three Guinea Pigs which Rice procured for
> him so that he desires me to say he will not trouble you to
> bring him any.[31]

The animals were part of God's family, and so they were also part of the
extended clan of the Lefroys.

Chapter 14

The Village School

Writing in the 1880s, the Reverend Thoyts made a conjecture about the ancient place-name in Ashe of 'Nursery'.

> May not also the word "Nursery" tell of the education of the children of the poor by the monks of old?[1]

It may have done, but by the time of the Lefroys, it would appear that even Ashe parishioners who acted as church volunteers were likely to be illiterate. We learn from Thoyts:

> John Goodall, being lame, but almost the only one who could read, was appointed Clerk on Sunday, April 5th, 1801.[2]

It may have been the sad state of education in the parish which inspired the Reverend George Lefroy to establish a school-house. In 1784, an exchange of land took place between the Reverend George and Joseph Portal, then the owner of the manor of Ashe. According to the arrangement, the Reverend George exchanged a cottage and garden, for the parcel of land next to the rectory. The Reverend George then had a cottage built on this block of land.

The cottage continued in the Lefroy family until 1837, and was generally occupied by the family's gardeners, who no doubt assisted Anne with Ben's garden.[3] But it also, according to Thoyts, was the original school-house of Ashe.[4]

We learn from the second earliest of her surviving letters (1801) that Anne operated a Sunday school:

> The morning was so wet that I could not stir out of doors not even to my Sunday School.[5]

In this, as with vaccination, once again Anne was an early adopter of an important, indeed revolutionary, reform. Sunday schools had been founded by Robert Raikes (1735–1811), starting with one in his own parish in Gloucestershire in 1780. Raikes was so concerned by the neglected state of the local children, and their behaviour on Sundays, that he set up a school. It operated on weekdays and Sundays, teaching Scripture, reading, and other basic skills.

Raikes promoted the system in a local newspaper, the *Gloucester Journal* (which he also founded). Despite opposition from some conservative critics who felt that education was likely to foment revolution, and also from strict observers of the Sabbath as a day of enforced non-activity, Raikes' system proved very successful. By the time of his death in 1811, a network of Sunday schools operated through England.[6] The system was also adopted on the Continent and in America.[7]

It seems that Anne's Sunday school took place in the afternoon, following the morning services.

> Mr Lefroy & I took a quiet walk after I had heard William
> Wild & Edward Goslett read & say the catechism…[8]

In the snows of winter, numbers of students were down, although Anne was ready to teach:

> This morning … Rice came up to fetch me to Deane we
> spent a quiet & comfortable day & about 10 o'clock William
> came to fetch me home as I wished to be ready to attend to
> the Sunday School children the next morning … the snow
> however was so deep that very few of them came & I might
> as well have saved myself the trouble of coming home…[9]

On weekdays, the school took place in the morning:

> This day was spent as most of the former have been about 10
> my School assembled & soon after 12 they were dismissed
> Amy Prior & Charlotte Field already write very legibly the
> others do not improve so fast but I hope they will all do
> tolerably well my great object is to make them understand
> their duty & to convince them it is both their interest & their

happiness to follow the precepts of that most excellent religion in the principles of which I endeavour to instruct them…[10]

Later in the spring, Anne apparently decided on an earlier start for her school. Breakfast for people of Anne's class was often around 10 a.m:[11]

> I am going tomorrow to begin here my School of a morning before breakfast & I shall then have my time to myself the rest of the day…[12]

Being the children's first theological educator was a grave responsibility, which Anne took very seriously. She writes in August 1802:

> My morning School goes on well. I followed your advice on Friday & read the boys an account of the Creation & the fall which they seemed to take great pains to understand…[13]

An uncertain note is struck before long:

> Our evening school goes on prosperously & I hope & trust the boys will be the better & the happier for the pains that is [*sic*] taken with them…[14]

Perhaps feeling that her own grasp of the finer points of Anglican doctrine was insufficient to support her lesson plans, Anne turned to acknowledged experts such as 'Dr Waldo', a writer whose *Admonitions for Children in Sunday Schools* (1799) was widely used.[15]

When the time came, the Reverend George took the older children aside to prepare them for Confirmation.

> In the evening your father had those children in to the study who are to be confirmed he took great pains to explain to them what they were going to promise & I hope & trust they understood the lecture.[16]

Given that the significance of Confirmation, as a secondary ritual to baptism, has continued to be debated for centuries within many churches, it was perhaps optimistic of Anne to have hoped that the Reverend George would have cleared up any issues for the students.[17] The Reverend George reinforced his teaching with another lesson on the following Friday.

At Anne's school, the children learned life skills as well as basic reading, writing and Scripture:

> Peter Rogers & Will Prior have each of them learnt to knit stockings & do it very tolerably.[18]

Stockings (the term covered also what we would now call socks) were required wear for both boys and girls, so being able to knit their own was an important way of not only helping to clothe themselves, but also to occupy the long winter evenings.

As well as teaching them skills to help themselves, Anne encouraged the students to assist those of even more humble stations in life. As with her vaccination program, Anne emphasised practical charity. It appears that she had the students make needle-cases and pin-cushions for a local woman to re-sell:

> At noon the little old woman to furnish [whom] we made the needle books & pin cushions, came to say she had sold them all, & with the produce had bought herself an apron, & replenished her stock of needles, pins, garters which she had been accustomed to deal in; this gave me great pleasure – how easy is it my dear Boy to be charitable! Even those who have not money to bestow can sometimes give their time & attention to the poor & he who accepts the widows mite will reward them for their good deeds – the materials of which these needle books &c were made were not worth sixpence, & the only trouble was the work of a few hours, yet they afforded such comfort & support to this poor woman by producing to her more shillings than they cost pence to me…[19]

Anne seems to have had assistance from local woman Jenny Wilmot in running her school. In fact, whereas the Reverend Thoyts thought that the school-house was generally the home of gardeners, it would seem to have been, in earlier years, the home of Jenny Wilmot. Anne writes several times as though the school took place in Jenny's home:

> In the evening I went into Jenny Wilmots & read to the Children one of Mr Waldos most excellent Sermons to which they appeared to be extremely attentive...[20]

Poor Jenny was expected not only to accommodate the school, but a new male servant to replace 'John', who had proven to be quite unsatisfactory, including in his careless treatment of the horses. Anne writes in January 1803:

> Did I mention that John was going? He gave your father warning when we returned from Town knowing that your father would not keep him ... he was constantly out in our absence & once took my Mare out a whole day & locked up the other two Horses to shift for themselves till he returned at 11 o'Clock at night – we have not yet got a Servant in his room [vacancy] many have offered but not any that would do...[21]

Late in the month, however, the position was filled:

> Your father has taken [in place of John] a very steady middle aged man who lived 13 years with Mr Coulthard at Farley – he has a wife & I fear she must live in Jenny Wilmots cottage...[22]

In February 1803, there was concern lest Jenny have to leave her cottage. Anne seems mainly concerned about the loss to her school:

> Jenny Wilmot is certainly not to quit her cottage before Midsummer next at soonest she will be a great loss to me on account of my School.[23]

Luckily, Jenny did not move out, and the school continued into the following year:

> You cannot imagine how well my little evening school at Jenny Wilmots goes on, I've four scholars who only came to

Mr Knights at Michaelmas & already write good hands & seem extremely attentive to the instructions I endeavour to give them…[24]

Anne's teaching certainly seemed to have been of benefit to one boy, who pleased her greatly with an unprompted tribute.

I had last night the inexpressible pleasure of hearing one of the lads from Mr Knights say without any question being asked him he was much happier than before he used to spend his Sunday evenings as he now did to be permitted to be of essential service to any fellow creature appears to me the best blessing that can be bestowed upon us & I consider the endeavouring to be useful to others as the best return I can make to that merciful & gracious God who has hitherto preserved you & your Brothers & Sister from falling into those errors by which so many young people are undone.[25]

Anne thus considered as an integral whole her teaching of the village children, and her gratitude to God's assistance in guarding her own children from making poor life choices.

Part Four

Your Angel Mother

Chapter 15

Finale

In November 1804, Anne was looking forward to having both Christopher Edward and Ben at home for Christmas. Her letters were full of local and family news.

There had been the wedding, on 2 November, of Harris Bigg-Wither, the man who two years earlier had proposed to Jane Austen, been accepted, and then received her change of mind the following day. Consoling himself within a short time, Bigg-Wither had proposed to, and been accepted by, Anne Frith:

> I went to Manydown today to congratulate the family upon Harris's Marriage who brought his Bride to Quidhampton on Saturday last he has got leave of absence from the Regiment till after Christmas & I hope we shall see a good deal of them while they remain so near us.[1]

It is not clear whether Anne knew that Jane Austen had been Harris' first choice. It is unlikely that the Austens had publicised the debacle in December 1802, and the period falls into a long hiatus in Jane's surviving letters (between May 1801 and September 1804).[2]

Anne's grandchildren were at a delightful age. There was the upcoming christening of little Sarah Rice:

> 'I believe Sarah is to be Christened on Monday next Harry continues to talk of Uncle Edward [Christopher] very often he is grown very fond of Sarah who is handsomer than ever & uncommonly fat…'[3]
>
> 'Little Harry still talks of you very often he slept here last night & was very good & in high spirits Sarah is really beautiful & Harry is so fond of her he will give anything to his [sister].'[4]

'Sarah is more beautiful than ever & is quite the admiration
of the Neighbourhood...'[5]

The animal news, however, was less cheerful. Christopher Edward had
given his elder brother, George junior, a little dog called Chance:

> The little dog you gave George & of which I am very
> fond has been missing a week the men think she has been
> stolen ... I have not had courage to write George word of it
> in hopes we may yet find it again...[6]

Alas, this was not to be:

> I am very much mortifyed that poor little Chance is lost the
> servants think she was stolen by some Children who passed
> by soon after George went to Oxford.[7]

Christopher Edward had also ventured into purchasing a horse, with
some unsatisfactory result. It would appear that his proposed transaction
had not gone ahead, and that this was for the best:

> I am sorry you have had such bad success in Horsedealing
> tho' perhaps as it is generally to an honest man a losing
> trade it is fortunate that you met with a check so soon.

No doubt to help in cheering Christopher up after this mishap, Rice
added a mock-advertisement to his mother-in-law's letter:

> Mr Speculator, I have this inst. received an express informing
> me of a horse for sale I would strongly recommend you without
> delay to take your departure instantly from the Island as I think
> it a fit subject on which you may exercise your Judgment –
>
> 1. It is lame on all fours
> 2. It is blind
> 3. A defect in the wind
>
> In an incurable decline from old age. The price simply
> £7.0 – now if you can cure these trifling defects, I will give

you (for him) a draft on my Banker for a hundred, thirty
years after date

Signed H RICE
Veterinary Surgeon Nth Hants Yeom[anr]y Cavalry.[8]

After recovering from her broken ankle, Anne had become more cautious
about which horse she rode:

> I have just taken (as I am too great a coward to venture upon
> my Mare) to ride the Chair Horse & I do assure you she
> carrys me very well [tho'] not very expeditiously.

Similarly, in her next letter she again laments the slow speed of the chair
horse, that is the horse which would normally have pulled a 'chaise' (a
light vehicle).

> I have just taken to ride the Chair Horse & she goes very
> well but to be sure not very swift.[9]

Anne noted events in Gibraltar. As noted in Part Two, in 1800 Britain had
taken over Malta, and Gibraltar was also a key strategic location for the
control of the Mediterranean. During the summer of 1804 an epidemic
known as yellow fever (but possibly typhus) had broken out at Gibraltar.
Around 1,000 people belonging to the garrison of British troops and
their families were killed, with about 5,000 civilians also dying from
the disease.[10] Anne wrote of her relief that Christopher Edward had not
joined the regular army:

> I cannot help being inexpressibly thankful that you are not
> now in the Army. What would have become of me if you had
> been now at Gibraltar![11]

The immediate background to this sentiment had been that, in
October, Anne and George had had to deal with another application
from Christopher Edward to join the armed forces. As previously,
they called in the assistance of family friends to strengthen their
arguments:

I was pleased when I was at Debarys having a conversation respecting the Army which convinced me I had been right in objecting to your following that profession, & that you never will have reason to repent of your dutiful compliance with my entreaties: there was a boy of 15 or 16 staying at Mr Debarys, whose plans are still undetermined, upon Miss Debary asking him if he thought of being a Soldier, he said, no never, for that his two elder Brothers who were in the Army, had said so much of the hardships & slavery of their lives, that he would not subject himself to the same misery upon any account; D too mentioned a relation of his, who was very unhappy in his profession, & upon his applying to the Duke of York for leave to quit, the Duke refused to accept of his resignation, so that a man if he is ever so miserable may be obliged to remain; thank God my Child you have not subjected yourself to such slavery![12]

The Debarys were friends also of the Austens, and had been immortalised by Jane Austen four years previously: 'Miss Debary, Susan & Sally all in black … made their appearance, & I was civil to them as their bad breath would allow me.'[13]

His parents' intransigence was the cause of considerable unhappiness to Christopher Edward, but he later felt that he had not merited their kindness. Three years after this exchange, he annotated this letter from his mother, dating his note 15 November 1807:

Oh! That I could claim that promise! But my conscious heart is stung with deep conviction of the wrongs I've done my matchless parents. Oh! Can they see with what remorse my faults I now survey. Can I, a worthless worm, enjoy the love of spirits mingling with the saints above? – with Angel pleasure they will know, the tear I drop upon the sentence is sincere![14]

Returning to 1804, Christopher Edward's nineteenth birthday was on 24 November, and Anne had particular reason to be thankful:

Yesterday was a day that I trust I shall ever remember with gratitude not only in this short life but thro' all eternity –

may you continue many many years as great a comfort to your friends as you now are & be able to reflect upon your own conduct with as much satisfaction as you must now feel when you recollect the instance of duty & affection to us which you have lately shown.[15]

But Anne was trying to keep up her own spirits in the absence of her children and of the Reverend George, who was at Compton:

I have just made my solitary breakfast & tho' I try to keep up my spirits I cannot always succeed when I look back to the happy days when in your fathers absence I was surrounded by my Children the contrast is too much for my feelings & I feel forlorn & wretched beyond description but this I know to be very wrong & will not therefore dwell upon the subject.[16]

The next letter, with its emphases, indicates Anne's great anxiety to hear from her son:

I intreat a line at least by the return of the post...

A few days later, Anne's next letter is much more hopeful in tone.

Your letter was short & sweet I thank you from my heart for the comfort it afforded me...[17]

News of home follows, with plans for Christmas.

We expect George [junior] next week & Ben: on Monday sen'nite.[18]

Anne did not see the Christmas of 1804. The next, and last, letter in the collection is not from her to Christopher Edward, but from Charles Lyford to Richard Clarke, dated 16 December, and bearing terrible news.

Dear Sir
At the request of poor Mr Lefroy I have to impose on you the painful task of disclosing to his Son the melancholy

Event which has occurred this morning in the Death of Mrs Lefroy at Ashe. Riding out yesterday she was thrown from her horse between 3 and four o'Clock and received so violent a concussion of the Brain as to prove fatal soon after 3 o'Clock this morning. Mr Lefroy hopes to see his Son at home as soon as possible, & has desired me to direct my letter to you, that he might hear of it the less abruptly.

I am Dr Sir, your obed humble Servt Chas. Lyford.[19]

As it happens, we also have a much more detailed account of Anne's fatal accident. This was by Caroline Austen, younger daughter of James Austen, who was the last friend to see Anne before the event, and who was the minister who conducted her funeral:

December 16th. 'Died Mrs Lefroy of Ashe'. On the 21st my father buried her. She was greatly lamented and her end was a sad one. She was riding a very quiet horse [no doubt the Chair Horse whose lack of speed her recent letters had indicated], attended by a servant, as usual. My father saw her in Overton, and she observed the animal she rode was so stupid and lazy, she could scarcely make him canter. My father rode homeward, she staying to do some errands in Overton; next morning the news of her death reached Steventon. After getting to the top of Overton Hill, the horse seemed to be running away – it was not known if anything had frightened him – the servant, unwisely, rode up to catch the bridle rein – missed his hold and the animal darted off faster. He could not give any clear account, but it was supposed that Mrs Lefroy in her terror, threw herself off, and fell heavily on the hard ground. She never spoke afterwards, and she died in a few hours. She was a woman most highly gifted, and had the power of attaching and influencing all who came near her in an unusual manner. She had the happiest manners, and they truly expressed the benevolence of her heart.[20]

Caroline's knowledge of Anne Lefroy was of course only by hearsay and tradition (she was born in the year after Anne's death). Clearly Anne was remembered by both family and community as almost superhumanly impressive.

Even the self-obsessed Samuel Egerton Brydges was greatly affected by his sister's sudden death. It was probably he who provided the following obituary, which appeared in the *Gentleman's Magazine* for December 1804, in the popular section 'Obituary – with anecdotes, of Remarkable Persons'. Samuel is indicated as the source by the excessive detail about her Egerton forebears. He is also suggested as the author by the mention of the tragic death in a fire of (his and Anne's sister) Deborah Brydges Maxwell some years before, seeing both deaths as part of a gloomy pattern.

> At Ashe, in Hampshire, by a fall from her horse, which she survived only twelve hours in a state of insensibility, aged 56, Mrs Lefroy, wife of the Rev George L. rector of that parish, and of Compton, in Surrey, and eldest daughter of the late Edward Brydges, esq. of Wootton, in Kent, by Jemima daughter and coheir of William Egerton, LLD prebendary of Canterbury, &c and grandson of John second Earl of Bridgwater. By this marriage she has left three surviving sons, of whom the eldest [George junior] is student of Christ Church, Oxford; and one daughter, wife of the Rev. Henry Rice. This is the second time, within these few years, that a dreadful and fatal accident has fallen on this devoted family. Mrs L's sister, Mrs Maxwell, became a victim to her cloaths catching fire in Harley-street, in March 1789; a catastrophe too well remembered by the general sympathy and gloom which it caused, for some days, through the whole Western part of London, where the unhappy sufferer was distinguished for her beauty, elegance, and amiable disposition. (See vol. LIX, p. 374.) And no longer ago than August last a near relation (Mrs Egerton) met an almost similar doom by being thrown from her park chair (see this volume, p. 793).

To do justice to the character of Mrs L would require a command of glowing and pathetic expression far beyond the powers of the writer of this article. She was alike the delight of the old and the young, of the lively and of the severe, the rich and the poor. She received from Nature an intellectual capacity of the highest order; her perceptions were rapid; her memory was tenacious; her comprehension was extensive; her fancy was splendid; her sentiments were full of tenderness; and her language was easy, copious, and energetic. It may truly be said of her, that

'She lisp'd in numbers, for the numbers came.'[21]

At twelve years old she wrote a beautiful hymn, and other small poems; and two or three of her compositions, written nearly thirty years ago, are inserted in the first volume of the 'Poetical Register', pp. 32, 36, 112. These poems are easy, elegant, and full of those natural graces which form a charming contrast to that laboured and turgid style so lately fashionable. Yet they convey a very faint idea of the powers which, had she bestowed a little more effort and frequency on such occupations, she could have exhibited. But, possessed of various qualities to please, and capable of delighting by more general and social attractions, she never aspired to the fame of an author. It was only an accidental impulse that occasionally prompted her to seize the pen; when she wrote for private amusement a few glowing and unaffected lines with the same forcible and careless rapidity with which she talked: in these, however, a sagacious reader will see what a more constant and regulated attention to this art could have enabled her to perform. It was by the tenor of her amiable and virtuous life, by her lively and enchanting manners, by the overflowing benevolence of her disposition, by clothing the naked, by feeding the hungry, by instructing the ignorant, by healing the sick, and by comforting the mourner, that she has won a more noble wreath of fame, and drawn over her grave the lasting tears of her agonised friends and numerous acquaintances, and the heart-broken lamentations and earnest prayers of the poor!

It would be almost impossible to find an individual, in a private station, whose death will be more generally and deeply felt. And how much will that feeling be aggravated by the sudden and painful mode in which this sad event has taken place! It is a loss which, to her near relations, no earthly advantage can repair. Nor can the chasm be supplied, which this dreadful accident has occasioned in the wide circle she delighted, adorned, and illuminated. The Northern parts of Hampshire can attest that this character is not exaggerated; and the bleeding bosoms of a husband, children, mother, brothers, and sisters, will bear unfeigned testimony to her inimitable and angelic virtues.

Actuated by the warmth of her natural sensibility, and inspired by the elevated dictates of a Religion which predominated over her whole mind, she suffered neither the allurements of society, to which no one was so sensible, nor the attachments of blood and friendship, which no one ever felt more exquisitely, to seduce her from those more humble duties which she exercised in unwearied endeavours to ameliorate the condition of poverty and wretchedness. Whoever frequented her house, at which hospitality and benignity constantly reigned, has seen her at her daily task of instructing the village-children to read, to write, to work, to make baskets of straw; has seen her administer medicines to the sick, and consolation to the afflicted; and has seen the numerous resort from a wide-surrounding neighbourhood, of whom she communicated the important benefits of Vaccine Inoculation to upwards of 800 with her own hand.

Of such a character, so suddenly taken away, when neither age nor illness had yet arrived to impair her mind or constitution, even they who knew her not cannot blame this long memorial; for, where is such an union of admirable qualities to be found? In intellect, in heart, in temper, in manners, in strict and elevated principles, in pure and untainted conduct, she has left no second behind her. But who shall dare to arraign the decrees of Providence, however cruel they appear to the imperfect view of human beings![22]

Variations on this obituary appeared in a number of other outlets, including the *Reading Mercury* for 24 December.[23]

Information which Samuel's obituary gives in passing includes the fact that Anne spoke quickly: 'with forcible and careless rapidity'. There is an undertone of reproach in Samuel's assertion that Anne's verse could have been better, if she had given more effort to it. However, it is very likely that if Anne had, indeed, devoted more of her adult life to the writing of verse and prose, such critics as Samuel would have found this less praiseworthy than her devotion to traditionally social feminine accomplishments. It is definitely a case where a woman writer could not win.

It was sad that Charles Lyford, who had assisted so many members of Anne's community in their illnesses and injuries, and had set her broken leg bone only months before, could not help her in her final hours. A head injury such as Anne suffered, meaning she did not regain consciousness, was clearly very severe. It is noteworthy that even today, severe head injuries causing coma very often result in death. The outcome for recovery depends to some extent on the age of the patient: people under 20 are more than three times more likely to survive than people over 60, and Anne was in her mid-fifties.[24] Hospitals today can keep coma patients alive through intravenous sustenance, which could not be done in the early nineteenth century.

Friends such as Charles Lyford and James Austen helped poor George at this time. We do not know what Jane Austen's immediate reaction to the news was, as Anne's death occurred in the period of yet another hiatus in Jane's surviving letters, between September 1804 and January 1805.[25]

In August 1808, she wrote her tribute to Anne Lefroy:

> The day returns again, my natal day;
> What mix'd emotions with the Thought arise!
> Beloved friend, four years have pass'd away
> Since thou wert snatch'd forever from our eyes.
>
> The day, commemorative of my birth
> Bestowing Life & Light & Hope on me,
> Brings back the hour which was thy last on Earth.
> Oh! Bitter pang of torturing Memory!
>
> Angelic Woman! past my power to praise
> In Language meet, thy Talents, Temper, mind,

Thy solid Worth, thy captivating Grace! –
Thou friend & ornament of Humankind!

At Johnson's death, by Hamilton t'was said,
'Seek we a substitute – ah! vain the plan,
No second best remains to Johnson dead –
None can remind us even of the Man.'

So we of thee – unequall'd in thy race
Unequall'd thou, as he the first of Men.
Vainly we search around thy vacant place,
We ne'er may look upon thy like again.

Come then fond Fancy, thou indulgent Power,
Hope is desponding, chill, severe to thee! –
Bless thou, this little portion of an hour,
Let me behold her as she used to be.

I see her here, with all her smiles benign,
Her looks of eager Love, her accents sweet.
That voice & Countenance almost divine! –
Expression, Harmony, alike complete.-

I listen – 'tis not sound alone – 'tis sense,
'Tis Genius, Taste, & Tenderness of Soul.
'Tis genuine warmth of heart without pretence
And purity of Mind that crowns the whole.

She speaks, 'tis Eloquence – that grace of Tongue
So rare, so lovely! – Never misapplied
By *her* to palliate Vice, or deck a Wrong,
She speaks & reasons but on Virtue's side.

Her's is the Energy of Soul sincere.
Her Christian Spirit ignorant to feign,
Seeks but to comfort, heal, enlighten, chear,
Confer a pleasure, or prevent a pain. –

Can ought enhance such Goodness? – Yes, to me,
Her partial favour from my earliest years
Consummates all. – Ah! Give me yet to see
Her Smile of Love – the Vision disappears.

'Tis past & gone – We meet no more below.
Short is the Cheat of Fancy o'er the Tomb.
Oh! Might I hope to equal Bliss to go!
To meet thee Angel! In thy future home!

Fain would I feel an union in thy fate,
Fain would I seek to draw an Omen fair
From this connection in our Earthly date.
Indulge the harmless weakness – Reason, spare. [26]

As noted in Part One, the passionate tone of loss, grief and love expressed in this poem has no parallel in any other surviving non-fiction of Jane Austen. Unlike Samuel Egerton Brydges, Jane was not inclined to exaggerate or overstate: so it is difficult not to see this tribute as sincere.

The coincidence of Anne's death occurring on Jane's birthday is thus the framing device of the poem. The poet seeks to make the coincidence a sign ('an Omen') of their meeting in a future life, although she recognises that this has no basis in reason.

It is also likely to refer to Anne's own writing, in particular her verses expressing grief at the loss of her children. Jane Austen indicates that Anne is as prominent a woman among women ('thy race') as Samuel Johnson, who had died twenty years earlier in 1784 had been among men – male writers and personalities of great distinction.

Jane Austen also adds a local connection in alluding to the tribute to Johnson by 'Hamilton'. This was William Gerard Hamilton (1729–1796), a politician originally from Hampshire.[27] He had originally been elected for the seat of Petersfield in Hampshire, going on to hold a number of high offices, and was a lifelong friend of Johnson.

His utterance on Johnson's death, paraphrased by Jane Austen, was reported as:

He has made a chasm, which not only nothing can fill up, but nothing has a tendency to fill up. Johnson is dead. – Let us go to the next best: There is nobody. No man can be said to put you in mind of Johnson.[28]

In adopting and adapting this tribute for Anne, Jane Austen attempts to appropriate masculine celebrity status – uniqueness – for her friend. Jane Austen appears to be seeking on behalf of Anne Lefroy, writer and woman, those qualities which Jane Austen's own early biographers insisted she did not desire for herself: fame, applause, credit, celebrity. Austen is almost certainly taking the bold, feminist approach of positioning herself as the Boswell to Anne's Johnson. She also emphasises her personal connection with the deceased: 'Yes, to me, Her partial favour from my earliest years…'.

Considering the extent to which Austen's other surviving works have been studied, the lack of serious attention paid to this poem is surprising. R.W. Chapman included it in volume VI, the Minor Works, in his collected edition of the works of Jane Austen, first appearing in 1954, reprinted in 1958, and again with revisions in 1963. Chapman gave no date for the poem. His explanatory note is revealing of an era in which women writers were still the daughters, sisters, or wives of more important men:

> Mrs Lefroy was Anne, 1749 [*sic*] – 1804, sister of Sir Samuel Egerton Brydges and wife of Isaac Peter George Lefroy, Rector of Ashe. Ashe is very near Steventon, and Jane Austen was devoted to her friend, who was killed by a fall from her horse.

Chapman's extreme lack of interest is underscored:

> Two more stanzas [numbers 12 and 13] were published in Messrs. Sotheby's catalogue 25 April 1934, with a facsimile of the MS. The quotation about Johnson is adapted from Boswell, at 20 Dec. 1784. I do not know who owns either MS of this piece.[29]

This is the extent of his commentary.

In 1993, Margaret Anne Doody and Douglas Murray also found the manuscripts of Austen's poems generally uninteresting.

The manuscripts of the verses are not usually as interesting [as those of the juvenilia], and pose fewer problems – or at least fewer problems in relation to Jane Austen's central career. The verses themselves are problematic enough simply because some manuscripts have disappeared, so we have had to rely on printed versions…[30]

Doody and Murray noted that

Eleven quatrains of this poem were printed in J.E. Austen-Leigh's *Memoir* [1869], the author's nephew offering the verses 'not for their merits of poetry, but to show how deep and lasting was the impression made by the older friend on the mind of the younger' (p. 57).[31]

If Doody and Murray are correct, the copy certified by Jane Austen's great-nephew as being in her handwriting may well have been given by Jane to Lucy, or possibly to Anna and Ben. Sir John Lefroy reproduced a version in his 1868 family history, antedating by a year the version in James-Edward Austen-Leigh's memoir.[32]

David Selwyn, in *The Poetry of Jane Austen and the Austen Family* (1997), included the heading from the Winchester MS version, giving the date which Chapman omitted: 'To the Memory of Mrs Lefroy, who died Decr. 16 – my Birthday. – written 1808.'

Selwyn also appends the interesting information – not included by earlier editors – that there were variants at line 13. One version gives 'by Burke t'was finely' cancelled, and replaced with 'by Hamilton t'was.'[33] What is interesting is that Jane Austen originally either thought, or wished, that it had been the mighty orator Edmund Burke who had uttered the remark about Johnson. An appeal to the authority of Burke would have been a far more imposing claim than one to the lesser known Hamilton, but Jane Austen was nothing if not scrupulously careful about facts and attributions, so Hamilton it had to be.

The relative absence of attention which the poem has received may reflect our relative discomfort with a Jane Austen not 'light, and bright, and sparkling,' but subject to 'torturing Memory', and the sadness of bereavement.

Two months after Jane wrote her tribute to Anne, in October 1808, her sister-in-law Elizabeth Austen (the wife of Edward Austen Knight), died after giving birth to her eleventh child, Brook John.[34] Jane took an active role, taking turns at caring for her teenage motherless nephews Edward and George. In the coming weeks and months she may have reflected once again on George junior, Christopher Edward and Ben, the youths thrown suddenly into adulthood by Anne's death.

Chapter 16

Crisis

After the death of his wife, the Reverend George Lefroy found himself trying to be both parents to their surviving children.

From the surviving letters addressed to Christopher Edward, at 19 he appears to have gone through a crisis of confidence which aggravated his habitual doubts about his future career:

> My dearest Boy, do not harass yourself with the supposition that you left on my mind, from anything that pass'd, an unfavourable impression of your heart, or principles, or gratitude … [I] acknowledge that I fear you have too much vehemence, and enthusiasm in some of your notions … and I think also too much despondency & despair as to the position of comfort & happiness that may be within your reach in this life…[1]

Christopher Edward had proposed leaving the home of Mr Clarke and obtaining his own lodging, but had not mentioned this to Mr Clarke himself. His father was concerned both about the additional expense, and the rebuff to the ever-generous Mr Clarke:

> You tell me you have taken a Room, that the whole expense will be abt. 5/0 a week or £13 pr. ann[u]m. which I know you cannot pay out of your Allowance, but I will strive hard to discharge it, if it contributes in any degree to your improvement, your peace of mind & comfort…You are silent about Mr Clarke. Have you handsomely informed him of having taken the Room? I have no hesitation in saying you should…[2]

The Reverend George's patient tone had changed by the time of his next letter. Christopher Edward had apparently reacted rudely to Mr Clarke's inquiries:

> The alarming, I had almost said irreligious excess of that impracticable principle of Liberty & Free will, which you carry beyond all bounds, I give you my word preys deep on my heart. In my opinion it was clearly your duty, whether by way of advice, or not, to have communicated the plan to Mr Clarke, and as you had not done it, rather to soften the omission by pleading my consent, as an apology, than to have made the contemptuous answer you did. Well might Mr Clarke stare. I should have done as much if not more, in his situation. Indeed Edward you are to blame; and at least as much so, in the system of unmanageableness you have adopted for your conduct in the Office. The very idea of it stupefies me; surely you cannot be serious.[3]

The ensuing letters reveal a struggle between father and son to which the Reverend George increasingly felt unequal. It seems clear that Christopher Edward's rebellion was a reaction partly caused by his grief at his mother's death. His father, however, was trying to deal with the same grief, as well as cope with all the social responsibilities from which Anne had regularly shielded him. Christopher Edward had lashed out at his upbringing, and his father reacted with evident pain, deploying the memory of Anne as a potent emotional weapon:

> You charge me with putting an *harsh & gloomy* misconstruction upon all your *thoughts, words & deeds*, and assert you never act but upon the most mature deliberation, & that then you are *inflexible*, but, my beloved son, are you quite sure that you deliberate upon principles wise in themselves, & without that partiality to notions hastily preconceived, and now deeply rooted in your mind. You tell me, they have been imbibed from your infancy. I trust not from your parents – You add, you must struggle hard with your feelings. You must sacrifice your mental as well as corporeal feelings, and [?give] up the power of free agency; that you are by constitution prone to Idleness, have been reard with

196

the Ideas of Independence, – that for 15 years you have run wild both in Body and Mind, – that personal happiness you have long given up to hope for … Gracious Heaven, what a melancholy picture you draw of yourself. With what guilt you load me for having thus educated you! How bitter would this reflection have been to your departed Angel Mother![4]

Christopher Edward was remorseful, but the wrangling continued. His father could see the likeness between their tendencies to see the gloomy side of things:

My object in writing, as I have done, was to point strongly to you, the hazard that the warmth of your imagination, and the bias of your mind (alas! too like my own) to take the gloomy side in the affairs of the World, if not in the more important ones of the next, might subject you to…

Again, George recurred to Anne, who had been the intermediary between him and his children:

I have lost your Angel Mother whose very soul was so anxious to amend … And all of us have to encourage us in our best hopes.[5]

From Oxford, George junior, now qualified as a minister of religion, tried to convey tactfully to Christopher Edward that the situation at home was precarious. Both their father and their sister suffered from depression of spirits:

My Father is pretty well & I trust his Spirits are upon the whole tolerable tho' he does not recover them very fast. Lucy is yet low her reluctance to quit Dean[e] increases her depression.[6]

Just over a week later, George junior wrote to Christopher Edward from Ashe, because their father had suffered a serious medical episode, probably a stroke:

Our Father on Monday last fell asleep immediately after dinner. He had been very well in the morning & had rode his Poney as usual. After sleeping a very few minutes he awoke, perfectly lost as to recollection & without the power of Articulation.... In a short time he recovered in some degree the use of speech & was evidently better as to his Faculties.... This morning my Father is much better than he has ... [and] seems perfectly to have recovered his recollection & speech so that I hope in a very few days to have still more favourable accounts to send you.[7]

George senior had received some surgical interventions from Dr Lyford and the veteran Dr Littlehales. 'He has had a section put into his neck which will we think be of the greatest service.' This may have been an opening of the carotid artery to remove blockages which could lead to a stroke. One account suggests that this operation was first performed in the United States in 1807, while in the UK the noted surgeon Sir Astley Cooper described the procedure in 1808.[8] Either way, at little Ashe in 1805, George was receiving state-of-the-art stroke treatment.

Recovery from stroke, however, as from any serious medical episode, takes some time, particularly in someone of George's age (60). George junior found himself obliged to be at Ashe most of the time, managing the farm as well as his father's parochial duties.

What he did not need at this moment was a demand from Christopher Edward for a loan:

If you can *by any possible means avoid* (without doing anything dishonourable) *borrowing money of me or any other person* whilst you are at Mr Clarke's pray, for the sake of your own future comfort do it ... [but] if your wants are so pressing that money must be procured send me word what sum is *absolutely necessary* & I will endeavour to borrow it without having recourse to Mr Jeffreys who might perhaps put rather strange Constructions upon my being obliged to borrow money of him...I shall not abuse any Confidence you may chuse to place in me & will some day explain how my Father came to know that I had lent you Ten Guineas.[9]

Not content with offending his old employer and getting into debt, Christopher Edward soon afterwards appeared to have got involved with a young woman called Miss W (later revealed to be Winter), whose parents, while eminently respectable, were Dissenters, to the dismay of the Lefroys. Christopher Edward had consulted Mr Clarke, whose response was much as might be expected to his 19-year-old employee proposing to get married:

> I received your letter Wednesday Morning & I am not surprised at Mr Clarke's opinion. It is certainly what almost any man, at his time of life would express, for, generally speaking, a wife must be a clog to the progress of a very young man in any profession...

So wrote George junior, but it turned out that his own attitude to a young marriage was more sympathetic:

> [My] opinion is that a happy marriage is the greatest earthly blessing, & next to religion the most effectual spur to virtue & restraint from Vice, & that earthly matches founded upon sincere & mutual affection are the most likely to prove happy...

But here, in addition to Christopher Edward's youth and inexperience, there was the issue of religious difference:

> I will not conceal from you that I think the difference of religious tenets between yourself & Miss W – & her Parents, a very serious objection...

Again, however, George junior goes on to express a willingness to compromise which, while surprising in a Church of England clergyman, indicates the tone of sane and sensible tolerance which had characterised the Anglican outlook for much of the last hundred years:

> Though I feel assured that you will never sacrifice your present opinions but upon Conviction that they are erroneous & in justice to Mr W let me add that the letters which you have shown me breathe the spirit of a Christian & not of those whom we call perhaps harshly Schismaticks. Hitherto I have not much considered or enquired into the Principles of the

different Protestant dissenting Sects, convinced that the established worship of the Church of England has degenerated as little from the Apostolic Worship required in Scripture as any institution left in human hands for so many hundred years can have done, however I am aware that the Question before us is your attachment to Miss W – & not the merit of her *Principles* … in particular I should say for her *Principles* upon the most important points must be the same as yours.[10]

A number of letters follow from George senior, wishing Christopher Edward to obtain a room for him at Cowes on the Isle of Wight so that he could take the waters. His anxiety about details of rooms and situations is a pointer to his loss of confidence and possibly cognitive function from the stroke.[11] In addition, these were the kinds of matters which Anne would always have addressed.

Despite his father's final concession, 'I can do with only 2 Beds & 2 Servants, and one sitting room', Christopher Edward was obliged to report that there was no suitable accommodation in the Isle of Wight. (Presumably George senior's two servants were to share a bed between them.)[12]

At around the same time as this disappointment, it was left to George junior to break the news to their father about Christopher Edward's 'attachment' to Miss W:

> You will not be surprised that our Father raised objections on account of your extreme Youth.

George junior did not think it appropriate at this time to broach the next, perhaps more serious objection, of Miss W being a Dissenter. No doubt he thought his father could only cope with one difficulty at a time:

> The reason of my not acquainting him with that Circumstance at first was that I judged it better to familiarise him to the idea of your early marriage at any rate first as he has you know, strong objections to early marriages in general, objections which I would fain believe not altogether well founded…. [In] fact his spirits are extremely low & and he is so very feeble that I much fear to agitate him.[13]

George junior's patience with Christopher Edward in these trying circumstances was impressive, but the subtext of his letter is to underline the fact that the younger brother, through his worrying entanglements, was not helping with their father's recovery, but rather likely to hinder it.

Once George junior had broached the matter of Miss Winter's religion, it turned out that their father's reaction was surprisingly subdued:

> He objected a good deal to your so *very early* marriage at any rate & likewise to the connection with a Dissenter tho' he acknowledges Mr Winters letters as well as yours were very handsome. With regard to fortune he seems to think that probably Miss W may not have so much as you are led to suppose, & at any rate he says Mr W will probably expect a settlement equal to his Daughters fortune & that he cannot enable you to make such a Settlement. Such principally are my Father's objections & in a worldly point of view doubtless they are very strong.
>
> I have, as you know always been very much in favour of early marriages where it is possible they should take place. But perhaps my Father speaks & thinks too much as an Old *man* whilst You & I [are] biased a good deal by the [...] feelings & passions of *Young Men*. I am [confident] you will be guided by Principle & I heartily pray that the business may end in which ever way may be most conducive to your Happiness.[14]

George senior finally set off later in September 1805 for Southampton for sea bathing. He was to meet Christopher Edward at some point then, and George junior cautioned:

> You would consult our Father's present Comfort & of course your permanent Peace of mind, by abstaining, if possible, altogether from discussing the subject [of marriage] with him.[15]

By the time father and younger son met again, however, the subject was no longer distressing, because it appeared that Christopher Edward had given up the plan of marrying Miss Winter.

I am glad I confess Mr Clarke's & George's cogent arguments have induced you to give up a pursuit that would not have been satisfactory for either of us. If there was no other objection the different modes of Religion, the different principles, would, I should presume, have made you unhappy.[16]

Less satisfactorily, George senior was not experiencing the health benefits for which he had hoped.

I have not recovered the use of my right leg completely, or my right hand, as you may see by my writing…[17]

But later in the autumn Christopher Edward was again giving his father cause for concern, once more because of his spending:

I am not a little hurt that you want to anticipate so early on in this Quarter, your payment, that will become due on 5 January next. What are you to do for money upon your return? – Indeed Edward you somehow, or other, go on too fast in getting rid of your money before I am able to supply you. At this time of year especially, and had I not been more lucky than I expected, I should not have been able to send you even the 5 Guineas I now do, which I hope, will last you home.[18]

Christopher Edward, in his turn, might have been hurt that his father did not realise that the date of his letter, 24 November, was the date of his son's birthday: Anne had always marked the day.

His brother remembered, and wrote from Compton with good wishes.

I have not forgotten that today is a day of wishes for you…

Compton in Surrey was the Reverend George's other parish, where George junior had gone to carry out the rector's duties. The downside of collecting tithes from the local farmers was that they had to be entertained at a parish dinner, the prospect of which held no charms for George:

This part of the Ceremony I would fain have avoided but on the whole think it best to be acquainted with people who may perhaps even during my Father's life be my parishioners. You may therefore fancy my Reverence stuck up at the head of a table with some 18 Clodhoppers quite strangers drinking punch & smoking round me.[19]

The following March, as George junior was preparing to be ordained, the Reverend George died, perhaps from another stroke, or other cardio-vascular problem. George junior wrote to Christopher Edward on black-edged paper a letter mainly outlining the complicated situation as regarded inheritance by sons under age, as Christopher Edward still was:

Who will be entitled during the minority of Test[ator]'s Sons to receive & enjoy the Rents & Profits of the real & personal estates…[20]

The chronically short-of-money state of both sons led to considerable urgency in establishing who was entitled to what, and when. There were estates in Canterbury and in Wales. There was also the question of what, if anything, in addition to her marriage settlement, was owed to Lucy. Neither George junior or Christopher Edward had coherent ideas on the subject – as probably neither had their father before them – so they were entirely reliant on advisers such as Mr Jeffreys and a Mr Hughes:

With regard to the unsettled Freehold & Leasehold Estates (including that 1 / 4th part of the settled Estates which was repurchased of Lucy) the devises to us at the age of 25 will operate as Conditional limitations … and that the […] as well as the Rents of such parts as are freehold will in the mean time belong to the eldest Son [i.e. the writer, George] whilst the rents of the Leasehold will go as part of the Residuum to the younger Sons [i.e. Christopher Edward and Ben].[21]

Among the upheavals occasioned by the death of George senior, was the question of what would happen to Anne's old housekeeper and friend, Hester Boham. George writes:

Boham, as I supposed, declines Mr Holders offer not meaning ever to go again into Service of course she continues with me for the present.[22]

Perhaps it was a compliment to an old servant of the Lefroys for Mr Holder to offer her a position, but it is clear that Boham was far happier to remain at Ashe, less now as a servant than as a friend. Her position was likely to change again before long, as George was contemplating marriage with Sophia Cottrell, a sister of one of his friends.

Sir John Lefroy printed a letter from Hester Boham to George on the occasion of his marriage:

> The comfort and satisfaction of the *Home* I have for so many years enjoy'd is sufficiently evident from the great care I have taken to retain it, as well as the great pain I now feel in the near approach of my separation from it…You bid me attend intirely to my own convenience, my clothes and myself is all I have to attend to, but how to be convey'd, or where, I have not yet determined, in regard to the time I am to leave you, if you wish to make any change or alteration in your family or another servant to take place, my time is yours, if neither of this is the case, nor no other impediment in the way, my wish is to stay as near the time of your going from home as will be convenient…

Sir John adds:

> Mrs Boham … did not quit the family, but remained as housekeeper, the faithful servant, the attached friend, too often the comforter in sorrow, of two generations, and not rarely latterly the plague of a third. She died in her 77th year, May 28, 1834…[23]

In due form, an obituary of George senior appeared in the *Gentleman's Magazine:*

> 13. at Ashe, near Basingstoke, Hants, aged 60. The Revd. George Lefroy, rector of that parish, and of Compton, Surry [*sic*]. He was of All Souls college, Oxford, of founder's kin (see *Stemmata chicheleana*); MA 1771; and was a younger son of Anthony Lefroy, Esqre. an eminent merchant of Leghorn, and a great collector of virtu. He was a most valuable member of

society, and highly esteemed and respected by a numerous acquaintance for his strict principles of religion, the integrity of his conduct, his polite manners, and knowledge of the world, his sound understanding, the warmth of his affection and the firmness and activity of friendships. He suffered, about 15 months ago, one of the severest afflictions that can befall humanity in the death of the most accomplished and amiable of wives; an event which he never overcame, and which, after repeated paralytic Attacks, brought him to the grave.

The living of Ashe is in the gift of his family, and Compton in that of Mrs Brydges of Canterbury.[24]

By late April, George junior was effectively engaged to marry Sophia Cottrell. It also emerged that Christopher Edward was still 'seeing' Miss Winter, and wished George junior to make the acquaintance of the Winter family:

My Dear Fellow, we have both embarked on a hazardous Voyage & must have all our senses about us to conduct it but hazardous as it is I trust it will conduct us to increased Comfort here & certainly not lessen our Chance hereafter. I much wish my Connexion at Hadley [home of the Cottrells] to remain if possible a Secret because if any thing should break it off it is better for both parties that it should not be known…For the same reason I much hope that Mr & Mrs H[arris Bigg] Wither who are now in the Island may not discover your attachment to Miss W.[25]

George had the opportunity to meet the Winters in May, sharing their open carriage from Clapham to London, their servant riding George's horse:

Of course I could not have much opportunity of judging of your Adored, her person undoubtedly is very pleasing, her manner mild & interesting, & I doubt not her being every thing you imagine & wish her to be… The Winters (meaning the Father & Mother with whom I travelled) … spoke of you most highly & I endeavoured to say every thing handsome to them of you.

Alas, George believed that family friend Mr Maxwell disapproved of his proposed marriage, let alone Christopher Edward's.

> I therefore under all circumstances would just submit to you whether it is not better to say nothing to him for the present & should he, which is scarcely probable, find it out I will frankly acknowledge that its concealment from him was owing to my advice.[26]

Like his father before him, George found himself in an altercation by letter with Christopher Edward.

> I acknowledge my dear Fellow the justice of some of the charges brought against me in your Letter. It is I believe rather a Family failing to see things on the gloomy side...[27]

In the event, George and Sophia were married in July 1806. In other happy news, the execution of the estate was proceeding so as to allow George to provide his brother with ample funds.[28] Christopher Edward perhaps used these to move to London and commence work in a law office there under a Mr Sanders or Saunders. In November, George was writing to him at 4 Chapel Street, Lambs Conduit Street.[29]

George was also, before Christmas, able to set out what Christopher and Ben would inherit, the 'Residuum' of the estate. Elements included rent from the farm of Lwyn Lwyd in Wales (£110 yearly), freeholds in North Westgate, Canterbury (worth £28), and a share of 'the Douglas annuity' (£100), totalling £302 and 9 shillings, less about ten per cent for property tax.[30]

Despite George's strong desire for Christopher Edward's entanglement to remain secret, inevitably gossip got out:

> Mrs Cobham (a sister of Mrs Portals) told me the other day at Ashe Park that she had heard from some of the Maitlands who you know live in Berkshire of your intended Marriage & that it was a settled point. I hope you will not marry till you have the means of keeping a Wife & whenever your union with Miss W does take place may the Almighty bless you both.[31]

Now it was Ben's turn to desire a change of circumstances. He was 16, and keen to leave Winchester School. Typically, George and Mr Maxwell both wished him to remain, but admitted they were likely to lose the argument.[32]

Christopher Edward began to become involved in politics. In May 1807 he sought donations towards the election of William Wilberforce; George subscribed five guineas.[33]

In June, George and Sophia welcomed their first child, a boy, to be named George Henry after his grandfather and Mr Maxwell. Meanwhile, Christopher Edward decided to visit the family's holdings in Wales, a trip which George sarcastically called his 'grand Tour'.[34] Along the way, Christopher Edward met with an arm injury which had something to do with Welsh ponies:

> Should your arm be at all painful to you I hope you will go
> to a Surgeon about it & *implicitly* follow his Directions.

George adds:

> I know of no particular Hampshire news. No body married,
> no body hanged.[35]

In between the usual money worries, George received a letter out of the blue from Mr Winter:

> This mornings post brought me a *very handsome letter*
> from Mr Winter saying that the Connection between
> yourself & his Daughter was concluded owing to your
> answer to a remonstrance of hers on the visible alienation
> of your affections. Never having heard from you on the
> subject I cannot tell whether other grounds may have
> arisen.[36]

It would also seem as if Christopher Edward was trying to assuage his own doubts and concerns about Christian doctrine by writing at length to his brother, the rector, on doctrinal matters:

> I am most sensible my dear Fellow of the Christian
> benevolence & affection which dictate your Letters to me

on the subject of Religion. At present I can only say that it is my earnest wish & fixed intention to endeavour both to fashion my own life & to feed my flock according to the doctrine of Christ & that upon his mercy *only* I depend for knowledge & strength for that purpose.[37]

The brothers were also debating what to do about Anne's creative legacy:

I have written to our Uncle Egerton to say that our dearest Mothers poems were left in your hands & that I thought they might all be printed to be given as presents to the different Members of the Family (the expense attending which *We four* would be proud to bear amongst us) but that I thought as they were on private subjects & not intended to meet the publick eye they had better not be published. What think you on the subject?[38]

Both brothers acknowledged their family tendency to low spirits, and were aware of the need to take courage. Rice had evidently written to Christopher Edward of his concerns about George:

Rice's assertion is in some degree true. I am certainly nervous & frequently low spirited, but it is owing as far as it is independent of bodily health to *want* of Christian principles not to the possession of them. It is owing to want of that resolution & self Command which I do hope by the Grace of God vouchsafed to me, to attain in time but which I dare not hope will be afforded me till after a long & painful struggle with my worldly Inclinations & feelings, a struggle rendered more difficult from natural weakness & irresolution….You are so much my Superior in a religious point of view, Edward, that I cannot hope to enforce any thing that Mr Brooks has said but I do perfectly agree with him that you are too apt to give way to despair…[39]

It had been Anne who had kept up the spirits of the Lefroy family, and the loss of her bright personality continued to be felt.

Chapter 17

Generations

Both Ben and Christopher Edward attended Oxford at the same period. Christopher Edward had decided belatedly to attend university, and with commendable commitment, enrolled as a comparatively mature-aged student.[1] Ben, after leaving Winchester and studying with a private tutor, had attended Merton College.[2]

Christopher Edward was to marry neither Miss Winter nor anyone else. It was Ben who was next to marry, at the age of 23. His marriage to Anna Austen, elder daughter of the Reverend James Austen and the eldest niece of Jane Austen, took place in November 1814. Caroline Austen, Anna's young half-sister, aged 9 at the time, later described the occasion:

> Weddings were then usually very quiet. The old fashion of festivity and publicity had quite gone by, and was universally condemned as showing the great bad taste of all former generations…. The bridegroom came from Ashe Rectory where he had hitherto lived with his brother, and Mr and Mrs Lefroy [George and Sophia] came with him, and another brother, Mr [Christopher] Edward Lefroy. Anne Lefroy, the eldest little girl [of George's], was one of the bridesmaids, and I was the other…. The season of the year, the unfrequented road of half a mile to the lonely old church, the grey light within of a November morning making its way through the narrow windows, no stove to give warmth, no flowers to give colour … all these circumstances and deficiencies must, I think, have given a gloomy air to our wedding.[3]

Ben, like George, was to enter the church. He was ordained in 1817. A family story published in 1952 indicates that Ben's examination by his ordaining bishop was cursory in the extreme:

> The Bishop asked him only two questions. 'Are you the son of Mrs Lefroy of Ashe?' and 'Did you marry a Miss Austen?' That was enough. He qualified.[4]

Christopher Edward took his BA and was admitted to the Middle Temple, in 1815, and his MA in the following year. We get a pleasing glimpse of him and Ben from a letter of Jane Austen's in this period:

> [Christopher] Edward & Ben called here on Thursday. Edward was in his way to Selborne. We found him very agreable [sic]. He is come back from France, thinking of the French as one cd wish, disappointed in every thing.[5]

He was called to the Bar in 1819, a conclusion no doubt a great relief to George.[6] Soon after his call to the Bar, Christopher Edward took on the post of British Commissary Judge of the Mixed Court, established by a treaty with the government of the Netherlands for the suppression of the slave trade in Surinam, at this time a Dutch colony (but which had prior to 1667 been a British one).

Surinam, on the north-eastern coast of South America, was a plantation colony, its principal exports coffee and sugar. After 1815, slavery was illegal for Dutch subjects, but it still operated in Dutch colonies, even though in theory the Dutch government supported the English ban on the trade.[7] The result was a mix of blind eyes being turned, corruption and semi-corruption, and the inevitable persistence of slave ships arriving. Christopher Edward wrote an incendiary novel about his experiences, published anonymously in 1826: *Outalissi: a tale of Dutch Guiana*.[8]

It turned out that Christopher Edward, so long frustrated by his parents and his brother in every direction that he sought – whether his desire to join the Army or to marry – was a very talented writer. *Outalissi* is a philosophical novel. It is a novel about slavery and race relations. It is about the role of Christianity in the developing world. It is also a shocking book, featuring the rape and murder of a teenage slave girl, as well as the unjust torture and execution of a blameless missionary as well as the slave hero, Outalissi. The book is a page-turner, despite its frequent philosophical and religious digressions.

The hero, Edward Bentinck, is an officer in the Dutch army. His moral dilemmas appear early on: he is in love with a Creole woman, Matilda Cotton, whose father owns a slave-worked plantation. Mr Cotton holds religion in contempt, and English law in defiance – it is a Dutch colony, after all.

An English sailor confides in Edward that he has witnessed a slave ship, with a French captain, arrive. Edward passes this information to the authorities, thus betraying his beloved's father. One of the group of slaves, Outalissi, manages to escape his bonds. The action of the novel climaxes in a revolt led by Outalissi, resulting in the destruction by fire of much of the capital Paramaribo, an event which actually took place in January 1821.

The resulting trial of Mr Schwartz, the Moravian missionary, for having incited the revolt through encouraging the slaves to become Christians, and Outalissi for his role, allowed Christopher Edward to showcase the moral debates of the day around slavery. He considered it particularly unjust that marriage, the institution most identified with Christianity, was forbidden to the slaves. The view of the novel is that this prohibition was a key factor preventing the slaves from settling down and advancing in life. Interestingly, given his family background, Christopher Edward also discussed the Church of England, and whether it was really fulfilling Christian principles, or simply going through the motions.

Writing anonymously allowed Christopher Edward to express himself with blazing honesty. The *Gentleman's Magazine* reviewer trod delicately around the issues, but found that the author of the novel was likely to bring religion into disrepute:

> We know that we are treading on tender ground, and subject ourselves to aspersions. But it is our solemn and decided opinion, that if the Religionists of the present day could execute their wild theories, Religion would be turned into a jest at home, and a mischief abroad … The Author, though we do not approve his principles, has the merit of being a very able sentimentalist.[9]

Correspondence from around 1819 survives between Christopher Edward and Dutch authorities such as the judge Adriaan Lammens. According to one analysis:

> Lefroy is a burning idealist with little regard for realities, particularly proud of the attitude of England as a champion of the rights of the Negro slaves. The realist [Dutch judge Adriaan] Lammens points him to the attitude of England towards the East Indies and the people living there. Lefroy blames Lammens for not arguing as a person in these matters, but as a white man. Lefroy is a very interested [sc. Interesting?] man. He tries to learn Dutch and repeatedly asks to read speeches, to which he then delivers his criticism...[10]

Sir John Lefroy, writing in the 1860s, pointed out that some aspects of the novel would have been unpublishable at that later date.[11] Christopher Edward was convinced that it was because of *Outalissi* that he failed to receive some £150 from his stipulated pension, and he blamed the Duke of Wellington, in 1829 the First Lord of the Treasury, for this outcome.[12]

Christopher Edward returned to England at the time of his brother Ben's death, at only 38, in 1829. George, too, had died young, in 1823, upon which Ben and Anna had succeeded to the rectory at Ashe. On Ben's death, his widow Anna and their seven children had to leave the rectory. Christopher Edward, in a final act of sacrifice and love for his family, purchased a property at Westham near Basingstoke, and took on the role of father to Ben and Anna's children.[13]

Christopher Edward's nephew, Sir John, reflected on his uncle's unusual personality:

> There was about him all his life a Quixotry of character, a generosity, and an oddity, which while it endeared him to his family, made him a source of amusement, and sometimes of uneasiness.[14]

He concluded:

> This honest indignation at fraud and cruelty; this fearless and simple assertion of the truth of revelation and of the

judgment to come, [Christopher] EDWARD LEFROY carried [with] him to the close of life. His conversation was always forcible and original, with a character of humour which was often exceedingly quaint.[15]

Christopher Edward, like his father, suffered a stroke in 1852. He never recovered from the partial paralysis, and died, aged 70, in 1856.[16]

Lucy's life with Rice proved particularly challenging. After Sarah, the Rices had another daughter, Anne. Over several years, Lucy's mother-in-law Mrs Rice paid for many of their expenses. In 1812, Christopher Edward had sued Rice for debt (apparently Mrs Rice settled this debt), and in 1819 Rice fled to France to avoid his creditors.[17]

Tragedy hit their family when son Henry – Anne's beloved grandson Toddy – after travelling to Germany in 1820 as a student or teaching assistant, fell ill and died. Some years later the Rices returned to England, with Henry Rice taking up the living of Great Holland in Essex, but the family remained financially dependent on Mrs Rice's interventions until that lady died in 1841.[18] Lucy and Henry Rice died in the early 1860s.

Anne Brydges Lefroy's daughters-in-law, Anna and Sophia, had passed upon their marriages into a perpetual round of childbearing. Not long before her death, in March 1817, during only the third pregnancy of her niece Anna, Jane Austen commented:

Poor Animal, she will be worn out before she is thirty.[19]

For her part, in 1823, Sophia was widowed with eleven children. Ironically, the generation of women after Anne had less opportunity than she did to write, paint, or carry out community activities: with only four surviving children, Anne had been comparatively free in comparison with her Victorian daughters-in-law.

George and Sophia's sixth child and third son was John Henry, later Sir John Henry Lefroy, scientist, soldier and explorer, who was promoted to general in the British Army. As a junior officer, Sir John had made a speciality of measurement of magnetic activity. In 1843–44, he undertook a ground-breaking survey of magnetic and meteorological events in North America. During the Crimean War, he made the acquaintance of Florence Nightingale and supported her work. In 1871 he was appointed Governor of Bermuda, and in 1880–81 he was an active and popular governor of Tasmania.[20] In 1868, as we have seen, he assembled the first comprehensive history of the Lefroy family, drawing in part from documents provided by Anna and no doubt his uncle Christopher Edward.

The intelligent, numerous, dutiful, affectionate, but often gloomy Lefroys carried on the legacy of Anne Brydges Lefroy. George and Sophia's next child after Sir John Henry was Henry Maxwell Lefroy (1818–1879), who first arrived in Western Australia in 1840, but had little success with farming (the perennial Lefroy concerns about money followed him to the colonies). After a return to England and a stint teaching navigation in the Royal Navy, Maxwell, as he was known, returned to Australia in 1854 to become Assistant Superintendent of convicts at Fremantle. His cousins, Irish Lefroys descended from the Reverend George's brother Anthony, also settled in Western Australia.

One of Henry Maxwell Lefroy's younger sons with his wife Annette was another John Henry Maxwell Lefroy (1865–1936, similarly known as Maxwell), a surveyor, eventually appointed Assistant Surveyor General. His youngest son was Cuthbert George Lefroy. It was *his* elder daughter I have had the pleasure of meeting, Annette Rowlands (b. 1938). Annette is therefore the great-great-great-granddaughter of Anne Brydges Lefroy, a very short chain of generations in a period covering over 250 years.

Annette is an historian in a family of keen family-historians, and has been kind enough to share much of her knowledge. She has transcribed family records and had them deposited in the State Library of Western Australia, an appropriate monument to a numerous and prominent clan which has contributed a great deal to that state.

To conclude Anne's story, I travelled to the UK in April 2018 to visit places which she knew during her life. I began in Canterbury, where the Brydges and Lefroys owned property during the eighteenth century.

In preparing his 1868 family account, Sir John Lefroy himself tried to establish where in the city centre of Canterbury the main Lefroy estate had been. He had been advised by Anna Austen Lefroy:

> There was a tradition in my family…which must have come from yours [the Lefroys], that the great Fountain Inn at Canterbury had been the family residence of the Lefroys, and I have heard that your Grandfather [the Reverend

George senior] was used to speak of his own and his Brother's holydays as very dull, and that they passed them in a large old house where there was only an old woman to look after it and them.[21]

Sir John noted that at his time of writing, the Fountain Inn bore the date 1723. The Fountain Inn appears to have survived until the German air raids of 1942.[22]

In 1857 Sir John called upon a Mr Charles Miette, who with his brother Matthew, had purchased 'the last of the Lefroy property in Canterbury'. Charles Miette believed that the main Lefroy family residence had been a house opposite All Saints Church in High Street, Canterbury.

This house, Sir John found at that time, had a 'modern stucco front'. Further, the son of the current owner, who had been three times Mayor of Canterbury, was rude and unhelpful:

His son … was a most uncivil person, [who] refused to give any information, not even his father's address.[23]

All Saints Church, opposite which Charles Miette believed the Lefroy house had stood, was demolished in about 1938.[24] A plaque records its existence, and a small enclosed park remains from the church grounds, slightly offset from High Street.

If Charles Miette was correct, then the Lefroy home occupied the site opposite, where a Georgian-style building from the late nineteenth century now stands. It would have been from an earlier house on this site that George Senior and his brother Anthony, as boys, every morning left for The King's School just a few blocks away.

On the other hand, the Reverend George's will mentioned property in 'North Westgate'. The north side of High Street would be the *same* side as the former All Saints Church; the property opposite will have been on the south side.

Vague enough even by the mid-nineteenth century, the location of the Lefroy property, therefore, remains uncertain today. It would have been more helpful if Sir John's informant had located the site in relation to the ancient Eastbridge Hospital, which still stands on the southern side of the road. But of course he was not to know that All Saints Church would not survive as a landmark.

I was very hospitably shown around The King's School by archivist Peter Henderson. Very few really ancient parts of the school survive, but the Norman gateway and stairs are outstanding. The green square where Anne watched the boys play survives intact, carefully tended and mown.

The King's School scholars have always gone into Canterbury Cathedral, just across the green square, to attend service. It was a great privilege to enter the ancient shrine through the cloisters as the boys would have done.

I spent a morning in search of Wootton, the village some half hour's drive east of Canterbury, where Anne, Samuel and their siblings grew up, and neighbouring Denton, where Samuel eventually settled. The old Dover road passes through little Denton, and Samuel's property, Denton Court, still stands adjoining the churchyard; it is now privately owned. I visited on a Sunday, but it appears that Denton and Wootton alternately hold a church service, and it was Wootton's turn that day.

Wootton, up a precipitous hill from Denton, is another tiny village whose roads are barely wide enough for two small vehicles (let alone the ubiquitous Range Rovers) to pass one another. It is much today as Edward Hasted described it in 1800: 'The parish of Wootton lies very obscurely and unfrequented, among the high mountainous hills of the eastern part of Kent.' Here, alas, Wootton Court no longer stands, having been demolished in 1952.[25] The utter peace and quiet of Wootton and Denton is very striking.

The same can be said of the villages which form the scene of Anne's married life: Ashe, and its environs. For the Jane Austen fan, it is a surprising fact that Steventon and Ashe are as far as it is possible to be from being tourist destinations. Bath, a city which Jane Austen disliked, is full of Austen-related kitsch, the tourist coaches rolling in, but the beloved scenes of her childhood and youth are pretty well unvisited. On the basis that if tourist buses were to come, the roads would have to be considerably upgraded, it is understandable that the local authorities seem to be happy to leave things as they are.

Steventon does boast a red telephone box, presumably no longer functional, which bears the legend 'Jane Austen', and the signs at each end of the village mention her name, but this appears to be all. Ashe is even more remote; the church of Holy Trinity and St Andrew was locked up on the day I visited, but closer view, a notice beside the door indicated that in

2015, the Bishop of Winchester had determined that presentations would no longer be made at Ashe. It was not clear why. The whole scenario – the matter of the 'presentation' – sounded a strangely dated echo.

I later emailed the office of the Bishop, to ask for some more information. His representative advised me that while the formal process for appointing a permanent rector is currently suspended, the parishes of Ashe, Steventon, North Waltham and Deane are being serviced by an acting minister.[26] It would appear that one person is acting in the role that George Senior and two of his sons occupied from the mid-1780s until Ben's death in 1829.

I was able to gain access to the church by way of a key stored in a green box on the wall of the Glebe Cottages. Inside, it appeared little used; dust lay over the pews and cushions. My husband photographed the Lefroy monuments on the wall, then we left.

It seems sad that the church of Ashe, where Dr Russell, George Senior, George Junior and Ben read the Sunday services, christening, marrying and burying their parishioners, and which the Reverend Thoyts took the trouble and expense to restore in the 1880s, looks so unloved today.

The Rectory, where the Lefroys lived, still stands just past the Glebe Cottages; a graceful Georgian house, privately owned. Over these hills and past these fields, the Miss Austens walked to visit Anne Lefroy and Lucy, and in turn Anne returned the visit on a 'Donky' or a horse. The peace of these beautiful villages allows the visitor more readily to imagine the gossip and laughter which must have taken place during those visits.

Acknowledgements

I am grateful to the Hunter Branch of the Jane Austen Society of Australia, who first invited me to speak in 2015, and to whom I gave a talk about Anne Lefroy. That talk formed the seed which has eventually grown into this book.

I owe particular thanks to Adrienne Bradney-Smith, who has provided helpful thoughts, material, and support throughout all my Jane Austen related projects.

Joanna Penglase, of the Jane Austen Society of Australia, read some chapters in draft form and saved me from committing some errors. Those remaining errors are of course my own.

Thanks are due to The King's School, Canterbury and its archivist Peter Henderson, who was most helpful in giving me a guided tour of the school.

Annette Rowlands, a direct descendant of Anne Brydges Lefroy, and her husband Jim, hosted me for an afternoon, permitting me to view and photograph precious family materials. I will be forever grateful. If this book is at all useful to Jane Austen readers, it will be because of Annette.

Other members of the extended Lefroy diaspora helped point me in the right directions: particular thanks to Ann Lefroy of Murdoch University, and Mike and Joy Lefroy.

I am grateful to the staff of the State Library of Western Australia.

Special thanks are due to Jonathan Wright, Laura Hirst and all the staff of Pen and Sword Books, for making this book a reality and thanks to editor Karyn Burnham, who wrestled with my manuscript.

Last but not least, heartfelt thanks to my husband Stuart Wilson, who cheerfully accompanied me to Anne Lefroy sites, and took many of the photographs for this book.

Bibliography

Key works

Brydges, Samuel Egerton, *Arthur Fitz-Albini, A Novel* (London: J. White, second edition, 1799)

Brydges, Samuel Egerton (ed.), Arthur Collins, *Collins' Peerage of England: Genealogical, Biographical, and Historical*, nine vols (London: for C. and J. Rivington, 1812)

Brydges, Samuel Egerton, *The Autobiography, times, opinions and contemporaries of Sir Egerton Brydges*, two vols (London: Cochrane and McCrone, 1834)

Chapman, R.W. (ed.), *The Works of Jane Austen* vol. VI Minor Works (London: Oxford University Press, 1954, reprinted 1958, and with revisions 1963)

Doody, Margaret Anne and Douglas Murray, [Jane Austen] *Catharine and Other Writings* (Oxford: Oxford University Press, 1993)

Jones, Hazel, *Jane Austen and Marriage* (London: Hambledon Continuum, 2009)

Le Faye, Deirdre, Caroline Austen, *Reminiscences of Caroline Austen* (The Jane Austen Society, 1986)

Le Faye, Deirdre, *Jane Austen: A Family Record* (Cambridge University Press, second edition, 2004)

Jane Austen's Letters (Oxford University Press, fourth edition, 2011)

A Chronology of Jane Austen and her Family: 1600 to 2000 (Cambridge University Press, 2013)

[Lefroy, C.E.L.], *Outalissi: A Tale of Dutch Guiana* (London: J. Hatchard and Son, 1826)

Lefroy, Helen, and Gavin Turner, *The Letters of Mrs Lefroy: Jane Austen's Beloved Friend* (Winchester: The Jane Austen Society, 2007), appearing in notes as LT (2007)

Lefroy, Helen, MS, unpublished letters of the Lefroy family (no date)

Lefroy, John Henry, *Notes and Documents relating to the Family of Loffroy, of Cambray prior to 1587, of Canterbury 1587-1779, now chiefly represented by the Families of Lefroy of Carriglass, Co. Longford, Ireland, and of Itchel, Hants; with branches in Australia and Canada, being a contribution to the History of Foreign Protestant Refugees, by a Cadet* (Woolwich: Royal Artillery Institution, 1868)

Lefroy, Mrs (ed. C.E.L. Lefroy), *Carmina Domestica: or poems on several occasions* (London: Law and Gilbert, 1812)

Spence, Jon, *Becoming Jane Austen* (London: Hambledon Continuum, 2003)

Thoyts, Rev. F. W., *A History of Esse or Ashe, Hampshire* (London: William Clowes and Sons, 1888)

Tomalin, Claire, *Jane Austen: A Life* (London: Penguin, 1997)

Selected other works

Anonymous, Review, *Outalissi: A Tale of Dutch Guiana, Gentleman's Magazine* January – June 1827, vol. XCVII (20th of a new series, Part the First), 612–613

Aspinall, Arthur, 'Barry, Richard, 7th Earl of Barrymore [1] (1769–1793), of Wargrave-on-Thames, Berks,' in R. Thorne (ed.), *The History of Parliament: the House of Commons 1790–1820* (1986), http://www.historyofparliamentonline.org/volume/1790-1820/member/barry-richard-1769-93 accessed 8 May 2018

Bates, Cristina, 'The role of British merchants in Livorno in the marble trade between Italy and Britain during the eighteenth century,' 2007, in *Archeologia Postmedievale* 19 (2015), 61–69

Baxby, Derrick, 'Jenner, Edward (1749–1823)', *Oxford Dictionary of National Biography*, Oxford University Press, 2004; May 2009 [http://www.oxforddnb.com/view/article/14749, accessed 15 June 2018]

Beltz, G.F. *A Review of the Chandos Peerage Case, adjudicated 1803, and of the pretensions of Sir Samuel Egerton Brydges, baronet, to designate himself* per legem terrae *Baron Chandos of Sudeley* (London: R. Bentley, 1834)

Bettenson, Henry (ed.), *Documents of the Christian Church* (London: Oxford University Press, 1967)

Black, Maggie, and Deirdre Le Faye, *The Jane Austen Cookbook* (London: The British Museum, 1995)

Black, Peter M., Patricio C. Gargallo, and Adam C. Lipson, The Dana Foundation, 19 June 2009, http://www.brainline.org/content/2009/06/brain-trauma-concussion-and-coma_pageall.html accessed 15 June 2018

Blumberg, Arnold, 'The accurate and deadly Baker rifle,' http://warfarehistorynetwork.com/daily/military-history/the-accurate-and-deadly-baker-rifle/ accessed 12 June 2018

Boys, John, in Marshall (1817), 415-452

Brand, John (ed.) W. Carew Hazlitt, *Popular antiquities of Great Britain* (London: John Russell Smith, 1870)

Brayley, Edward, *The Beauties of England and Wales; or, original delineations, topographical, historical, and descriptive, of each county,* vol. VIII (London, 1808)

Breasted, B. 'Comus and the Castlehaven Scandal,' *Milton Studies*, 3 (1971), 201-224

Brooke, John, 'Lowther, Sir James, 5th Bt. (1763-1802), of Lowther, nr. Penrith, Westmld.,' http://www.historyofparliamentonline.org/volume/1754-1790/member/lowther-sir-james-1736-1802 accessed 4 May 2018

Brumwell, Stephen, *Paths of Glory: the life and death of General James Wolfe* (London: Hambledon Continuum, 2006)

Bruun, Geoffrey, 'The balance of power during the wars, 1793–1814, in Crawley (ed., 1980), 250–274

Burke, John, *A general and heraldic dictionary of the peerages of England, Ireland, and Scotland, extinct, dormant, and in abeyance* (London: H. Colburn and R. Bentley, 1831)

Burke, John, and John Bernard Burke, *A Genealogical and Heraldic Dictionary of the Landed Gentry of Great Britain and Ireland*, vol. I A-L, (London: Henry Colburn, 1846)

Byrne, Paula, *The Genius of Jane Austen: her Love of Theatre and why she is a Hit in Hollywood* (London: William Collins, 2017)

Chipulina, N. '1804 – yellow fever – an accumulation of dirt and filth,' http://gibraltar-intro.blogspot.com.au/2013/01/1804-yellow-fever-accumulation-of-dirt.html accessed 25 January 2018

Cibber, Colley, *The Dramatic Works of Colley Cibber, Esq. in five volumes* vol. V (London: J. Rivington and Sons, 1777)

Clayton, Tim, and Sheila O'Connell, *Bonaparte and the British: prints and propaganda in the age of Napoleon* (London: The British Museum, 2015)

Crawley, C.W. (ed.), vol. IX, War and Peace in an Age of Upheaval 1793–1830,' *The New Cambridge Modern History* (Cambridge University Press, 1980)

Creaser, J. 'Milton's *Comus*: the irrelevance of the Castlehaven scandal,' *Milton Quarterly,* vol. 21, no.4, Comus: Contexts (December 1987), 24–34

Cross, F.L. (ed.), *The Oxford Dictionary of the Christian Church* (Oxford University Press, 1961)

Davenport, R., L. Schwartz, J. Boulton, 'The decline of adult smallpox in eighteenth-century London,' http://www.geog.cam.ac.uk/people/davenport/davenport8.pdf accessed 3 April 2018

Debrett, John, *The Baronetage of England* (London: for F.C. and J. Rivington, third edition, 1815)

DeRitter, Jones, 'Wonder not, princely Gloster, at the notice this paper brings you': women, writing, and politics in Rowe's 'Jane Shore', *Comparative Drama* vol. 31, no. 1, Drama and Opera of the Enlightenment (Spring, 1997), 86–104

Doody, Margaret, *Jane Austen's Names: Riddles, Persons, Place* (University of Chicago Press, 2015)

Earle, Peter, *The Earles of Liverpool: a Georgian merchant dynasty* (Liverpool University Press, 2015)

Evenden, Michael, 'Flora's descent; or Hob's Re-re-re-resurrection,' *Eighteenth Century Studies* vol. 44, no. 4, Summer 2011, 565–567, summary at Project Muse, https://muse.jhu.edu/article/446584/ summary accessed 8 May 2018

Fawcett, Kirstin, 'Trepanation: the history of one of the world's oldest surgeries,' 1 January 2016, http://mentalfloss.com/article/70309/trepanation-history-one-worlds-oldest-surgeries accessed 15 June 2018

Fedorak, Charles John, 'In Defence of Great Britain: Henry Addington, the Duke of York and Military Preparations against Invasion by Napoleonic France,' in Mark Philp (ed.) *Resisting Napoleon: the British Response to the Threat of Invasion, 1797–1815* (Aldershot: Ashgate, 2006), 91-110

Fisher, David R. 'Temple Nugent Grenville (afterwards Temple Nugent Brydges Chandos Grenville), Richard (1776–1839), of Stowe, Bucks. and Avington Park, Hants,' in R. Thorne (ed.), *The History of Parliament: the House of Commons 1790–1820* (1986), digitized at http://www. historyofparliamentonline.org/volume/1790-1820/member/temple-nugent-grenville-%28afterwards-temple-nugent-brydges-chandos-grenville- accessed 12 June 2018

Galway, Elizabeth A. *From Nursery Rhymes to Nationhood: Children's Literature and the Construction of Canadian Identity* (London: Routledge, 2008)

Gardner, Percy, 'A stone tripod at Oxford,' *Journal of Hellenic Studies* vol. XVI (1896), 275–284

Garrett, Martin, 'Mitford, Mary Russell (1787–1855)', Oxford Dictionary of National Biography, Oxford University Press, 2004 [http://www. oxforddnb.com/view/article/18859, accessed 8 May 2018]

Gibbs, N.H. 'Armed forces and the art of war,' in Crawley (1980), 61–76

Gillan, Thomas, 'From the History of Medicine Artifacts Collection: Perkins' Tractors,' 26 January 2017, https://blogs.library.duke.edu/ rubenstein/2017/01/26/perkins-tractors/ accessed 15 June 2018

Grenby, M. O. 'Moral and instructive children's literature,' 15 May 2014, The British Library, https://www.bl.uk/romantics-and-victorians/articles/ moral-and-instructive-childrens-literature accessed 6 March 2018

Gruber, Jacob W. 'Hunter, John (1728–1793)', Oxford Dictionary of National Biography, Oxford University Press, 2004; online edn, May 2010 [http://www.oxforddnb.com/view/article/14220, accessed 15 June 2018]

Hall, Augusta (ed.), *The Autobiography and Correspondence of Mary Granville, Mrs Delany* (Cambridge University Press, 2011)

Hammond, M. 'Jemima-Lucy Lefroy,' *Persuasions* 14 (1992), 57–61

Harman, Claire, *Jane's Fame: How Jane Austen Conquered the World* (Edinburgh: Canongate, 2009)

Hasted, Edward, *The History and Topographical Survey of the County of Kent* (Canterbury: W. Bristow, 1800), reproduced at British History Online https://www.british-history.ac.uk/search/series/survey-kent accessed 2 October 2018

Herrup, Cynthia B. 'The patriarch at home: the trial of the 2nd Earl of Castlehaven for rape and sodomy,' *History Workshop Journal*, no. 41 (Spring, 1996), 1–18

A House in Gross Disorder: sex, law, and the 2nd Earl of Castlehaven (New York: Oxford University Press, 1999)
'Touchet, Mervin, second earl of Castlehaven (1593–1631), convicted rapist and sodomite' (2004). Oxford Dictionary of National Biography. Retrieved 5 March 2018

Hoffman, Stephanie B. 'Behind closed doors: impotence trials and the trans-historical right to marital privacy,' *Boston University Law Review* 89 (2009), 1725–1752

James, William, *The Naval History of Great Britain, from the declaration of war by France in 1793, to the accession of George IV*, in 6 vols (London: Richard Bentley, 1837)

Johnson, Ben, 'Riding side-saddle,' http://www.historic-uk.com/CultureUK/Riding-SideSaddle/ accessed 15 June 2018

Johnson, Ben, 'The last invasion of Britain', www.historica-uk.com/HistoryofWales/The-Last-Invasion-of-Britain accessed 12 June 2018

Kewes, Paulina, 'The State is out of Tune: Nicholas Rowe's 'Jane Shore' and the succession crisis of 1713–1714,' *Huntingdon Library Quarterly*, vol. 64, no. 3 / 4 (2001), 283–308

The Rev A.G. L'Estrange, ed. *The Life of Mary Russell Mitford, related in a selection from her letters to her friends*, 3 vols (London: Richard Bentley, 1870)

Le Faye, Deirdre, *Jane Austen's Country Life* (London: Frances Lincoln Ltd, 2014)

Leasure, R. 'Milton's queer choice: Comus at Castlehaven,' *Milton Quarterly*, vol. 36, no. 2 (May 2002), 63–86

Lees, R.E. 'Epidemic disease in Glasgow during the nineteenth century,' Scott Med J. 1996 Feb;41(1):24–7. Abstract at https://www.ncbi.nlm.nih.gov/pubmed/8658120 accessed 15 June 2018

Lockhart, John Gibson, 'Autobiography of Sir Egerton Brydges,' *Quarterly Review* 51 (June 1834), 342–65, http://spenserians.cath.vt.edu/BiographyRecord.php?action=GET&bioid=4840 accessed 12 June 2018

Manley, K.A. 'Brydges, Sir (Samuel) Egerton, first baronet, styled thirteenth Baron Chandos (1762–1837).' Oxford Dictionary of National Biography, Oxford University Press, 2004 [http://www.oxforddnb.com/view/article/3809, accessed 12 June 2018]

Marchand, Leslie A. *Byron: A Portrait* (London: Futura, 1971)

Markham, Felix, 'The Napoleonic adventure', in Crawley (1980), 307–336

Marland, H. *Dangerous Motherhood: Insanity and Childbirth in Victorian Britain* (Palgrave Macmillan, 2004), revised 28 November 2006, https://warwick.ac.uk/fac/arts/history/chm/events/dangerous/ accessed 15 June 2018

Marmontel, Jean-François (in anonymous English translation), *Belisarius by M. Marmontel, member of the French Academy* (London: for C. Nourse, a new edition, 1783)

Marquis of Carmarthen against the Marchioness of Carmarthen, libel given in the 26th of January, 1779, in *Trials for Adultery: or, the History of Divorces. Being select Trials at Doctors Commons, for Adultery, Fornication, Cruelty, Impotence, &c., from the year 1760 to the present time* [1779] ... *taken in short-hand, by a CIVILIAN*, vol. I (reissued Clark, New Jersey, by The Law Book Exchange, 2006), section XIV

Marshall, William, *A review (and complete abstract) of the Reports to the Board of Agriculture; from the southern and peninsular departments of England: comprising Hertfordshire, Berkshire, Middlesex, South Essex, South Wiltshire, Southeast Somerset, Dorsetshire, Hampshire, Surrey, Kent, Sussex, Cornwell, Devonshire, West Somersetshire* (York: Thomas Wilson and Sons, for Longman, Hurst, Rees, Orme, and Brown, London, 1817)

Martin, E.D. 'Depression in the Clergy,' *Christianity Today* Winter 1982, http://www.christianitytoday.com/pastors/1982/winter/ depressioninclergy.html accessed 15 June 2018

McDonald, Kelly, 'Madam Lefroy in her own words,' *JASNA News*, vol. 24, no. 2, Summer 2008

McNairn, Alan, *Behold the hero: General Wolfe and the arts in the eighteenth century* (Liverpool University Press, McGill-Queens University Press, 1997)

Memes, John S. (ed.), *The Poems of William Cowper, with a Life and notes*, 3 vols (Edinburgh: Fraser & Co, 1835)

Milner, J. *Milner's Historical Account of Winchester Cathedral, with a supplement,* eleventh edition (Winchester: Robbins and Wheeler, 1808)

Mundhenk, R.K. 'Dark scandal and the sun-clad power of chastity: the historical milieu of Milton's Comus,' *Studies in English Literature, 1500–1900,* vol. 15, no. 1, The English Renaissance (Winter, 1975), 141–52

Nall, Rachel, 'History of Stroke,' https://www.healthline.com/health/stroke/history-of-stroke 'medically reviewed by University of Illinois-Chicago, College of Medicine on 21 March 2016', accessed 3 April 2018

Namier, Sir Lewis, 'Powlett, Lord Harry (1720–94),' http://www.historyofparliamentonline.org/volume/1754-1790/member/powlett-lord-harry-1720-94 accessed 4 May 2018

Namier, Sir Lewis, 'Powlett, Sir Charles (c. 1718–65),' http://www.historyofparliamentonline.org/volume/1754–1790/member/powlett-sir-charles-1718-65 accessed 4 May 2018

Orde, Denis, *Nelson's Mediterranean Command* (Barnsley: Pen & Sword Books, 1997)

Pasquin, Anthony, Esq. (= John Williams), *The Life of the late Earl of Barrymore, third edition* (London: H.D. Symonds, 1793)

Probert, Rebecca, *Marriage Law and Practice in the Long Eighteenth Century: A Reassessment* (Cambridge University Press, 2009)

Reid, Stuart, 'Wolfe, James (1727–1759)', Oxford Dictionary of National Biography, Oxford University Press, 2004; Oct 2008 [http://www.oxforddnb.com/view/article/29833, accessed 3 April 2018]

Renwick, John, 'Marmontel, Voltaire, and the Bélisaire affair,' *Oxford University Studies in the Enlightenment 121* (The Voltaire Society in association with Liverpool University Press, 1974)

Roberts, Benjamin, *Through the keyhole: Dutch child-rearing practices in the seventeenth and eighteenth century: three urban elite families* (Hilversum Verloren, 1998)

Robicsek, F., T.S. Roush, J.W. Cook, M.K. Reames, 'From Hippocrates to Palmaz-Schatz, the history of carotid surgery', *European Journal of Vascular and Endovascular Surgery,* vol. 27, issue 4, April 2004, 389–397, https://www.sciencedirect.com/science/article/pii/S107858840400005X#BIB7 accessed 3 April 2018

Robinson, J.R. *The Last Earls of Barrymore* (London: Sampson Low, Marston, & Company, 1894)

Rodger, N. 'Nelson, Horatio, Viscount Nelson (1758–1805), naval officer.' Oxford Dictionary of National Biography, 2004. Retrieved 12 June 2018

Rose, H.J. 'Cotys, Cotyt(t)o,' *The Oxford Classical Dictionary* (Oxford University Press, 1957), 238

Rowney, Jane, 'Samphire: the next superfood?', *Weekend Notes* 16 March 2013, https://www.weekendnotes.com/samphire-the-next-superfood/ accessed 15 June 2018

Scott, Bruce, 'Flora – an 18th century British invasion', 20 May 2011, http://www.npr.org/2011/05/20/136469565/flora-an-18th-century-british-invasion accessed 8 May 2018

Selwyn, David (ed.), *The Poetry of Jane Austen and the Austen Family* (Iowa City: University of Iowa Press, 1997)

Seward, Marc, 'The Health Benefits of Samphire', 25 September 2017, https://healthyfocus.org/the-health-benefits-of-samphire/ accessed 15 June 2018

Seymour, Edward J. *The Nature and Treatment of Dropsy: considered especially in reference to the diseases of the internal organs of the body which most commonly produce it,* Parts I and II (London: Longman, Rees, Orme, Brown, Green, and Longman, 1837)

Smollett, Tobias, *The Adventures of Roderick Random*, two vols (sixth edition, London, 1763)

Southam, Brian, *Jane Austen and the Navy* (London: The National Maritime Museum, second edition, 2005)

Stove, Judy, *The Missing Monument Murders* (Basingstoke: Waterside Press, 2016)

Thirsk, Joan. 'Hasted, Edward (1732–1812), county historian.' Oxford Dictionary of National Biography, Oxford University Press, 2004, accessed 2 October 2018

Usborne, Margaret, 'Jane Austen – the Lefroys', *The Spectator* 29 February 1952, p. 9, http://archive.spectator.co.uk/article/29th-february-1952/9/jane-austenthe-lefroys accessed 10 April 2018

Vetch, R. (2004) revised by Roger T. Stearn (2012), 'Lefroy, Sir John Henry (1817–1890), army officer and meteorologist.' Oxford Dictionary of National Biography. Retrieved 21 Jun. 2018

Weiner, Gaby (ed.), *Harriette Wilson's Memoirs* (1825; London: Virago, 1985)

Woodman, Richard, *The Sea Warriors: The Fighting Captains and their Ships in the Age of Nelson* (Seaforth Publishing, Pen & Sword Books, 2014)

Notes

I – Jane/Anne

1. Helen Lefroy and Gavin Turner, *The Letters of Mrs Lefroy* (2007), hereafter LT (2007), p. 215. Jon Spence, *Becoming Jane Austen* (London: Hambledon Continuum, 2003), p. 99.
2. Spence (2003), p. 95. Lincoln's Inn: Lefroy (1868), p. 105.
3. John Henry Lefroy, *Notes and Documents relating to the Family of Loffroy, of Cambray prior to 1587, of Canterbury 1587-1779, now chiefly represented by the Families of Lefroy of Carriglass, Co. Longford, Ireland, and of Itchel, Hants; with branches in Australia and Canada, being a contribution to the History of Foreign Protestant Refugees, by a Cadet* (Woolwich, Royal Artillery Institution, 1868), hereafter Lefroy (1868), p. 105.
4. Letter 1, to Cassandra, 9-10 January 1796, Deirdre Le Faye, *Jane Austen's Letters* (Oxford University Press, fourth edition, 2011), hereafter Le Faye (2011), p. 1.
5. Letter 1, to Cassandra, 9-10 January 1796, Le Faye (2011), p. 2.
6. Quoted in Le Faye (2011), p. 369, n. 16, from Fielding's first (1749) edition in 6 vols, Book vii, ch. 14.
7. Hazel Jones, *Jane Austen and Marriage* (2009), p. 11.
8. Letter 1, to Cassandra, 9-10 January 1796, Le Faye (2011), p. 1.
9. Le Faye (2011), p. 3.
10. Spence (2003), p. 109.
11. Letter 2, to Cassandra, 14-15 January 1796, Le Faye (2011), p. 3.
12. Letter 2, to Cassandra, 14-15 January 1796, Le Faye (2011), p. 4.
13. Le Faye (2011), p. 533.
14. Le Faye (2011), p. 564.
15. SEB *Collins' Peerage* (1812), vol. 8, p. 558. SEB does not give Charles' birth year, but it was post-1787 (the year of birth of the Orde-Powletts' fourth child, Thomas). Charles d. 1806.
16. Le Faye (2011), p. 582.

17. Letter 2, to Cassandra, 14-15 January 1796, Le Faye (2011), p. 4.
18. Le Faye (2011), p. 370, n. 2.
19. Spence (2003), p. 98.
20. Spence (2003), p. 110.
21. Letter 3, to Cassandra, 23 August 1796, Le Faye (2011), p. 5.
22. Le Faye (2011), p. 5.
23. Letter 11, to Cassandra, 17-18 November 1798, Le Faye (2011), p. 19.
24. Letter 11, to Cassandra, 17-18 November 1798, Le Faye (2011), p. 19.
25. Le Faye (2011), p. 375, n. 5 gives the identification, p. 498 his dates.
26. Spence (2003), p. 109.
27. Letter 11, to Cassandra, 17-18 November 1798, Le Faye (2011), pp.19-20.
28. Shakespeare, *Richard III* Act I Scene 2.
29. Le Faye (2011), p. 549.
30. *Jane Austen: A Family Record* (Cambridge University Press, second edition, 2004), p. 93.
31. Claire Tomalin, *Jane Austen: a Life* (Penguin, 1997), p. 119.
32. Spence (2003), p. 110.
33. Caroline's letter (1868 or 1869) and Anna's letter quoted in Le Faye (2004), pp. 277-278.
34. Spence (2003), pp. 111–112.
35. Spence (2003), p. 111.
36. Jones, (2009), pp. 11–12.
37. Le Faye (2011), p. 544.
38. Letter 1, 29 September 1800, LT (2007), p. 29.
39. Letter dated (probably erroneously) December 1799, quoted in Lefroy (1868), pp. 138-139.
40. Letter 4, 17 June 1801, LT (2007), p. 37.
41. SEB *Autobiography* (1834), vol. II, p. 40.
42. Tomalin (1997), p. 39.
43. Quoted in LT (2007), p. 22.
44. Le Faye (2011), p. 1.
45. Le Faye (2011), pp. 19-20.
46. Le Faye (2011), p. 27.
47. Le Faye (2011), pp. 27–28.
48. Le Faye (2011), pp. 30–31.
49. Le Faye (2011), p. 33.
50. Le Faye (2011), pp. 498, 517.
51. Le Faye (2011), p. 38.
52. Le Faye (2011), p. 45.
53. Le Faye (2011), pp. 55-56.

54. Le Faye (2011), p. 522.
55. Le Faye (2011), p. 77.
56. Milles family: Le Faye (2011), p. 554.
57. LT (2007), p. 206.
58. Le Faye (2011), p. 262, adding in a note that Le Mere Beauté is a reference to a description in the letters of Madame de Sévigné (p. 433, n. 4).

2 – Anne/Jane

1. Letter 8, 23 September – 2 October 1801, LT (2007), p. 44.
2. Deirdre Le Faye, *A Chronology of Jane Austen and her Family: 1600 to 2000* (Cambridge University Press, 2013), hereafter Le Faye (2013), pp. 260, 262.
3. Letter 9, 3 October 1801, LT (2007), p. 45; Le Faye (2013), p. 262.
4. Letter 91, 20 October 1803, LT (2007), pp. 139-140.
5. Letter 3, 4 June 1801, LT (2007), p. 33.
6. J. Milner, *Milner's Historical Account of Winchester Cathedral, with a supplement* 11th edition (Winchester: Robbins and Wheeler, 1808), p. 163.
7. Letter 73, 27 July 1803, LT (2007), p. 121.
8. Letter 2, 29 May 1801, LT (2007), pp. 30–31.
9. Letter 38, to Cassandra, 26-27 May 1801, Le Faye (2011), p. 95.
10. Letter from Sir Thomas Williams, Commander *Endymion*, to Evan Nepean, 17 May 1800; *The London Gazette* issue 15258, p. 486. https://www.thegazette.co.uk/London/issue/15258/page/486 accessed 12 June 2018.
11. Letter 20, 3-16 March 1802, LT (2007), p. 63.
12. Jones (2009), p. 84; banns: p. 78.
13. Letter 20, 3-16 March 1802, LT (2007), p. 62.
14. Account in *Hampshire Chronicle* 15 March 1802, quoted in LT (2007), p. 188.
15. Letter 20, 3-16 March 1802, LT (2007), p. 63.
16. Benjamin Langlois, 'Instructions to his Execs.', quoted in Lefroy (1868), p. 112.

3 – Egertons and Brydges

1. Herrup, C. (2004-09-23). Touchet, Mervin, second earl of Castlehaven (1593–1631), convicted rapist and sodomite. Oxford Dictionary of National Biography. Retrieved 5 March 2018, from http://www.oxforddnb.com/view/10.1093/ref:odnb/9780198614128.001.0001/odnb-9780198614128-e-66794.
2. 'A Mask presented at Ludlow Castle,' lines 55–77. 1645 edition, version at https://www.dartmouth.edu/~milton/reading_room/comus/text.shtml accessed 27 February 2018.

3. Stage direction at line 93.

4. H.J. Rose, 'Cotys, Cotyt(t)o,' *The Oxford Classical Dictionary* (Oxford University Press, 1957), p. 238; also N.P.M. Nilsson, 'Mysteries,' pp. 593–94, section 3.

5. Edmund Spenser, *The Faerie Queene* (1590), II.13-14, 17, 19.

6. B. Breasted, 'Comus and the Castlehaven Scandal,' *Milton Studies*, 3 (1971), 201-224; R.K. Mundhenk, 'Dark scandal and the sun-clad power of chastity: the historical milieu of Milton's Comus,' *Studies in English Literature, 1500–1900*, vol. 15, no. 1, The English Renaissance (Winter, 1975), pp. 141–52.

7. J. Creaser, 'Milton's *Comus*: the irrelevance of the Castlehaven scandal,' *Milton Quarterly*, vol. 21, no.4, Comus: Contexts (December 1987), pp. 24–34, Austen: p. 29; 'invidious issue' and victim-blaming: p. 32.

8. R. Leasure, 'Milton's queer choice: Comus at Castlehaven,' *Milton Quarterly*, vol. 36, no. 2 (May 2002), pp. 63–86, Comus' ambiguity: p. 69.

9. C. Herrup, 'The patriarch at home: the trial of the 2nd Earl of Castlehaven for rape and sodomy,' *History Workshop Journal*, no. 41 (Spring, 1996), pp. 1–18, and subsequently her book *A House in Gross Disorder: sex, law and the 2nd Earl of Castlehaven* (New York: Oxford University Press, 1999).

10. Leasure (2002), p. 79.

11. Herrup (2004).

12. A. Collins, S.E. Brydges, *Collins' Peerage* (1812), 9 vols, vol. III, p. 202.

13. Ibid., p. 202.

14. These birth years are approximate only; Jemima's birth month is given as September 1728 on the website https://www.geni.com (accessed 3 March 2018), but the source for this is unclear.

15. SEB, *Collins' Peerage* (1812), 9 vols, vol. III, p. 202.

16. Reference in *Gentleman's Magazine* to marriage in September 1791 of Mrs Beauvoir, widow of 'Osmond Beauvoir, D.D. (LIX.672), formerly master of the free-school at Canterbury': *GM* v. 70, Part the Second, October 1791, p. 968.

17. *Collins' Peerage* (1812), vol. III, p, 203.

18. Ibid. p. 204.

19. SEB, *Autobiography* (1834), vol. I, p 40.

20. SEB, *Autobiography* (1834), vol. II, p. 11.

21. Edward Braylcy, *The Beauties of England and Wales; or, original delineations, topographical, historical, and descriptive, of each county*, vol. VIII (London, 1808), p. 1073. The volume is dedicated by the author to SEB.

22. John Burke, *A general and heraldic dictionary of the peerages of England, Ireland, and Scotland, extinct, dormant, and in abeyance* (London: H. Colburn and R. Bentley, 1831), p. 92.

23. G.F. Beltz, *A Review of the Chandos Peerage Case, adjudicated 1803, and of the pretensions of Sir Samuel Egerton Brydges, baronet, to designate himself*

per legem terrae *Baron Chandos of Sudeley* (London: R. Bentley, 1834), hereafter Beltz (1834), Pedigree II.

24. "England, Kent, Canterbury Parish Registers, 1538-1986," database with images, *FamilySearch*(https://familysearch.org/ark:/61903/1:1:QGNV-SCJP:24 February 2018), Ann Brydges, 22 Mar 1747; from "Kent, Canterbury Archdeaconry Parish Registers Browse, 1538–1913," database and images, *findmypast* (http://www.findmypast.com : n.d); citing Baptism, Wootton, Kent, England, United Kingdom, Citing Canterbury Cathedral Archives, England. However, the marriage of Anne's parents is also said to have taken place in March 1747 (see Debrett, *The Baronetage of England* vol. II London, 1815, p. 1365); both cannot be correct. Elsewhere Anne's birth year is listed as 1748, possibly because of the perennial confusion between Old Style and New Style dates (LT 2007), p. ix and *passim*; 1749 on various websites (e.g. https://www.janeausten.co.uk/madam-anne-lefroy/ accessed 3 June 2017).

25. Edward Timewell baptism 18 June 1748 (https://search.findmypast.co.uk/record?id=GBPRS/CANT/B/96432436 8 August 2017), 1749 according to his own testimony (Beltz,1834, pedigree II).

26. Dates from LT (2007), p. 206, also Beltz (1834), pedigree II.

27. Beltz (1834), p. 185.

28. Edward Hasted, *The History and Topographical Survey of the County of Kent* (Canterbury, 1800), vol. IX, hereafter Hasted (1800), pp. 365–6.

29. Ibid., quoting '*Saxonum codicelli*, in the Surrenden Library.'

30. 'Parishes: Wootton,' in *Hasted* (1800), pp. 364–73.

31. 'J. Plaw delin., T. Morris sculp., Wootton Court in Kent, the seat of the Revd. Edward Timewell Bridges,' late eighteenth century: http://www.alamy.com/stock-photo-wootton-court-kent-the-seat-of-the-reverend-edward-tymewell-bridges-105317331.html accessed 4 March 2018.

32. John Boys, in William Marshall, *A review (and complete abstract) of the Reports to the Board of Agriculture; from the southern and peninsular departments of England: comprising Hertfordshire, Berkshire, Middlesex, South Essex, South Wiltshire, Southeast Somerset, Dorsetshire, Hampshire, Surrey, Kent, Sussex, Cornwell, Devonshire, West Somersetshire* (York, 1817), hereafter Boys (1817), pp. 413ff.

33. Letter 90, to Francis Austen, 25 September 1813, Le Faye (2011), p. 239.

34. Boys (1817), footnote to p. 418, qualified: 'Perhaps more fanciful than true. – Editor.'

35. Boys (1817), p. 420.

36. Boys (1817), p. 428.

37. Boys (1817), p. 424.

38. Boys (1817), p. 424.

39. Boys (1817), p. 426.
40. Boys (1817), p. 430.
41. Boys (1817), p. 432.
42. Boys (1817), p, 434.
43. Boys (1817), p. 434.
44. Wootton Historical Society, *Wootton, Selsted and Denton History,* http://woottonselsteddentonhistory.blogspot.com.au/2015/04/wootton-court-part-3.html 25 April 2015, accessed 5 March 2018.
45. Transcription originally by antiquary Rev. Bryan Faussett (1720–1776), 1758; added to website 8 June 2007: http://www.kentarchaeology.org.uk/Research/Libr/MIs/MIsWootton/01.htm accessed 5 March 2018.
46. SEB, *Autobiography* (1834) vol. I, p. 5.
47. Letter from Lady Jane Head to niece Anne Brydges Lefroy, 25 February 1779, quoted in Lefroy (1868), p. 111.
48. Lefroy (1868), p. 111.
49. LT (2007), p. 5.
50. Lefroy (1868), p. 112.
51. SEB *Autobiography*, vol. I, p. 137.
52. Lefroy (1868), footnote to p. 114.

4 – Poems of a Sister

1. Title page. London: Law and Gilbert, 1812. Thanks to staff of The British Library, who in October 2016 assisted me to examine their copy, inscribed: 'The gift of Christopher Edward Lefroy to Mr Brooks April 22nd 1812.'
2. Letter 92, to Cassandra, 14-15 October 1813, Le Faye, (2011), p. 250.
3. Letter 107, to Anna Austen, 9-18 September 1814, Le Faye, (2011), p. 288.
4. Footnote to Eclogue the Third, 'Abbra; or the Georgian Sultana.'
5. Eclogue the Fourth, 'Agib and Secander; or the Fugitives,' lines 1–2.
6. 'History,' http://www.kings-school.co.uk/about/history/a-brief-history accessed 6 March 2018.
7. King's School, Canterbury, Register 1750–1859, Indexhttps://www.kings-school.co.uk/wp-content/uploads/2017/08/KSC_register_index_1750-1859.pdf accessed 6 March 2018.
8. King's School, Canterbury, Register 1750–1859, Indexhttps://www.kings-school.co.uk/wp-content/uploads/2017/08/KSC_register_index_1750–1859.pdf accessed 6 March 2018.
9. M. O. Grenby, 'Moral and instructive children's literature,' 15 May 2014, The British Library, https://www.bl.uk/romantics-and-victorians/articles/moral-and-instructive-childrens-literature accessed 6 March 2018.

10. John Debrett, *The Baronetage of England*, 3rd edition 1815, vol. I, pp. 325–326.
11. Annual Register for 1777, reported in Marriage: Canterbury births, marriages, deaths: http://www.machadoink.com/Birth%20Marriage%20Death.htm accessed 6 March 2018; death of Sandys: Debrett (1815), p. 326.
12. William F. Shortz, 'British word puzzles 1700–1800,' article from 1973, pp. 131–138, digitalcommons.butler.edu/cgi/viewcontent.cgi?article=1737&context=wordways accessed 6 March 2018.
13. *London Magazine* XVII, October 1748, p. 471, quoted in *Shortz* (1973), pp. 133–134. Solution: glass-lass-ass.
14. Milton, *Paradise Lost* IV. 596–602.
15. LT (2007), p. 5 and p. 24, n. 7.
16. Burke and Burke, *A Genealogical and Heraldic Dictionary of the Landed Gentry of Great Britain and Ireland*, vol. I A-L, (London: Henry Colburn, 1846), p. 532.
17. LT (2007), letter 94 (13 November 1803), p. 142.
18. Burke and Burke, *Landed Gentry* (1846), vol. I, p. 532; website: https://www.geni.com/people/Catherine/6000000050430627931 accessed 6 March 2018.

5 – Anne and the Belisarius Affair

1. Albert Boime, 'Marmontel's *Bélisaire* and the pre-Revolutionary progressivism of David,' http://www.albertboime.com/Articles/37.pdf accessed 9 March 2018.
2. Marmontel (English translation 1783), p. 18.
3. Marmontel (1783), p. 52.
4. Marmontel (1783), p. 209.
5. Marmontel (1783), p. 205. 'There is no good spirit without God…Between good men and God there is a partnership, fostered by virtue' (my translation).
6. Renwick (1974), p. 123. Pelagian doctrine about infants: teaching ascribed to Pelagius' disciple Coelestius, *ap.* Aug. *De gestis Pelagii* 23, in Henry Bettenson (ed.), *Documents of the Christian Church* (London: Oxford University Press, 1967), pp. 53-54.
7. Marmontel (1783), p. 210.
8. Renwick (1974), pp. 95–109.
9. Renwick (1974), p. 155.
10. Quoted in Martin Myrone, *Reforming Masculinities in British Art 1750–1810* (New Haven and London: Yale University Press, 2005), p. 121.

11. Anonymous translator's preface, *Belisarius by M. Marmontel, member of the French Academy* (London: for C. Nourse, a new edition, 1783); preface dated 2 March 1767, pp. v–vi.
12. Renwick (1974), p. 48.
13. 'Calvinism,' in F. L. Cross (ed.), *The Oxford Dictionary of the Christian Church* (London: Oxford University Press, 1961), p. 221.
14. C.E.L. Lefroy, *Outalissi: a tale of Dutch Guiana* (London: J. Hatchard and Son, 1826), pp. 4–5.

6 – Marrying George Lefroy

1. LT (2007), p.6; King's School register, see references in Chapter 3.
2. Lefroy (1868).
3. Lefroy (1868), p. xxxix.
4. In Lefroy (1868), p. xxx.
5. Lefroy (1868), p. xlvi.
6. Lefroy (1868), p. 13.
7. Lefroy (1868), p. 16.
8. Lefroy (1868), p. 29.
9. Quoted in Lefroy (1868), pp. 31–32.
10. Lefroy (1868), p. 31.
11. Lefroy (1868), p. 25.
12. Lefroy (1868), p. 35.
13. Lefroy (1868), p. 45.
14. Lefroy (1868), pp. 43ff.
15. The following account follows Cristina Bates, 'The role of British merchants in Livorno in the marble trade between Italy and Britain during the eighteenth century,' 2007, in *Archeologia Postmedievale* 19 (2015), 61–69. See also the website on the Leghorn Merchants maintained by Matteo Giunti, https://leghornmerchants.wordpress.com.
16. Bates (2015), p. 63.
17. Bates (2015), p. 64.
18. Lefroy (1868), p. 51.
19. See its website, http://www.accademia-etrusca.org/la-storia/ accessed 22 March 2018.
20. Wortley-Montague to Lord Bute, 8 April 1763, quoted in Lefroy (1868), p. 52.
21. Lefroy (1868), p. 59.
22. Letter from Anthony Lefroy to Benjamin Langlois, 18 May 1763, quoted in Lefroy (1868), pp. 56–57.
23. *New Oxford Guide* (Oxford, Munday and Slatter, 1818), pp. 22–23.

24. Anonymous article XIX in *The Topographer, for the year 1789* (London, Robson and Clarke), vol. I, 1789, pp. 513–514.

25. P. Gardner, 'A stone tripod at Oxford,' *JHS* vol. XVI (1896), 275–284, p. 276.

26. Gardner (1896), p. 277.

27. Gardner (1896), p. 280.

28. Email from Gaye Morgan, Librarian in Charge and Conservator, The Codrington Library, All Souls College, to author, 5 Sep 2017. Ashmolean ref: LI16.1, Department of Antiquities.

29. Letter dated 29 April 1763, quoted in Lefroy (1868), pp. 55–56.

30. Bates (2015), p. 64.

31. Peter Earle, *The Earles of Liverpool: a Georgian merchant dynasty* (Liverpool University Press, 2015), p. 143.

32. Letter dated 5 August 1763, quoted in Lefroy (1868), pp. 70–71.

33. Earle (2015), p. 143; Bates (2015), p. 64, n. 26 re Phoebe's marriage.

34. Lefroy (1868), p. 72.

35. Lefroy (1868) gives the pedigree, *Stemmata Chicheleana*, which provided evidence of George's descent, via Hammonds and Digges, pp. 27–29.

36. LT (2007), p. 6.

37. Le Faye (2013), p. 24.

38. Commission registered 21 August 1778, quoted in Lefroy (1868), p. 110.

39. The Marquis of Carmarthen against the Marchioness of Carmarthen, libel given in the 26th of January, 1779, in *Trials for Adultery: or, the History of Divorces. Being select Trials at Doctors Commons, for Adultery, Fornication, Cruelty, Impotence, &c., from the year 1760 to the present time* [1779] … *taken in short-hand, by a CIVILIAN*, vol. I (reissued Clark, New Jersey, by The Law Book Exchange, 2006), section XIV, pp. 3–4.

40. *Trials for Adultery: or, the History of Divorces. Being select Trials at Doctors Commons, for Adultery, Fornication, Cruelty, Impotence, &c., from the year 1760 to the present time* [1779]…*taken in short-hand, by a CIVILIAN*, vol. I (reissued Clark, New Jersey, by The Law Book Exchange, 2006), section XIV.

41. *Autobiography and Correspondence of Mary Granville, Mrs Delany*, ed. Augusta Hall (Cambridge University Press, 2011), vol. 6, p. 165.

42. Leslie A. Marchand, *Byron: a Portrait* (Futura, 1971), p. 130.

43. Lefroy and Turner (2007), p. 7.

44. "England Marriages, 1538–1973," database, FamilySearch (https://familysearch.org/ark:/61903/1:1:NNNS-C43 : 10 December 2014), The Rev. George Lefroy and Anne Brydges, 28 Dec 1778; citing Wootton, Kent, England, reference item 4 p 6, index based upon data collected by the Genealogical Society of Utah, Salt Lake City; FHL microfilm 1,866,580. Also Lefroy and Turner (2007), p. 7.

45. LT (2007), p. 8.

46. L'Estrange (1870), vol. I, p. 215

47. M. Plumptre to Anne's sister Deborah Brydges, 18 Jan 1779, quoted in Lefroy and Turner (2007), p. 8.

48. "England Births and Christenings, 1538–1975," database, FamilySearch (https://familysearch.org/ark:/61903/1:1:NKG6-FBW : 6 December 2014, Jemima Lucy Lefroy, 09 Dec 1779); citing BASINGSTOKE, HAMPSHIRE, ENGLAND, index based upon data collected by the Genealogical Society of Utah, Salt Lake City; FHL microfilm 1,041,201. Interestingly, in this parish record, Anne's name is given as Anna (later to be more generally associated with her daughter-in-law Anna Austen Lefroy).

49. Lefroy and Turner (2007), p. 8.

50. Lefroy and Turner (2007), pp. 8–9.

51. Lefroy (1868), p. 93.

52. Elizabeth Langlois Lefroy, Livorno, to Rev. George Lefroy, 14 May 1781, quoted in Lefroy (1868), pp. 92-93.

53. LT (2007), p. 9.

54. "England Deaths and Burials, 1538–1991," database, FamilySearch (https://familysearch.org/ark:/61903/1:1:JZGZ-72B : 24 December 2014), Edward Esqr. Brydges, burial 26 Nov 1780; citing Wootton, Kent, England, index based upon data collected by the Genealogical Society of Utah, Salt Lake City; FHL microfilm 1,866,580

55. LT (2007), p. 9.

56. "England Births and Christenings, 1538–1975," database, FamilySearch (https://familysearch.org/ark:/61903/1:1:JQFH-V2G:6 December 2014, Anthony Bridges Lefroy, 19 Oct 1784); citing BASINGSTOKE, HAMPSHIRE, ENGLAND, index based upon data collected by the Genealogical Society of Utah, Salt Lake City; FHL microfilm 1,041,201. But cf. Anthony's memorial plaque in Ashe church, which gives his birth date as 21 September 1785 (author visit April 2018).

57. LT (2007), p. 9.

58. R. Davenport, L. Schwartz, J. Boulton, 'The decline of adult smallpox in eighteenth-century London,' http://www.geog.cam.ac.uk/people/davenport/davenport8.pdf accessed 3 April 2018.

59. Report of the physician to the Small-Pox and Vaccination Hospital, St Pancras, 1 February 1839, in *London Medical Gazette* new series, vol. I, 1838-1839 (London, 1839), p. 762.

60. Rev. W. Bingley *History of Hampshire* vol. II (1807-1813), quoted at https://austenonly.com/2012/09/21/the-parish-church-of-holy-trinity-and-st-andrew-ashe-part-one/ accessed 3 April 2018. But in Rev. F.W. Thoyts, *A History of Esse or Ashe, Hampshire* (1888), p. 119, Russell's age at death is recorded as 88.

61. SEB *Autobiography*, quoted in Lefroy (1868), pp. 114-115.
62. In *GM* 1789, p. 374, quoted in Lefroy (1868), pp. 122-123.

7 – Jane Shore at Hackwood Park I: Miss L- and Captain Whiffle

1. Paula Byrne, *The Genius of Jane Austen: her Love of Theatre and why she is a Hit in Hollywood* (London: William Collins, 2017), pp. 57, 215–216, 226–227.
2. https://www.the-saleroom.com/en-gb/auction-catalogues/chiswick-auctions/catalogue-id-srchis10108/lot-12e4f59f-6211-4774-a1ca-a44c00ef584e accessed 4 May 2018.
3. Lefroy (1812), pp. 46–47.
4. Jane Austen, *Mansfield Park* (1814), ch. 13.
5. Reissued in 2017 as *The Genius of Jane Austen* (London: William Collins).
6. D. Le Faye, *Chronology* (2013), pp. 119–120.
7. Sir Lewis Namier, 'Powlett, Sir Charles (c. 1718–65),' http://www.historyofparliamentonline.org/volume/1754–1790/member/powlett-sir-charles-1718-65 accessed 4 May 2018.
8. Sir Lewis Namier, 'Powlett, Lord Harry (1720–94),' http://www.historyofparliamentonline.org/volume/1754-1790/member/powlett-lord-harry-1720-94 accessed 4 May 2018. Slightly differing dates given for Lord Harry's first marriage in E. Burke (ed.), *Annual Register* (1794), 2nd ed. (London, 1806), p. 56.
9. Confusingly, the biographical note on 'Lady Bolton' in LT (2007), p. 205, refers not to this person, but to a later Lady Bolton, the wife of Admiral Harry's successor in the dukedom. See Chapter 9. Separating and identifying the numerous Powletts, Paulets, and Boltons is, however, a difficult task.
10. Harry Powlett: Sir Lewis Namier, 'Powlett, Lord Harry (1720–1794),' http://www.historyofparliamentonline.org/volume/1754–1790/member/powlett-lord-harry-1720-94 accessed 12 Sep 2017; James Lowther: John Brooke, 'Lowther, Sir James, 5th Bt. (1736-1802), of Lowther, nr. Penrith, Westmld,' http://www.historyofparliamentonline.org/volume/1754-1790/member/lowther-sir-james-1736-1802 accessed 12 Sep 2017.
11. John Brooke, 'Lowther, Sir James, 5th Bt. (1763-1802), of Lowther, nr. Penrith, Westmld.,' http://www.historyofparliamentonline.org/volume/1754-1790/member/lowther-sir-james-1736-1802 accessed 4 May 2018.
12. Stuart Reid, 'Wolfe, James (1727–1759)', Oxford Dictionary of National Biography, Oxford University Press, 2004; online edn, Oct 2008 [http://www.oxforddnb.com/view/article/29833, accessed 3 April 2018]

13. Stuart Reid, 'Wolfe, James (1727–1759)', Oxford Dictionary of National Biography, Oxford University Press, 2004; online edn, Oct 2008 [http://www.oxforddnb.com/view/article/29833, accessed 3 April 2018]

14. Quoted in Reid (2008).

15. Poetical Essays in *GM,* vol. XXVIII, November 1759, p. 613.

16. Brumwell (2006), p. 297.

17. Alan McNairn, *Behold the hero: General Wolfe and the arts in the eighteenth century* (Liverpool University Press, McGill-Queens University Press, 1997), p. 53.

18. James Adams, 'A James Wolfe portrait up for auction reveals the general's off-battlefield romance,' *The Globe and Mail* 21 November 2014, https://beta.theglobeandmail.com/arts/art-and-architecture/a-james-wolfe-portrait-up-for-auction-reveals-the-generals-off-battlefield-romance/article21690122/?ref=http://www.theglobeandmail.com accessed 3 April 2018.

19. Reid (2008).

20. Stephen Brumwell, *Paths of Glory: the life and death of General James Wolfe* (Hambledon Continuum, 2006), p. 186.

21. Brumwell (2006), p. 298.

22. https://www.ancestry.com.au/genealogy/records/sarah-timmings_10199340 accessed 3 April 2018.

23. 'Natasha,' 4 March 2001, http://www.genealogy.com/forum/surnames/topics/timmins/77/ accessed 3 April 2018.

24. "England Marriages, 1538–1973," database, FamilySearch (https://familysearch.org/ark:/61903/1:1:NK37-SWP : 10 December 2014), Joseph Nash and Sarah Timmins, 6 Nov 1784; citing Saint Thomas, Dudley, Worcester, England, reference, index based upon data collected by the Genealogical Society of Utah, Salt Lake City; FHL microfilm 378,762, 378,763, 378,764, 378,765, 378,766, 378,767, 378,768, 378,769, 378,770. Accessed 12 Sep 2017.

25. *The Athenaeum, a Magazine of Literary and Miscellaneous Information (published Monthly),* conducted by J. Aikin, M.D., vol. V, January to June, 1809, p. 455.

26. B. Longmate (ed.), *Collins' Peerage* (supplement to 5th edition, London, 1784), p. 349.

27. [Tobias George Smollett], *The Adventures of Roderick Random*, (sixth edition, London, 1763), 2 vols, vol. I, pp. 270-271.

28. Elizabeth A. Galway, *From Nursery Rhymes to Nationhood: Children's Literature and the Construction of Canadian Identity* (Routledge, 2008), p. 80.

29. Christine L. Krueger, 'Green, Mary Anne Everett (1818–1895)', Oxford Dictionary of National Biography, Oxford University Press, 2004; online edn, May 2008 [http://www.oxforddnb.com/view/article/11395, accessed 1 May 2018]

30. "intimate, adj. and n.". OED Online. March 2018. Oxford University Press. http://www.oed.com.ezproxy.sl.nsw.gov.au/view/Entry/98506? rskey=UTSjeI&result=1&isAdvanced=false (accessed 4 May 2018).
31. "possession, n.". OED Online. March 2018. Oxford University Press. http://www.oed.com.ezproxy.sl.nsw.gov.au/view/Entry/148352? rskey=yQKSWV&result=1&isAdvanced=false (accessed May 4, 2018).
32. *The Oxford Magazine or, University Museum*, vol. II (London: 1769), p. 234. Also, *inter alia*, in similar terms: *The London Magazine, or Gentleman's Monthly Intelligencer*, vol. 38 (1769), p. 330.
33. 'The Classic Domino', 2 August 2011, http://www.historicalfancydress. com/2011/08/the-classic-domino.html accessed 1 May 2018.
34. David Selwyn, *Jane Austen and Leisure* (London and Rio Grande: The Hambledon Press, 1999 and digital reprint 2004), p. 248.

8 – Jane Shore at Hackwood Park II: Featuring Hellgate and Billingsgate

1. Paulina Kewes, 'The State is out of Tune: Nicholas Rowe's 'Jane Shore' and the succession crisis of 1713–1714,' *Huntingdon Library Quarterly*, vol. 64, no. 3 / 4 (2001), 283–308, p. 284.
2. Tate Gallery no. 05898, *The Penance of Jane Shore in St Paul's Church*, ink, watercolour, and gouache on paper; http://www.tate.org.uk/art/artworks/ blake-the-penance-of-jane-shore-in-st-pauls-church-n05898 accessed 8 May 2018.
3. Jones DeRitter, 'Wonder not, princely Gloster, at the notice this paper brings you': women, writing, and politics in Rowe's 'Jane Shore', *Comparative Drama* vol. 31, no. 1, Drama and Opera of the Enlightenment (Spring, 1997), 86–104, p. 92.
4. DeRitter (1997), p. 93.
5. DeRitter (1997), p. 96.
6. *Pride and Prejudice* (1813), ch. 40.
7. Lot 103, Single Sheet Playbill advertising a performance of Jane Shore, auction date 18 March 2015, https://www.the-saleroom.com/en-gb/auction-catalogues/chiswick-auctions/catalogue-id-srchis10108/lot-12e4f59f-6211-4774-a1ca-a44c00ef584e accessed 8 May 2018
8. J.R. Robinson, *The Last Earls of Barrymore* (London: Sampson Low, Marston, & Company, 1894), pp. 6–7.
9. Robinson (1894, p. 9.
10. Robinson (1894), p. 10.

11. Anthony Pasquin, Esq. *The Life of the late Earl of Barrymore, 3rd edition* (London: H.D. Symonds, 1793), p. 68.

12. Pasquin (1793), p. 73.
13. Robinson (1894), p. 20; Pasquin (1793), p. 74.
14. Austen's visit: Le Faye (2013), p. 185.
15. Robinson (1894), p. 21.
16. Robinson (1894), p. 22–23.
17. *The Dramatic Works of Colley Cibber, Esq. in five volumes* (London: J. Rivington and Sons, 1777), vol. V contains shorter works associated with Cibber's name but not necessarily by him. *Flora, or Hob in the Well*: pp. 77–109.
18. Michael Evenden, 'Flora's descent; or Hob's Re-re-re-resurrection,' *Eighteenth Century Studies* vol. 44, no. 4, Summer 2011, 565–567, summary at Project Muse, https://muse.jhu.edu/article/446584/summary accessed 8 May 2018.
19. Evenden (2011).
20. Bruce Scott, 'Flora – an 18th century British invasion', 20 May 2011, http://www.npr.org/2011/05/20/136469565/flora-an-18th-century-british-invasion accessed 8 May 2018.
21. 'Diphthongs', English Language and Linguistics Online, www.ello.uos.de/field.php/EarlyModernEnglish/Diphthongs accessed 8 May 2018.
22. Cibber (1777), p. 80.
23. Cibber (1777), p. 80.
24. Cibber (1777), p. 85.
25. Cibber (1777), p. 89.
26. Cibber (1777), pp. 99-100.
27. Cibber (1777), p. 106.
28. Cibber (1777), p. 109.
29. Robinson (1894), pp. 11, 16.
30. Robinson (1894), p. 47.
31. Mrs Inchbald, *The Midnight Hour; a petite comedy* (Boston: Wells and Lilly, 1823), p. 11.
32. Robinson (1894), pp. 48–49.
33. Robinson (1894), p. 54.
34. Robinson (1894), p. 23.
35. Rebecca Probert, *Marriage Law and Practice in the Long Eighteenth Century: a Reassessment* (Cambridge UP, 2009), pp. 296–297.
36. Probert (2009), p. 301.
37. Stephanie B. Hoffman, 'Behind closed doors: impotence trials and the trans-historical right to marital privacy,' *Boston University Law Review* 89 (2009), 1725–1752, p. 1727.
38. Hoffman (2009), p. 1727.

39. Hoffman (2009), p. 1737, n. 96.
40. Hoffman (2009), p. 1736.
41. Robinson (1894), pp. 104–105.
42. Robinson (1894), p. 109.
43. Arthur Aspinall, 'Barry, Richard, 7th Earl of Barrymore [1] (1769–1793), of Wargrave-on-Thames, Berks,' in R. Thorne (ed.), *The History of Parliament: the House of Commons 1790–1820* (1986), http://www. historyofparliamentonline.org/volume/1790-1820/member/barry-richard-1769-93 accessed 8 May 2018.
44. Robinson (1894), p. 119.
45. Aspinall (1986).
46. Robinson (1894), pp. 217–219.
47. Robinson (1894), p. 200.
48. Robinson (1894), p. 216.
49. Aspinall (1986).
50. Robinson (1894), pp. 221-222.
51. Robinson (1894), p. 224.

9 – Samuel's Claim (a Genealogical Digression)

1. John Gibson Lockhart, 'Autobiography of Sir Egerton Brydges', *Quarterly Review* 51 (June 1834), 342–65, http://spenserians.cath.vt.edu/ BiographyRecord.php?action=GET&bioid=4840 accessed 12 June 2018.
2. K. A. Manley, 'Brydges, Sir (Samuel) Egerton, first baronet, styled thirteenth Baron Chandos (1762–1837)', Oxford Dictionary of National Biography, Oxford University Press, 2004 [http://www.oxforddnb.com/view/article/3809, accessed 12 June 2018]
3. Letter 12, to Cassandra, 25 November 1798, Le Faye (2011), pp. 22–23. Claire Harman, *Jane's Fame: How Jane Austen Conquered the World* (Edinburgh: Canongate), 2009, pp. 29–30.
4. *Arthur Fitz-Albini, a Novel* (London: J. White), 2nd edition, 1799, vol. I, pp. 37–38.
5. Preface to the Second Edition, (1799), vol. I, p. vii.
6. Preface to the Second Edition, (1799), vol. I, p. x.
7. K. A. Manley, 'Brydges, Sir (Samuel) Egerton, first baronet, styled thirteenth Baron Chandos (1762–1837)', Oxford Dictionary of National Biography, Oxford University Press, 2004 [http://www.oxforddnb.com/view/article/3809, accessed 12 June 2018]
8. Chandos, first Baron Leigh of the second creation, 1791–1850. See Judy Stove, *The Missing Monument Murders* (Basingstoke: Waterside Press), 2016, p. 168.

9. *Legacies of British Slave Ownership* website (University College London), s.v. 'Duchess of Chandos Anna Eliza Brydges (née Gamon), 1737–1813, https://www.ucl.ac.uk/lbs/person/view/2146640763 accessed 12 June 2018.

10. Ibid.

11. Beltz,(1834), p. 5.

12. Beltz (1834), pp. 9–10.

13. Jemima met costs: Beltz (1834), p. 9.

14. SEB *Autobiography* (1834), vol. II, p. 135.

15. SEB (1799), pp. xiii–xiv.

16. Beltz (1834), p. 1.

17. Beltz (1834), p. 2.

18. Beltz (1834), Pedigree 1, section (b).

19. Beltz (1834), Pedigree I.

20. Beltz (1834), Pedigree I.

21. Beltz (1834), p. 5.

22. Beltz (1834), p. 6.

23. Beltz (1834), p. 9; will: pp. 3–4.

24. Opinion of Attorney-General, Spencer Perceval,in 1802 hearing, Beltz (1834), p. 50.

25. Beltz (1834), p. 158. This John Bridges died in 1656 unmarried.

26. Quoted in Beltz (1834), p. 87.

27. Quoted in Beltz (1834), p. 83.

28. Beltz (1834), pp. 92–93.

29. Beltz (1834), p. 104.

30. Thirsk, Joan. "Hasted, Edward (1732–1812), county historian." Oxford Dictionary of National Biography. 11 Jun. 2018.

31. Hasted (1800), p. 368.

32. Beltz (1834), p. 123.

33. Beltz (1834), p. 124.

34. Beltz (1834), p. 123.

35. Beltz (1834), Pedigree III.

36. Beltz (1834), pp. 130–131.

37. Beltz (1834), p. 135.

38. Beltz (1834), p. 187.

39. Beltz (1834), p. 143.

40. Beltz (1834), p. 144.

41. 'A manifest interpolation': Beltz (1834), Appendix VIII, viii.

42. The notorious 'Best receipt,' supposedly 'found' at Wootton by Samuel and his brother: Beltz (1834), pp. 171–173.

43. Beltz (1834), pp. 181–182.

44. Beltz (1834), footnote, p. 130.

45. Letter 49, 23 January 1803, LT (2007), p. 101.

46. Letter 60, 8 May 1803, LT (2007), p. 113. SEB's sons: Manley, K. (2004-09-23). Brydges, Sir (Samuel) Egerton, first baronet, styled thirteenth Baron Chandos (1762–1837), writer and genealogist. Oxford Dictionary of National Biography. Retrieved 11 June 2018

47. Letter 84, 13 September 1803, LT (2007), p. 133.

48. Letter 87, 23 September 1803, LT (2007), p. 135.

49. Letter 24, 27 April – 11 May 1802, LT (2007), p. 72.

50. Letter 25, 11-24 May 1802, LT (2007), p. 73.

51. Letter 26, 25 May – 9 June 1802, LT (2007), p. 75.

52. Letter 31, undated, July 1802, LT (2007), p. 79.

53. Beltz (1834), p. 128.

54. Kelly McDonald, 'Madam Lefroy in her own words,' JASNA News, vol. 24, no. 2, Summer 2008, p. 17.

55. LT (2007), p, 195.

56. Letter 65, 15 June 1803, LT (2007), p. 117.

57. Title page of SEB *Autobiography* (two vols, 1834).

58. Beltz (1834), p. vii.

59. David R. Fisher, 'Temple Nugent Grenville (afterwards Temple Nugent Brydges Chandos Grenville), Richard (1776–1839), of Stowe, Bucks. and Avington Park, Hants,' in R. Thorne (ed.), *The History of Parliament: the House of Commons 1790–1820* (1986), digitized at http://www.historyofparliamentonline.org/volume/1790-1820/member/temple-nugent-grenville-%28afterwards-temple-nugent-brydges-chandos-grenville- accessed 12 June 2018.

60. Fisher (1986).

61. Fisher (1986).

62. Letter 6, to Cassandra, 15/16 September 1796, Le Faye (2011), p. 10.

63. Margaret Doody, *Jane Austen's Names: Riddles, Persons, Places*, University of Chicago Press, 2015, p. 4.

10 – Ashe: Home, Family, Neighbours

1. Rev. F.W. Thoyts, *A History of Esse or Ashe, Hampshire* (London: William Clowes and sons, Limited), 1888.

2. Thoyts (1888), p. 59.

3. Beaufiz: p. 51.

4. Thoyts (1888), p. 1.

5. Thoyts (1888), p. 2.

6. Thoyts (1888), p. 6.

7. Thoyts (1888), p. 63.

8. Thoyts (1888), pp. 52–53. It is unclear who the Bishop of Cardica [*sic*] may have been.
9. Thoyts (1888), p. 99.
10. Thoyts (1888), pp. 108–109.
11. Thoyts (1888), p. 117.
12. Thoyts (1888), p. 118.
13. Thoyts (1888), p. 119; cf. Le Faye (2011), who gives dates for Dr Russell of 1695–1783, hence an age at death of 88 (p. 568).
14. CEL: Thoyts (1888), p. 120; Francis Russell Midford: Thoyts (1888), p. 121.
15. Thoyts (1888), p. 122.
16. Martin Garrett, 'Mitford, Mary Russell (1787–1855)', Oxford Dictionary of National Biography, Oxford University Press, 2004 [http://www.oxforddnb. com/view/article/18859, accessed 8 May 2018].
17. Christopher Edward: Thoyts (1888) p. 120; William Thomas: p. 121; Benjamin: p. 123. Mystery surrounds the birth dates of Anthony and his brother Christopher Edward. Their joint memorial plaque in Ashe Church gives Anthony's birth date as 21 September 1785, and Christopher Edward's as 24 November 1785. One is, or both are, almost certain to be incorrect.
18. Beltz (1834), p. 215.
19. Lefroy and Turner (2007), p. 14.
20. Photographed by S. Wilson, April 2018. The Book of Wisdom, or Wisdom of Solomon, was traditionally part of the Greek Septuagint, but not of the collection transmitted as the Hebrew Bible; it remained, however, highly influential on the Christian church ('Wisdom of Solomon, The' in F. L. Cross (ed.), *The Oxford Dictionary of the Christian Church* (OUP, 1961), p. 1471.
21. Thoyts (1888), p. 1245.
22. Thoyts (1888), p. 126.
23. D. Le Faye, *Jane Austen's Country Life* (London: Frances Lincoln Ltd, 2014), p. 135.
24. Quoted in Lefroy (1868), p. 138. Sir John notes that Anthony's death did not, in fact, take place until 27 January 1800, which seems to make the dating of Benjamin Langlois' letter erroneous.
25. Photographed by S. Wilson, April 2018.
26. Notice of death of Rev. John Faithfull, 1824: *Gentleman's Magazine* 136, July–December 1824, vol. XCIV, pp. 380–381.
27. LT (2007), p. 14.
28. LT (2007), p. 207.
29. LT (2007), p. 14.
30. See some points summarized by Benjamin Roberts, *Through the keyhole: Dutch child-rearing practices in the seventeenth and eighteenth century: three urban elite families* (Hilversum Verloren, 1998), pp. 33–35.

31. Letter 2, LT (2007), p. 30.
32. Letter 7, 15 September 1801, LT (2007), pp. 41–42.
33. Boham: LT (2007), p. 205.
34. Letter 17, 15 February 1802, LT (2007), pp. 58-59.
35. Letter 17, LT (2007), p. 59.
36. Le Faye (2011), p. 566.
37. LT (2007), p. 220.
38. M. Hammond, 'Jemima-Lucy Lefroy,' *Persuasions* 14 (1992), 57–61, p. 58.
39. Le Faye (2011), p. 566.
40. Hazel Jones, *Jane Austen and Marriage* (London and New York: Hambledon Continuum, 2009), p. 87.
41. John Brand, (ed.) W. Carew Hazlitt, reissued as *Popular antiquities of Great Britain* (London: John Russell Smith, 1870), vol. II, p. 58. Text clearly a facsimile of an eighteenth-century edition.
42. John William Cunningham, *Pneumanee: or, the Fairy of the Nineteenth Century* (Philadelphia: Edward Earle, 1815), pp. 214–215.
43. Quoted in Jones (2009), p. 87.
44. Letter 6, 20 July 1801, LT (2007), p. 41.
45. Jones (2009), p. 97.
46. Letter 3, 4 June 1801, LT (2007), p. 33.
47. Notice in *The Athenaeum*, vol. 5, January – June 1809, p. 357.
48. Denis Orde, *Nelson's Mediterranean Command* (Barnsley: Pen & Sword, 1997), p. 217. Variant Jane Mary Powlett: *The Legal Observer, or Journal of Jurisprudence*, vol. XXIV, May – October 1842 (London: Edmund Spettigue, 1842), p. 356.
49. *Collins' Peerage of England; genealogical, biographical, and historical. Greatly augmented, and continued to the present time, by Sir Egerton Brydges, K.J. In nine volumes* (London: 1812), vol. VIII, pp. 557–558.
50. Letter 13, to Cassandra, 1–2 December 1798, Le Faye (2011), p. 26.
51. Letter 22, 29 March – 12 April 1802, LT (2007), p. 66.
52. Letter 25, 11–24 May 1802, LT (2007), p. 73.
53. Letter 29, 29 June 1802, p. 77.
54. Orde at Eton, Cambridge: SEB *Collins' Peerage* (1812), vol. VIII, p. 556.
55. Letter 24, to Cassandra, 1 November 1800, Le Faye (2011), p. 55.
56. Letter 47, 5 January 1803, LT (2007), p. 98.
57. LT (2007), p. 219. Huguenot background: Le Faye (2011), p. 562.
58. http://research.hgt.org.uk/item/ashe-park/ accessed 1 June 2018; but see 'Joseph Portal by will of Mrs Jones' as owner of Ashe Park from 1763, in Thoyts (1888), p. 8.
59. Letter 1, to Cassandra (at Kintbury), 9–10 January 1796, Le Faye (2011), p. 2.
60. Letter 21, to Cassandra (at Steventon), 11 June 1799, Le Faye (2011), p. 46.
61. LT (2007), p. 214.

62. Le Faye (2011), p. 563; LT (2007), p. 219.
63. Letter 8, 23 September – 2 October 1801, LT (2007), p. 44.
64. Letter 12, 27 October – 7 November 1801, LT (2007), p. 51.
65. Letter 33, 27 August – 4 September 1802, LT (2007), p. 81.
66. Letter 24, to Cassandra, 1 November 1800, Le Faye (2011), p. 55.
67. Letter 13, 9–17 November 1801, LT (2007), p. 53.
68. Letter 14, 18–25 December 1801, LT (2007), p. 54.
69. LT (2007), p. 213.
70. Letter 25, to Cassandra, 8–9 November 1800, Le Faye (2011), pp. 57–58.
71. Letter 25, to Cassandra, 8–9 November 1800, Le Faye (2011), pp. 57–58.
72. Letter 2, 29 May 1801, LT (2007), p. 31.
73. Letter 14, 18–25 November 1801, LT (2007), p. 55.
74. W. James, *The Naval History of Great Britain, from the declaration of war by France in 1793, to the accession of George IV*, in 6 vols (London: Richard Bentley, 1837), vol. II, pp. 115–116.
75. Richard Woodman, *The Sea Warriors: The Fighting Captains and their Ships in the Age of Nelson* (Seaforth Publishing, Pen & Sword Books, 2014), pp. 90–91.
76. Brian Southam, *Jane Austen and the Navy* (National Maritime Museum, London; second edition, 2005), pp. 211–212.

11 – Mentioning the War

1. Ben Johnson, 'The last invasion of Britain', www.historica-uk.com/HistoryofWales/The-Last-Invasion-of-Britain accessed 12 June 2018.
2. Tim Clayton and Sheila O'Connell, *Bonaparte and the British: prints and propaganda in the age of Napoleon* (London: The British Museum, 2015) p. 60.
3. Rodger, N. (2004-09-23). Nelson, Horatio, Viscount Nelson (1758–1805), naval officer. Oxford Dictionary of National Biography. Retrieved 12 June 2018
4. Felix Markham, 'The Napoleonic adventure', in C.W. Crawley (ed.), *The New Cambridge Modern History* (Cambridge University Press), 1980, vol. IX, War and Peace in an Age of Upheaval 1793–1830, 307–336, p. 323.
5. Markham (1980), p. 323.
6. Geoffrey Bruun, 'The balance of power during the wars, 1793–1814, in Crawley (ed., 1980), 250–274, p. 263.
7. John Roach, 'Education, and public opinion,' in Crawley (ed., 1980), 179–208, p. 181.
8. Clayton and O'Connell (2015), p. 28.
9. Clayton and O'Connell (2015), p. 15.

10. Markham (1980), p. 324.
11. N.H. Gibbs, 'Armed forces and the art of war,' in Crawley (ed., 1980), 61–76, p. 80. Charles John Fedorak, 'In Defence of Great Britain: Henry Addington, the Duke of York and Military Preparations against Invasion by Napoleonic France,' in Mark Philp (ed.) *Resisting Napoleon: the British Response to the Threat of Invasion, 1797–1815* (Aldershot: Ashgate, 2006), 91-110, p. 94.
12. Clayton and O'Connell (2015), p. 109.
13. Clayton and O'Connell (2015), p. 133.
14. Fedorak (2006), p. 103.
15. Letter 54, 14 March 1803, LT (2007), p. 108.
16. Letter 55, 18 March 1803, LT (2007), p. 108.
17. Letter 61, 15 May 1803, LT (2007), p. 114.
18. Letter 61, 15 May 1803, LT (2007), p. 114.
19. Stephen and John Terry: biographical notes in LT (2007), p. 223.
20. William Cowper, *The Task* Book IV, in John. S. Memes (ed) *The Poems of William Cowper, with a Life and notes*, 3 vols (Edinburgh: Fraser & Co, 1835), vol. III, p. 252.
21. From *The Salisbury & Winchester Journal* 17 October 1803, quoted in notes to Letter 91, 20 October 1803, LT (2007), p. 139, and n. p. 198.
22. Arnold Blumberg, 'The accurate and deadly Baker rifle,' http://warfarehistorynetwork.com/daily/military-history/the-accurate-and-deadly-baker-rifle/ accessed 12 June 2018.
23. Letter 92, 26 October 1803, LT (2007), p. 140.
24. Letter 105, 2 March 1804, LT (2007), p. 151.
25. LT (2007), p. 199.
26. Letter 73, 27 July 1803, LT (2007), p. 121.
27. Letter 91, 20 October 1803, LT (2007), p. 139.
28. Letter 93, 1 November 1803, LT (2007), p. 141.
29. LT (2007), p. 222.
30. *Harriette Wilson's Memoirs* (1825; London: Virago, 1985), pp. 141–142; 307.
31. Letter 75, 3 August 1803, LT (2007), p. 123.
32. Letter 61, 15 May 1803, LT (2007), p. 114.
33. Anonymous, 'Vent contraire' ('Contrary wind'), November – December 1803, reproduced in Clayton and O'Connell (2015), p. 132.
34. Quoted in Clayton and O'Connell (2015), p. 59.
35. Letter 21, 17–28 March 1802, LT (2007), p. 65.
36. *GM* October 1802, Part the Second, pp. 894–895.
37. *GM* October 1802, Part the Second, p. 895.
38. James Gillray, 'The hand-writing upon the wall,' 24 August 1803, reproduced in Clayton and O'Connell (2015), p. 126.
39. Letter 41, 3 November 1802, LT (2007), p. 90.

40. Letter 51, 14 February 1803, LT (2007), p. 103.
41. Letter 58, 14 April 1803, LT (2007), p. 111.
42. 'Number of the Beast, The,' in F.L. Cross (ed.), *The Oxford Dictionary of the Christian Church* (Oxford University Press, 1961), p. 969.
43. Cross (1961), p. 969.
44. Letter 102, undated but February 1804, LT (2007), p. 148.
45. Burns' poem: numerous versions online, including www.online-literature. com/robert-burns accessed 12 June 2018. Anne's version: Letter 75, 3 August 1803, LT (2007), pp. 124–125.
46. Markham (1980), p. 325.
47. Markham (1980), p. 326.
48. Gibbs (1980), p. 80.

12 – In Sickness and in Health

1. Jacob W. Gruber, 'Hunter, John (1728–1793)', Oxford Dictionary of National Biography, Oxford University Press, 2004; online edn, May 2010 [http://www. oxforddnb.com/view/article/14220, accessed 15 June 2018]
2. Gruber (2010).
3. Gruber (2010).
4. History of Royal Hampshire Hospital, Winchester: https://h2g2.com/edited_ entry/A87827241 accessed 15 June 2018.
5. Derrick Baxby, 'Jenner, Edward (1749–1823)', *Oxford Dictionary of National Biography*, Oxford University Press, 2004; online edn, May 2009 [http://www. oxforddnb.com/view/article/14749, accessed 15 June 2018]
6. Derrick Baxby, 'Jenner, Edward (1749–1823)', Oxford Dictionary of National Biography, Oxford University Press, 2004; online edn, May 2009 [http://www. oxforddnb.com/view/article/14749, accessed 15 June 2018]
7. Letter 21, 17–28 March 1802, LT (2007), p. 64.
8. Letter 5, 1 July 1801, LT (2007), p. 40. Anne almost invariably spells 'inoculating/inoculation' with two n's, but I have used the modern spelling to avoid the distraction of inserting '[*sic*]' on a regular basis.
9. Letter 50, 29 January 1803, LT (2007), p. 103.
10. Letter 51, 14 February 1803, p. 104.
11. Letter 52, 19 February 1803, p. 106.
12. Letter 45, 27 November 1802, LT (2007), p. 94.
13. Letter 51, 14 February 1803, LT (2007), p. 104.
14. Thomas Gillan, 'From the History of Medicine Artifacts Collection: Perkins' Tractors,' 26 January 2017, https://blogs.library.duke.edu/rubenstein/2017/01/ 26/perkins-tractors/ accessed 15 June 2018.

15. Letter 9, 3–14 October 1801, LT (2007), p. 46.

16. Quoted in Gillan (2017).

17. LT (2007), p. 222.

18. https://www.nhs.uk/conditions/oedema/ accessed 15 June 2018.

19. Letter 3, 4 June 1801, LT (2007), p. 33.

20. See, e.g., Edward J. Seymour, *The Nature and Treatment of Dropsy: considered especially in reference to the diseases of the internal organs of the body which most commonly produce it,* Parts I and II (London: Longman, Rees, Orme, Brown, Green, and Longman, 1837), p. 93.

21. Letter 7, 15 September 1801, LT (2007), p. 42.

22. Letter 12, 27 October – 7 November 1801, LT (2007), p. 50.

23. Seymour (1837), p. 93.

24. Letter 50, 29 January 1803, LT (2007), p. 102.

25. Letter 75, 3 August 1803, LT (2007), p. 123.

26. Letter 83, 13 September 1803, LT (2007), p. 133.

27. Letter 93, 1 November 1803, LT (2007), p. 141.

28. NSW Health, *Communicable Diseases Factsheet: Measles*, updated 6 March 2014, http://www.health.nsw.gov.au/Infectious/factsheets/Factsheets/Pages/measles_factsheet.aspx accessed 15 June 2018.

29. NSW Health (2014).

30. R.E. Lees, 'Epidemic disease in Glasgow during the nineteenth century,' Scott Med J. 1996 Feb;41(1):24–7. Abstract at https://www.ncbi.nlm.nih.gov/pubmed/8658120 accessed 15 June 2018.

31. Letter 94, 13 November 1803, LT (2007), p. 142.

32. Letter 98, 2 December 1803, LT (2007), p. 146.

33. Marc Seward, 'The Health Benefits of Samphire', 25 September 2017, https://healthyfocus.org/the-health-benefits-of-samphire/. 'Superfood': Jane Rowney, 'Samphire: the next superfood?', *Weekend Notes* 16 March 2013, https://www.weekendnotes.com/samphire-the-next-superfood/ both accessed 15 June 2018.

34. Letter 82, undated but September 1803, LT (2007), p. 132.

35. Letter 83, 13 September 1803, LT (2007), p. 133.

36. Letter 83, 13 September 1803, LT (2007), p. 132.

37. Letters 93–94, 1–13 November 1803, LT (2007), pp. 140–142.

38. Letter 88, 24 September enclosed with letter of 1 October 1803, LT (2007), p. 137.

39. Letter 88, 24 September enclosed with letter of 1 October 1803, LT (2007), p. 137.

40. Letter 117, 6 June 1804, LT (2007), p. 162.

41. Letter 119, 11 June 1804, LT (2007), p. 163.

42. Letter 120, 20 June 1804, LT (2007), p. 163.

43. Letter 122, 13 July 1804, LT (2007), p. 165.

44. Letter 125, 5 August 1804, LT (2007), p. 167.

45. Warwick University Centre for the History of Medicine, abstract of H. Marland, *Dangerous Motherhood: Insanity and Childbirth in Victorian Britain* (Palgrave Macmillan, 2004), revised 28 November 2006, https://warwick.ac.uk/fac/arts/history/chm/events/dangerous/ accessed 15 June 2018.
46. Letter 11, 17–27 October 1801, LT (2007), p. 50.
47. Letter 10, 14 October 1801, LT (2007), p. 48.
48. Letter 11, 17–27 October 1801, LT (2007), p. 50.
49. Letter 18, 16 February – 1 March 1802, LT (2007), p. 60.
50. E.D. Martin, 'Depression in the Clergy,' *Christianity Today* Winter 1982, http://www.christianitytoday.com/pastors/1982/winter/depressioninclergy.html accessed 15 June 2018.
51. Letter 23, 12–24 April 1802, LT (2007), p. 69.
52. Letter 24, 27 April – 11 May 1802, LT (2007), p. 71.
53. Letter 31, undated, July 1802, LT (2007), p. 79.
54. Letter 40, 25 October 1802, LT (2007), p. 89.
55. Letter 49, 23 January 1803, LT (2007), p. 101.
56. Letter 99, 16 January 1804, LT (2007), p. 146.
57. William Heberden, quoted in LT (2007), pp. 198–9.
58. From *Hampshire Chronicle,* 6 July 1802, quoted in LT (2007), notes to Letter 33, p. 190.
59. Letter 33, 27 September – 4 August 1802, LT (2007), p. 82.
60. Kirstin Fawcett, 'Trepanation: the history of one of the world's oldest surgeries,' 1 January 2016, http://mentalfloss.com/article/70309/trepanation-history-one-worlds-oldest-surgeries accessed 15 June 2018.

13 – Animals and Plants

1. Letter 4, 17–30 June 1801, LT (2007), p. 37.
2. Letter 18, 16 February – 1 March 1802, LT (2007), p. 61.
3. Letter 14, 18-25 November 1801, LT (2007), p. 54.
4. Letter 35, 12 September 1802, LT (2007), p. 84.
5. Ben Johnson, 'Riding side-saddle,' http://www.historic-uk.com/CultureUK/Riding-SideSaddle/ accessed 15 June 2018.
6. Letter 43, 16 November 1802, p. 92.
7. Letter 49, 23 January 1803, LT (2007), p. 101.
8. Letter 50, 29 January 1803, LT (2007), p. 102.
9. LT (2007), colour illustrations between pages 114 and 115.
10. LT (2007), p. vi. This collection is apparently unpublished.
11. Benjamin Langlois, *Instructions to his Execs.*, quoted in Lefroy (1868), p. 112.
12. Letter 2, 29 May 1801, LT (2007), p. 30.

13. Letter 13, 9–17 November 1801, LT (2007), p. 53.
14. Letter 9, 3–14 October 1801, LT (2007), pp. 46–47.
15. Letter 57, 7 April 1803, LT (2007), p. 110.
16. Letter 58, 14 April 1803, LT (2007), p. 111. 'Banstickle' is an old term for a three-spined stickleback, a small river fish.
17. Letter 25, 11–24 May 1802, LT (2007), p. 73.
18. Letter 20, 3–16 March 1802, LT (2007), p. 63.
19. Letter 22, 29 March – 12 April 1802, LT (2007), p. 67.
20. *Gentleman's Magazine* January 1802, vol. LXXII, Part the First, May 1802, p. 415.
21. Letter 29, 29 June 1802, LT (2007), p. 77.
22. Letter 23, 12–24 April 1802, LT (2007), p. 70.
23. Letter 24, 27 April – 11 May 1802, p. 71
24. Letter 35, 12 September 1802, LT (2007), p. 85.
25. Letter 50, 29 January 1803, LT (2007), p. 103.
26. Letter 52, 19 Februrary 1803, LT (2007), p. 106.
27. Enclosed in Letter 88, 1 October 1803, LT (2007), p. 137.
28. Letter 58, 14 April 1803, LT (2007), pp. 111–112.
29. Letter 59, 27 April 1803, LT (2007), p. 112.
30. Letter 123, 20 July 1804, LT (2007), pp. 165–166.
31. Letter 124, 27 July 1804, LT (2007), p. 166.

14 – The Village School

1. Thoyts (1888), p. 3.
2. Thoyts (1888), p. 73.
3. Thoyts (1888), p. 80.
4. Thoyts (1888), p. 80.
5. Letter 2, 29 May 1801, LT (2007), p. 31.
6. 'Raikes, Robert (1735–1811),' in F.L. Cross (ed.), *The Oxford Dictionary of the Christian Church* (London: Oxford University Press, 1961), p. 1136.
7. 'Sunday schools,' in Cross (ed, 1961), p. 1305.
8. Letter 4, 17–30 June 1801, LT (2007), p. 36.
9. Letter 16, 28 November – 8 December 1801, LT (2007), p. 56.
10. Letter 18, 16 February – 1 March 1802, LT (2007), p. 60.
11. Maggie Black and Deirdre Le Faye, *The Jane Austen Cookbook* (The British Museum, 1995), p. 8.
12. Letter 23, 12–24 April 1802, LT (2007), p. 70.
13. Letter 32, 28 August 1802, LT (2007), p. 80.
14. Letter 33, 27 August – 4 September 1802, LT (2007), p. 82.

15. LT (2007), p. 190. 'Peter Waldo' would seem to be a pseudonym for this writer, as it was actually the name of a twelfth-century religious and social reformer of Lyons in France (d. 1217, hence 'Waldensians', followers of the same, subject to persecutions: 'Waldenses', in Cross, 1961, pp. 1434–1435). My research has to date not yet found a more likely name for this writer.
16. Letter 34, 5 September 1802, LT (2007), p. 83.
17. 'Confirmation', in Cross (ed., 1961), pp. 327–328.
18. Letter 43, 16 November 1802, LT (2007), p. 92.
19. Letter 2, 29 May 1801, LT (2007), p. 31.
20. Letter 35, 12 September 1802, LT (2007), p. 84.
21. Letter 47, 5 January 1803, LT (2007), p. 98.
22. Letter 50, 29 January 1803, LT (2007), p. 102.
23. Letter 52, 19 February 1803, LT (2007), p. 105.
24. Letter 111, 30 April 1804, LT (2007), p. 157.
25. Letter 54, 14 March 1803, LT (2007), pp. 107–108.

15 – Finale

1. Letter 136, 9 November 1804, LT (2007), p. 177. Wedding: Le Faye (2013), p. 276.
2. Le Faye (2011), p. 96 (hiatus).
3. Letter 136, 9 November 1804, LT (2007), p. 177.
4. Letter 137, 18 November 1804, LT (2007), p. 179.
5. Letter 140, 7 December 1804, LT (2007), p. 181.
6. Letter 135, 2 November 1804, LT (2007), p. 176.
7. Letter 136, 9 November 1804, LT (2007), p. 178.
8. Letter 137, 18 November 1804, LT (2007), p. 178.
9. Letters 136 9 November, and 137, 18 November, LT (2007), pp. 177 and 179.
10. N. Chipulina, '1804 – yellow fever – an accumulation of dirt and filth,' http:// gibraltar-intro.blogspot.com.au/2013/01/1804-yellow-fever-accumulation-of-dirt.html accessed 25 January 2018.
11. Letter 137, 18 November 1804, LT (2007), p. 179.
12. Letter 131, 8 October 1804, LT (2007), p. 173.
13. Letter 27, to Cassandra, 20–21 November 1800, Le Faye (2011), pp. 63–64.
14. Notes to Letter 127, LT (2007), p. 201.
15. Letter 138, 25 November 1804, LT (2007), p. 179.
16. Letter 138, 25 November 1804, LT (2007), p. 180.
17. Letters 139, 27 November, and 140, 7 December 1804, LT (2007), p. 180.
18. Letter 140, 7 December 1804, LT (2007), p. 181.
19. Letter 141, 16 December 1804, LT (2007), p. 181.

20. Caroline Austen, *Reminiscences of Caroline Austen* (completed 1873: ed. Deirdre Le Faye, The Jane Austen Society, 1986), pp. 6–7.

21. A reference to Alexander Pope, *Epistle to Dr Arbuthnot* (1735), line 128.

22. Probably SEB, *GM* December 1804, vol. LXXIV, Part the Second, pp. 1178–1179. The accident to 'Mrs Egerton' to which SEB refers, which took place the previous August, is described on p. 793 of the same volume: Mrs Egerton was the wife of William Tatton Egerton of Tatton Park, Cheshire, and a Hammond relation of the Brydges; '[her] death was occasioned by precipitately jumping from a low chair (in which she was taking her usual airing in the park), in consequence of the horse becoming restive. By the fall she became senseless, and expired without uttering a word.' The similarity of her death to her cousin Anne's is certainly striking.

23. Clearly an abridgement of the *GM* account; quoted at https://austenonly.com/2012/10/17/madame-lefroy-the-obituarie/ accessed 15 June 2018.

24. Peter M. Black, Patricio C. Gargallo, and Adam C. Lipson, The Dana Foundation, 19 June 2009, http://www.brainline.org/content/2009/06/brain-trauma-concussion-and-coma_pageall.html accessed 15 June 2018.

25. The gap is between letters 39, to Cassandra, 14 September 1804, and 40, to Frank, 21 January 1805: Le Faye (2011), pp. 96–100.

26. Text here as given in LT (2007), pp. 21–23. This is from David Selwyn (ed.), *The Poetry of Jane Austen and the Austen Family* (Iowa City: University of Iowa Press, 1997), pp. 8–9. The August dating is in Selwyn, reproducing the MS signature as: 'JA. – Aug;st 26. – 1808' (p. 66).

27. John Brooke, Hamilton, William Gerard (1729–1796), of Hampton Court, Mdx.
Published in The History of Parliament: the House of Commons 1754–1790, ed. L. Namier, J. Brooke., 1964 http://www.historyofparliamentonline.org/volume/1754-1790/member/hamilton-william-gerard-1729-96#offices-held accessed 15 June 2018.

28. The final passage in James Boswell, *The Life of Samuel Johnson, LLD* (1791). Boswell does not name Hamilton as the author, as noted by Selwyn (1997), p. 66.

29. R.W. Chapman (ed.), *The Works of Jane Austen* (London, Oxford University Press), vol. VI, Minor Works, 1954, reprinted 1958, and with revisions 1963, pp. 440–442. The basis for the 1749 birth date given for Anne is unclear.

30. Jane Austen, ed. Margaret Anne Doody and Douglas Murray, *Catharine and Other Writings* (Oxford, Oxford University Press, 1993), pp. xx–xxi.

31. Doody and Murray (1993), pp. 277–78.

32. Lefroy (1868), pp. 117–18. Sir John updated some typography, e.g. made some initial letters of nouns lower–case, from his family MS version.

33. David Selwyn (1997), pp. 8–10; notes at p. 66.

34. Le Faye (2013), p. 358.

16 – Crisis

1. Letter 203, 24 January 1805, Rev GL to CEL, Helen Lefroy MS (n.d.), p. 128.
2. Letter 205, 7 February 1805, Rev GL to CEL, Helen Lefroy MS (n.d.), p. 130.
3. Letter 206, 24 February 1805, Rev GL to CEL, Helen Lefroy MS (n.d.), p. 131.
4. Letter 207, 6 March 1805, Rev GL to CEL, Helen Lefroy MS (n.d.), p. 132.
5. Letter 208. 20 March 1805, Rev GL to CEL, Helen Lefroy MS (n.d.), pp. 133–134.
6. Letter 209. 20 March 1805, IGHL to CEL, Helen Lefroy MS (n.d.), p. 135.
7. Letter 210, 28 March 1805, JGHL to CEL, Helen Lefroy MS (n.d.), p. 135.
8. US: 'In 1807 … Dr Amos Twitchell performed the surgery in New Hampshire' (Rachel Nall, 'History of Stroke,' https://www.healthline.com/health/stroke/history-of-stroke 'medically reviewed by University of Illinois-Chicago, College of Medicine on 21 March 2016, accessed 3 April 2018). UK: F. Robicsek, T.S. Roush, J.W. Cook, M.K. Reames, 'From Hippocrates to Palmaz-Schatz, the history of carotid surgery', *European Journal of Vascular and Endovascular Surgery,* vol. 27, issue 4, April 2004, 389–397, https://www.sciencedirect.com/science/article/pii/S107858840400005X#BIB7 accessed 3 April 2018.
9. Letter 212, 16 April 1805, IGHL to CEL, Helen Lefroy MS (n.d.), pp. 136–137.
10. Letter 221, IGHL to CEL, 9 August 1805, Helen Lefroy MS (n.d.), p. 142.
11. Letters 222–224, Rev GL to CEL, pp. 143ff.
12. Letters 224–225, Rev GL to CEL, September 1805, p. 145.
13. Letter 225, IGHL to CEL, Ashe, 5 September 1805, pp. 144–145.
14. Letter 226, IGHL to CEL, Ashe, 12 September 1805, p. 143–144.
15. Letter 227, IGHL to CEL, Ashe, 17 September 1805, p. 146.
16. Letter 228, Rev GL to CEL, Southampton, 21 September 1805, p. 146.
17. Letter 228, Rev GL to CEL, Southampton, 21 September 1805, p. 146.
18. Letter 231, Rev GL to CEL, Ashe, 24 November 1805, p. 147.
19. Letter 232, IGHL to CEL, Compton, 24 November 1805, p. 148.
20. Letter 236, IGHL to CEL, Ashe, 12 March 1806, p. 150.
21. Letter 236, IGHL to CEL, Ashe, 12 March 1806, p. 151.
22. Letter 235, IGHL to CEL, Ashe, 1 March 1806, p. 150.
23. Letter of 28 June 1806, quoted in Lefroy (1868), p. 141. Re 'plague': does Sir John mean that Boham was strict on the youngest generation?
24. Appended to letter 238, 'Extract from the Obituary of the Gents. Magazine January [–June?] 1806,' IGHL to CEL, Ashe, 21 March 1806, p. 152.
25. Letter 240, IGHL to CEL, Ashe, 29 April 1806, p. 153.
26. Letter 241, IGHL to CEL, The White Hart in Bagshot, 16 May 1806, p. 154.
27. Letter 243, IGHL to CEL, Ashe, 18 June 1806, p. 155.
28. Letter 248, IGHL to CEL, Ashe, 2 September 1806, p. 158.
29. Letter 250, IGHL to CEL, Ashe, 14 November 1806, p. 159.

30. Letter 253, IGHL to CEL, Ashe, 2 December 1806, p. 161.
31. Letter 259, IGHL to CEL, Ashe, 2 February 1807, p. 165.
32. Letter 260, IGHL to CEL, 12 February 1807, p. 165.
33. Letter 273, IGHL to CEL, 25 May 1807, p. 173.
34. Letter 277, IGHL to CEL, 25 June 1807, p. 175.
35. Letter 285, IGHL to CEL, 10 September 1807, p. 179.
36. Letter 287, IGHL to CEL, 20 September 1807, p. 181.
37. Letter 296. IGHL to CEL, 14 January 1808, p. 186.
38. Letter 299, IGHL to CEL, 26 February 1808, pp. 187–88.
39. Letter 307, IGHL to CEL, 2 May 1808, p. 192.

17 – Generations

1. LT (2007), pp. 16–17.
2. LT (2007), p. 16.
3. *Reminiscences of Caroline Austen* (ed. D. Le Faye, Jane Austen Society, 1986), pp. 39–40.
4. Margaret Usborne, 'Jane Austen – the Lefroys', *The Spectator* 29 February 1952, p. 9, http://archive.spectator.co.uk/article/29th-february-1952/9/jane-austenthe-lefroys accessed 10 April 2018.
5. Letter 145, to Cassandra, 8/9 September 1816, Le Faye (2011), p. 335.
6. LT (2007), p. 17.
7. https://www.rijksmuseum.nl/en/rijksstudio/timeline-dutch-history/1700-1830-surinam accessed 22 June 2018.
8. London: J. Hatchard and Son, Piccadilly, 1826.
9. Review, *Outalissi: a Tale of Dutch Guiana, Gentleman's Magazine* January – June 1827, vol. XCVII (20th of a new series, Part the First), pp. 612–613.
10. Date after 12 May 1819, summary in Johannes Lamens, 'Lam(m)ens part 9 (Research),' family history research page, https://sites.google.com/site/fiscaalcompleet/familie/lam-m-ens-deel-9 accessed 10 April 2018, translated by Google, accessed 17 June 2018.
11. Lefroy (1868), p. 113.
12. Lefroy (1868), p. 113.
13. LT (2007), p. 18.
14. Lefroy (1868), pp. 162–163.
15. Lefroy (1868), p. 165.
16. Lefroy (1868), pp. 165–166.
17. LT (2007), p. 15.
18. M.C. Hammond, 'Jemima Lucy Lefroy', *Persuasions* 14 (1992), 57–61.
19. Letter 155, to Fanny Knight, 23–25 March 1817, Le Faye (2011), p. 351.

NOTES

20. Vetch, R. (2004-09-23). Lefroy, Sir John Henry (1817–1890), army officer and meteorologist. Oxford Dictionary of National Biography. Retrieved 21 Jun. 2018.
21. Quoted in Lefroy (1868), p. 18.
22. Lefroy (1868), p. 18. 'The Royal Fountain Hotel', Historic Canterbury, http://www.machadoink.com/Royal%20Fountain%20Hotel.htm accessed 18 June 2016.
23. Lefroy (1868), p. 19.
24. http://www.machadoink.com/All%20Saints%20Church.htm accessed 18 June 2018.
25. http://woottonselsteddentonhistory.blogspot.com/2015/04/wootton-court-part-3.html accessed 22 June 2018.
26. Mat Phipps, email to author, 24 April 2018.

Index